Photoshop 7 and Illustrator 10

Create Great Advanced Graphics

Dave Cross
Barry Huggins
Vicky Loader
Ian Tindale

friendsof

DESIGNER TO DESIGNER™

Photoshop 7 and Illustrator 10:
Create Great Advanced Graphics

© 2002 friends of ED

First printed July 2002

Trademark Acknowledgements

friends of ED has endeavored to provide trademark information about all the companies and products mentioned in this book by the appropriate use of capitals. However, friends of ED cannot guarantee the accuracy of this information.

Published by **friends of ED**
30 – 32 Lincoln Road, Olton, Birmingham,
B27 6PA, UK.

Printed in USA.

ISBN 1-903450-93-4

Credits

Authors
Dave Cross
Barry Huggins
Vicky Loader
Ian Tindale

Technical Reviewers
Denis E. Graham
Michael Walston
Jan Badger
Vibha Roy
Steve Cox

Proof Readers
Cathy Succamore

Managing Editor
Chris Hindley

Commissioning Editor
Luke Harvey

Technical Editors
Libby Hayward
Victoria Blackburn

Author Agent
Mel Jehs

Project Manager
Simon Brand

Graphic Editor
Katy Freer

Indexer
Simon Collins

Dave Cross

Dave Cross is an author and trainer based in Ottawa, Canada. He is the author and co-author of several Photoshop books and is a contributing writer to Photoshop User Magazine. Over the past 12 years Dave has trained thousands of users in graphics, publishing and web design. He is a member of the Photoshop World Instructor Dream Team, teaches for the Photoshop Seminar Tour and was named as one of Wacom's Top 40 Photoshop Experts. Dave is an Adobe Certified Expert, Certified Technical Trainer, Adobe Certified Training Provider and is often referred to by his students as "The Photoshop Coach".

Barry Huggins   www.matrixtraining.com

Barry left behind his days in international Commerce and jumped enthusiastically onboard the Internet at a time when it was a vague notion in the public imagination. He saw the potential of the Internet as a golden opportunity to marry his passion for art, design and creativity with the new developing technologies. His computer generated design however soon brought him back to the international arena, creating designs for clients in Japan, the USA, Italy and Portugal.

Barry now has his own training and consultancy company in London; Matrix Training, where he specializes in graphics and multimedia applications for both the Internet and print publishing. On the increasingly rare occasions when he is not working, he indulges in his other passions of scuba diving in warm waters and playing saxophone. But as he readily admits, the distinction between work and play is becoming increasingly hazy and he wouldn't change that for the world.

Vicki Loader   www.vickiloader.com

Vicki's early years were spent in South Africa. Now she is resident in rural village England, a stone's throw from the heart of London, where she divides her days between freelance training (to private companies or through a select number of high-profile London-based training concerns), and writing instructional books with friends of ED.

Whenever possible she pushes the boundaries of creative software on a laptop computer, while sitting in the sun at a Mediterranean street café or on a tropical beach. During these difficult times, Cava, champagne, cocktails, foreign movies, music and tapas bars sit tantalisingly close by.

Ian Tindale

Ian is married to a beautiful Jamaican - Deloris, and they live in a beautiful house, in the beautiful Dockands of London. He asks himself: "Well, how did I get here?"

Originally an artist and photographer, then designer, then typographer, Ian rode the crest of the DTP and PostScript(tm) wave, ending up as art editor of many major UK magazines including Mayfair Magazine. Ian frequently tutored others in QuarkXpress, Illustrator and Photoshop to an advanced level.

Currently, Ian is involved in XML media technologies, such as SVG, XSL-FO, SMIL2 and XHTML (and a lot of Linux). He sees the smart designers of the future recognising that they will effectively become document template and style-sheet designers, and concludes that this is an intelligent direction to be heading.

Welcome

As you are reading this, you probably know all about Adobe Photoshop and Illustrator – two of the most essential programs used in the graphics industry today – but are you getting the most out of them? Many designers use these favorites on a daily basis without ever harnessing their true efficiency. This book aims to change all that – focusing on using the two in conjunction to improve your workflow and produce stunning results for both the Web and print. We will take a critical look at each one to help guide you through any pitfalls and make an informed choice when selecting the right tool for the job.

This book divides into two sections – theory and practice. In the first half we examine the strengths and weaknesses of Photoshop 7 and Illustrator 10 to understand how they can work in perfect harmony. We'll refine your existing knowledge of both applications, look at why some functions are best handled by one application rather than the other; cover the correct settings and preferences to be used for efficient collaboration, and discover why each is indispensable to the other when developing advanced design skills. Although these sections are theory-based, they also include specific demonstrative examples.

The second half of the book covers practical demonstrations of projects you are likely to encounter in your work, allowing you to try out your newly acquired knowledge. The tutorials are backed up with theory and additional information to help you make the right decision when deciding on the workflow that suits you best. We hope to help you make the most of your skills and talents, so you can go further and achieve more...

Platform specifics

Photoshop and Illustrator users are as likely to be Mac-based as they are to be Windows-based, and for this reason, screenshots will be relevant to both platforms. Throughout the book, you will find the majority of the parts have Windows screenshots, although, Part 5, Creating a Product, was produced using a Mac. Regardless of this, any keyboard shortcuts will be written with the Mac one first, for example:

- SHIFT+CMD/CTRL+OPT/ALT is the keyboard shortcut to reset your preferences. SHIFT+CMD+OPT is the Mac shortcut and SHIFT+CTRL+ALT is the PC shortcut.

All about this book

As stated earlier, the book basically falls into two halves. Within each of these halves, there are three parts, which are then broken down into smaller sections. Some of these parts are quite large so we have clearly marked new sections to allow you to work through from start to finish or pick out the sections you think will be most useful to you.

To keep things as simple as possible we've only used a few layout styles to avoid confusion.

A few of the chapters have practical exercises included, and these will all appear under headings in this style:

Creating in Illustrator

In the time-honored fashion we have numbered the steps of each tutorial, like this:

1. Do this

2. Then do this

3. Do this next, etc...

When you come upon an important word or tool for the first time it will be in bold type:

■ Select the **Move** tool and ...

We've used different fonts to highlight filenames, and URL's too:

> `waterhole.psd` and friendsofed.com

All our menu commands are given in the following way:

> Image > Adjustments > Hue/Saturation

Finally, throughout the book, you may come across different boxes with information inside them.

> *If the box looks like this, this means the information contained is important for you to note. It may be a helpful tip or a warning about what you are doing, etc.*

If the box looks like this, the information is of a more background nature. It may be something you already know or simply an additional insight.

Files for download

To produce the results as shown, you may need to download the source files required for some of the exercises from our web site at www.friendsofed.com/code.html or you can use similar images of your own.

Support

If you have any queries about the book, or about friends of ED in general, visit our web site, you'll find a range of contact details there, or you can use feedback@friendsofed.com. The editors and authors will deal with any technical problems quickly and efficiently.

There's a host of other features on the site that may interest you; interviews with top designers, samples from our other books, and a message board where you can post your questions, discussions, and answers. Or you can take a back seat and just see what other designers are talking about. If you have any comments please contact us, we'd love to hear from you.

1 Knowing your Tools

Choosing which application to use for a particular design or publication used to be easy. It was essentially a case of *'Is it a graphic or a photographic image?'*; and the answer to that would determine whether Illustrator or Photoshop would be the chosen tool. However, in recent releases the boundaries have blurred - each application has progressively gained tools and functions previously the domain of the other. It would be wrong, however, to assume that either application perfectly replicates the other and that we can discount either one of them. Both applications have strengths and features that do not exist in the other; and for most designers, ownership of both is indispensable.

Further compounding the situation is the tighter integration of the applications with each other, allowing you to work effectively and more quickly between them. In addition to this, we seldom use just one application exclusively, but more typically use them both in tandem, swapping back and forth between the two to develop our project. The key to doing this really efficiently though, is being able to make a clear decision as to which is the most suitable tool for the task in hand.

OK, so we're all grown-ups here – we make informed and balanced decisions, we embrace change, we don't cling to our comfort zone – we like to push the envelope wherever possible...OK, maybe not. If you're anything like most designers I know then you will have a preference for either Photoshop or Illustrator, similar functionality may be present in both applications but you will choose the one that you are more comfortable with. This will probably produce acceptable end results, but acceptable isn't good enough – we want clean and powerful images. To vastly improve your workflow and efficiency it is clearly much better to have a thorough understanding of both applications, and to not let favoritism prevent you from choosing the best tool for the job.

In this chapter, and throughout the book, we'll examine Photoshop and Illustrator as companion tools, and you'll learn about different circumstances where the features of the applications can be used in tandem or individually to achieve that desired result with a minimum of fuss and greater productivity. Both product functionality and workflow will be explained so that you, as the designer, are in a position to make best use of the applications.

Resolution dependence and independence

Historically, one of the major divisions between Photoshop and Illustrator artwork has revolved around the issue of resolution, the distinction between vector and pixel-based images. At the simplest level, we could say that Illustrator images are resolution-independent, and that images created or manipulated in Photoshop are resolution-dependent. While this may have been true in the past, the continuing overlap between the applications now makes such a simple distinction misleading.

Essentially, Illustrator graphics are vector-based – they are defined by mathematical descriptions, and can be scaled up or down without any detrimental effect on their quality. However, not all components of an Illustrator graphic are vector-based: we can rasterize elements within the image, thereby converting them to pixel-based images; or we can import pixel-based images into the Illustrator document. Such pixel-based components are resolution-dependent, and so face the normal scaling restrictions and ppi considerations, despite the fact that they are in Illustrator they cannot be scaled vastly without affecting their visual appearance and quality.

Similarly, the majority of images generated in Photoshop and ImageReady are pixel-based and thus resolution-dependent which means that size and resolution play a primary role in the initial creation of the graphic – whether that be creating from scratch or scanning an image for use in the application. There are two exceptions to this rule: unrasterized text layers and shape layers, where the shape defines the edges of the visible image area – allowing for scalability because it is the vector outline and not the actual content which is being scaled to show more or less of the image area.

This vector data, including type, can be printed sharply from Photoshop if the **Include Vector Data** *option is checked at the base of the* File > Print with Preview *(CMD/CTRL+P) dialog box, and the target printer is a postscript printer. The result of this is that predominantly image based publications with a little text – for example a poster advertising an art exhibition – can now be created solely in Photoshop without the previous concerns over maintaining the sharpness of the type.*

Why all this fuss about resolution-dependence and independence when this is most likely a concept with which you are already familiar? The importance lies in remembering whether the component we are manipulating is a vector or bitmap image and thus how it might react when encompassed in another application. Take the situation where you are bringing pixel-based images from Photoshop into Illustrator, by any of the means described later on in this chapter, it is essential that you are aware of how these components will be interpreted by Illustrator, that the original resolution still applies, whether transparency will be retained; and how these concerns might affect the target media – be that print quality or appearance on the Web. Likewise, if you swap paths or graphics with Photoshop, whether they will be converted to pixels or remain as vector-based paths is important especially if the final print output will be from Photoshop but you wish to retain all the sharpness of the original vector shapes.

We'll discuss the various options for transferring both pixel and vector data between the two applications later in this chapter, allowing you to choose the most suitable option for your situation. Both applications can save in formats that retain both vector and pixel information, and the trick to using Photoshop and Illustrator together successfully lies in understanding these options and controlling this data exchange.

Designing for print and the web

As mentioned before, both applications natively handle information in different ways and this needs to be considered. Another factor to add to the equation is the fact that many publications are repurposed for both print and web today. This means that to eliminate duplication and unnecessary work it is important to consider both the differing resolutions and color modes required for these two different media whilst designing.

Imagine for instance that you are designing for print and will be including photographic images. After consultation with your printer who has told you that the desired output resolution is 300ppi, based on the fact that he will be using a 150 lpi screen to print and suggests that you multiply this value by two to get an optimum file size with sufficient pixel details for a good print. You also know that for the element to separate correctly at the press, the file needs to be created or converted in a CMYK color mode.

Once published, you learn that the design is to be repurposed for the web, this means that all images and graphics will have to be down-sampled to the accepted norm for web images – 72ppi; and converted to an RGB color mode. Unless you are preparing SVG (Scalable Vector Graphics) or graphics that will be used in a Flash animation, your lovely sharp resolution-independent vector shapes will have to be converted to pixel-based images and this can introduce some obvious loss of detail.

So does this mean that you have to recreate the entire file for the new media? Fortunately not - particularly if you have carefully planned your work. If the original logo was created in Illustrator it will be vector-based, and hence scalable without loss of quality, therefore there is nothing to stop you creating that original logo at its desired print size in CMYK; and then making another file with a small, scaled logo specifically for the web, using the File > Save for Web option. From within this dialog box you can choose the relevant file format to simplify the creation of the additional web graphic. Dependent on your choice of Color Table and the number of colors used, you may experience a color shift; and what you'll need to do is compromise between file size and color fidelity.

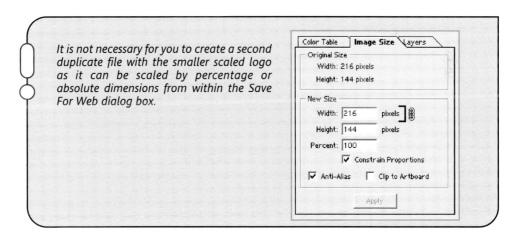

It is not necessary for you to create a second duplicate file with the smaller scaled logo as it can be scaled by percentage or absolute dimensions from within the Save For Web dialog box.

With careful planning, and an understanding of how the applications handle information and work together, you can get the best from each application to create those graphics – be they web or print.

Application integration

Recent releases in all the Adobe applications – not only Photoshop and Illustrator, but also InDesign, GoLive, and PageMaker – have seen a marked movement towards greater integration between the products. The result of this development has been that the interfaces are very similar in appearance making it easier for users to move from one application to the other. Because so many features of the individual file formats are supported in the other application, it has become markedly easier to use both products in tandem in order to achieve that final goal.

Having said that, and having also acknowledged that to some extent projects containing both vector and pixel information could be developed in either application, it is still important to remember that both Photoshop and Illustrator still have their specific strengths in the design process.

Advantages of Illustrator

Despite the introduction of more vector-based options in Photoshop in recent releases, Illustrator remains the tool of choice if the graphic is predominantly illustration based, or if exact measurement of graphics and building up to scale diagrams is important. The ease and accuracy with which vector shapes are created and manipulated within Illustrator means that the designer is more likely to create those shapes in Illustrator even if the remainder of the graphic will be developed in Photoshop.

Take for instance a situation where you wish to design a number of cogs and wheels for use in an illustration, but you wished to apply textures and subtle shading to the elements. Although the basic components could be created in either application, developing it in Illustrator using primitive shapes, Smart Guides, Scale, and Rotate options with repeat Transformation commands and finally using the Compound Shape palette would make the initial creation easier and more accurate.

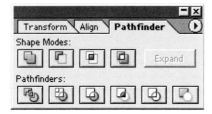

Having created the shape, it could be stored in the Symbols palette to be reused from within Illustrator, or the file could be exported into Photoshop, where the compound shape would be converted into a resolution-independent Shape layer.

The benefit in creating the initial cog in Illustrator begins to be shown in the following diagrams:

- The circle is created at the exact required measurement by clicking on the Artboard with the Ellipse tool and then specifying dimensions.

■ Accessing the Transform > Scale option or by choosing the **Scale** tool (S) and pressing ENTER creates the duplicate inner circle. The Preview and Copy options allow for the efficient creation of the duplicate.

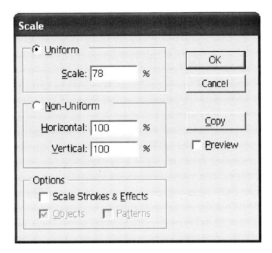

■ The smaller circle is placed exactly at the top of the circle by using Smart Guides, which indicate when the cursor is over the top center anchor.

■ The small duplicate circles are placed exactly around the circumference of the circle using the **Rotate** tool (R) and Smart Guides. OPT/ALT-clicking at the center of the larger circle displays the Rotate dialog box with the point of rotation remaining in the center of the large circle.

■ Preview options allow for accurate placement to be assessed before the Copy button is depressed.

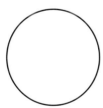

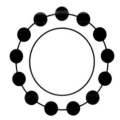

Circle with 1 in diameter created

Duplicate circle created using Scale dialog box. Smaller circle placed using Smart Guides.

Additional circles placed by numerically rotating copies around the centre of the larger circles.

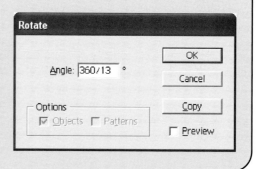

The correct rotation angle is determined by inputting 360° divided by the number of desired number of circles – 360/13 returns a value of 27.692° - the exact angle of rotation required to place thirteen equally spaced circles around the perimeter of the larger circle.

With the basic shape created, the enhanced Compound Shape options allow for the fine-tuning of its appearance.

- The smaller circles are created into a simple compound shape by selecting all of them and using the **Add to Shape Area** command on the Pathfinder palette.

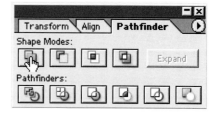

- Once the outer circles are one shape, they are easily subtracted from the outer circle by selecting both them and the outer circle and using the **Subtract from Shape Area** command. The inner circle may no longer be visible, but this is only because it is behind the newly created compound shape, and needs to be brought to the front.

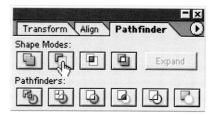

- The inner circle is then subtracted from the compound shape creating the transparent center. On completion it is evident that the inner circle was not scaled down sufficiently, but because Compound shapes are 'live shapes', selecting the circle with the **Group Selection** tool and then using the Scale command presents no problem.

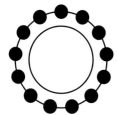

Smaller circles selected and converted to a Compound Shape using Add to Shape Area.

Compound small circles subtracted from the larger circle using Shape Mode - Subtract from Shape Area. Inner circle brought to front.

Inner circle subtracted from shape to create the transparent centre. Inner circle scaled to complete design.

This is Just one example of the strengths that Illustrator has for creating vector shapes simply and accurately, but this is not the only reason for using Illustrator to create either your entire graphic or at least the initial graphic for further manipulation in Photoshop.

- Although type is now handled very well in Photoshop, there is still no support for type on a path or within a shape and thus this would have to be created in Illustrator.

- Illustrator's powerful Gradient Mesh tool, Blend options, vector filters and effects, and the new Symbolism and Distortion tools introduced in Illustrator 10 allow for the creation of complicated illustrations which would be nearly impossible to create in Photoshop.

- Illustrator is not only powerful for print purposes. The web designer generating graphics to be exported for use in building vector-based animations in Macromedia Flash has at their disposal the Symbolism tools, the Release to Layers option, and support for exporting in the SWF file format; whilst SVG functionality allows for the creation of scalable web graphics.

As some, but not all, of the functions discussed above can be created in Photoshop, the idea is to use the strengths of each application to create the graphic as efficiently as possible.

Advantages of Photoshop

Photoshop is the tool of choice for any digitized photographic images and color correction. Its undisputed strength lies in the creation, processing, and manipulation of pixel-based images. Illustrator may have the ability to apply pixel-based filters to graphic components that have been rasterised, affect the transparency or blending mode of a rasterised image, or even colorize a black and white bitmap; but it cannot do any of the complex pixel-ased editing and retouching that Photoshop does.

Photoshop allows us to subtly change color casts in photographs, remove blemishes and unwanted elements. The new Painting engine and brush options introduced in Photoshop 7, also opens up a whole new area in creating and painting emulating real world media. In the previous example where the cog was developed initially in Illustrator as a flat graphic, bringing it into Photoshop and applying a few filters to create a metal texture starts to make it look a little more realistic.

Original graphic saved
as a PSD from Illustrator
with Compound shapes
retained.

Photoshop image with
filters and layer styles
applied to create
metallic effect.

Support for channels within Photoshop and the support for the Filmstrip file format also enables limited support for video manipulation.

Photoshop's companion application ImageReady provides further web support with the creation of animations and web rollovers.

Using the applications in tandem

The real power comes from using the strengths of both applications in tandem to create that ultimate graphic with the minimum of fuss. Granted that because there is an overlap in functionality as mentioned previously, there is not always the need to use both applications and much of it is dependent on the content of your particular design. Added to this, product knowledge and a certain sense of familiarity with an application often prescribes the way in which we work – but knowing both applications gives us the possibility to objectively assess which application to use at which stage of development.

For example in the sun illustration below, the use of both applications together in the development cycle, made the creation of the sun infinitely easier. The basic vector shapes – an ellipse and a triangle were created with primitive tools, and the basic face outline is made of bezier curves. The slightly irregular shape was then created using the new **Twirl** tool from the Liquify set of tools.

The larger petals were power-duplicated using a similar procedure to that described in the creation of the cog graphic above with a value of 360°/8. To place a smaller petal exactly between the larger front petals, the formula was changed to 360/16 to rotate a copy exactly half the amount of the previous rotations. Once in position, the petal was scaled and then power duplicated to create the remaining petals. The element stacking order was corrected to place the smaller petals at the base of the illustration; and then the petals and center were selected and refined using the **Trim** command on the Pathfinder palette to eliminate any overlapping elements. A copy of the outline was placed onto a separate layer before the gradient mesh was applied.

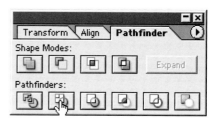

The Gradient mesh is a powerful tool for introducing subtle shading, but often actually managing those fine details can be very time-consuming and if our primary concern is not in retaining the vector attributes of the illustration, refining the shading is often achieved more easily in Photoshop. In this particular exercise, the shading on the face was done by manipulating by hand the placement of anchor points and color, but the shading applied to the petals is uniform and not manipulated.

In this illustration, it was essential to maintain the petals and the center as independent objects when the file was opened in Photoshop. This was achieved by using the Release to Layers option from the Layers palette menu. The file was then exported to Photoshop with Write Layers selected – the details of this option are discussed in the following sub-section.

In Photoshop, individual layers were targeted with Lock transparent pixels checked to safeguard the fidelity of the original shape.

The shading was enhanced by hand using Dodge and Burn tools, although other options were possible. Sometimes using the Gaussian Blur filter will help if any sharp edges remain from your original gradient mesh. Optional textures and filters could also be applied to further enhance the graphic. Once completed, the image could be placed in Illustrator again, bearing in mind that it has become resolution-dependent through its conversion into a PSD file. Alternatively, it could be used as a graphic in a web page design in Photoshop, Illustrator, or ImageReady, or as an animation or rollover in ImageReady.

Accepted, the graphic could have been generated totally in Photoshop, but the creation and power duplication of those original shapes, and the initial shading application would have been time-consuming and inefficient. Similarly the file could have been completely developed in Illustrator, but the attention to detail in the shading would have taken far longer with no Dodge and Burn tools to assist with the detailed build up. Thus it's often not a case of what each application can or cannot do individually, but which application can do it faster and more easily, to improve your overall efficiency.

Swapping information between Photoshop and Illustrator

It's all very well suggesting that as you develop your designs you use the applications in tandem, creating and then transferring those graphics or images to the sister application. What still remains very important is deciding the optimum way to swap the information between the two applications, and in many instances this will be dependent on the graphic and publication under development.

An important concept to grasp is the distinction between opening a file and placing a file.

Using Illustrator data in Photoshop

Once you have created your graphic in Illustrator, you have a number of methods by which you can port the graphics across to Photoshop and your choice of method is largely dependent on whether you wish to retain the vector information in the graphic.

Opening an Illustrator file from within Photoshop

Files created in Illustrator and saved as native AI files can be opened directly in Photoshop only if the Create PDF Compatible File option has been checked. With previous graphics you may have chosen to deselect this option to create a smaller file, and may thus have to re-check it for sharing Adobe graphics between applications.

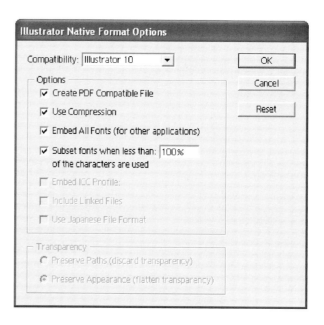

Failing to do this will result in the file opening with no visible graphic content and a text warning, part of which says, **This is an Adobe Illustrator file that has been saved without PDF content**.

Saving your file as either a PDF or EPS from Illustrator eliminates the possibility of such a warning being displayed, and the handling of the graphic is identical from this point on. From the Photoshop File menu, choose Open and navigate to the target graphic file. Once the file is selected, you will be presented with the following dialog box:

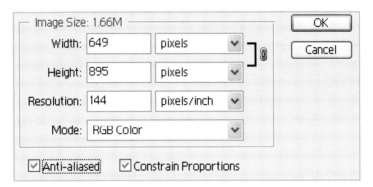

According to your own particular needs, you would indicate the required size, resolution, color mode, and anti-aliasing options and then click OK.

The image would be opened within Photoshop as a rasterised image with all the previous components from the Illustrator file placed on one layer irrespective of the structure of the Illustrator file. Note that any text included in the original Illustrator image will also have been rasterised.

Placing an Illustrator file in a Photoshop image

Similar in approach and final result is the option for placing an Illustrator within an existing Photoshop image using the File > Place command. Illustrator AI files can be placed if they have been saved as PDF compatible files as discussed above, and both the EPS and PDF format are also compatible.

Once the target file has been chosen using the Place command, the entire graphic will be placed on a new layer and is surrounded by a Transform bounding box. Once again, as with the original drag and drop method, the graphic can be scaled, rotated, or distorted without degrading the image quality before the transformation is accepted by pressing the ENTER key.

As soon as the initial transformation has been accepted, the vector information is discarded and the path becomes a pixel-based component of the illustration and is thus subject to the same constraints and considerations of original Photoshop components.

Copying and pasting an Illustrator file into Photoshop

The copy and paste method offers greater flexibility when transferring information from an Illustrator file to an open Photoshop file. After selecting and copying components of the Illustrator image, switch to Photoshop and choose Edit > Paste (CMD/CTRL+V). Photoshop displays the following dialog box, giving you the option of pasting the paths as Pixels, Paths, or as a Shape Layer.

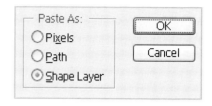

Let's have a look at these three options:

- If you select **Pixels** this means that the pixels will be placed on a new layer surrounded by a Transform bounding box allowing for freestyle transformation, similar to the drag and drop method. Once the transformation has been accepted, the Illustrator path is pixel-based and thus resolution-dependent.

- Pasting as **Path** will automatically paste the Illustrator paths into the Photoshop Paths palette as a work path, you then need to save the path in order for the information to be retained. However, as with all paths, they could be scaled or transformed as desired, but any fills or strokes applied to the paths would be resolution-dependent.

- Choosing the **Shape Layer** option pastes the information onto a new Shape layer allowing for the paths to be manipulated and transformed without affecting the crispness of the shapes outlines because of the inherent nature of Shape layers. Bear in mind though, that copying and pasting complex graphics and instance sets may be unpredictable.

Drag and drop method

With the applications side-by-side on your desktop, the selected Illustrator path can be dragged into the target Photoshop image. The path will be placed automatically on its own layer and surrounded by a Transform bounding box. At this stage, the path can be scaled, rotated, or distorted according to your needs before accepting the transformation by pressing the ENTER key.

Note that although you can initially distort the graphic without degrading the quality, once the transformation has been accepted, the path becomes a pixel-based component of the illustration and is thus subject to the same constraints and considerations of original Photoshop components. This would not be an option if you wished to retain the vector information in the path.

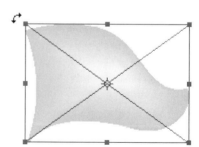

Dragging and dropping paths into the Photoshop Paths palette

There may be instances where you wish to adopt the simple drag-and-drop method, but don't wish for the path to be rasterized on a layer, but rather that it is placed directly into the Photoshop Paths palette.

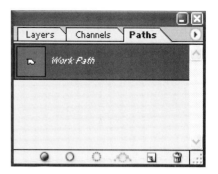

With the target path selected, drag it towards the Photoshop image and then depress the CMD/CTRL key. Once the path is in the desired position in the Photoshop image, release the mouse and then the modifier key and the path will automatically be created in the Paths palette as a **Work Path**.

Additional dragged paths can be added to this Work Path, but once the path has been converted to a saved path in the Paths palette, you will need to ensure that the saved path is not active if you wish to drag further paths across to be stored in the Paths palette. Alternatively, if you wanted to overwrite the original drag and drop path, then you would simply keep it selected in the Paths palette as you dragged a new path over.

Using this approach enables you to continue to scale and edit the path with the Direct Selection and Path Selection tools in Photoshop without degrading the resolution of the path as it is still vector-based, however any strokes or fills that are applied to the path are resolution-dependent and should only be modified bearing in mind the constraints of resolution-dependent graphics.

Exporting a file from Illustrator as a Photoshop (PSD) file

Illustrator also offers support for exporting an entire graphic complete with support for a number of features within the original graphic so that it can be imported as such into Photoshop and manipulated further.

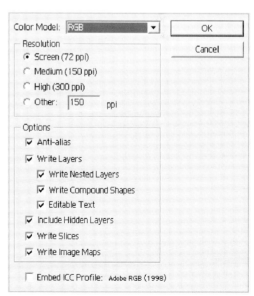

- Layers, including nested and hidden layers, are maintained if you check the option.

- Image resolution and Color Mode can be specified.

- Simple paragraph type is placed on its own layer and remains editable as type in Photoshop.

- Compound shapes are placed as Shape layers and also remain fully editable.

- All items other than type and compound shapes will be rasterized.

Thus if retaining the vector information of many of your image components is not required, but you wish to keep the layer information, web information, editable type, and compound shapes in addition to specifying the resolution and color mode of your graphic, exporting as a PSD would be the most reliable option. Note that if you use a Clipping Mask command from the Object menu, the clipped area will be visible when the file is opened in Photoshop, but the actual mask will have been applied and discarded. However, if you create a Clipping mask using the option from the Layers palette, the clipping mask will be maintained and will display in Photoshop as a Vector mask.

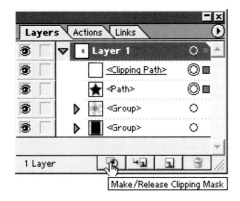
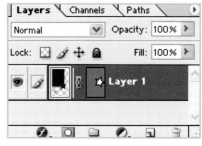

Using Photoshop data in Illustrator

Although usually you will be importing Photoshop images which are pixel-based into your Illustrator files, there may be times when you also wish to retain some of the vector information for manipulation in Illustrator. In the section below, we'll discuss the various ways of bringing your Photoshop files into Illustrator and how the different methods will affect the content.

Opening a Photoshop file from within Illustrator

As there are a number of different file formats that can be used in Photoshop and opened from within Illustrator. The strengths and weakness with regard to maintaining the fidelity of the original file will be discussed separately.

When you open a PSD file in Illustrator, you are faced with two options concerning how the Photoshop image will be imported:

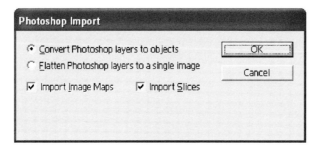

- Select **Convert Photoshop layers to objects** if you wish to further manipulate the positioning of certain aspects of the image, or manipulate some of those vector shapes that have been maintained in the conversion.

- Select **Flatten Photoshop layers to a single image** if you just wish to place the composite image into the Illustrator graphic.

Note that if Image Maps had been created in ImageReady, or Slices in either Photoshop or ImageReady, they will be imported if the options are checked.

Crop marks indicating the extent of the image are automatically created irrespective of whether the Photoshop layers were converted to objects, or the file was flattened and placed as a single image. These crop marks can be removed if desired by choosing Object > Crop Marks > Release.

Presuming that the option to convert layers to objects has been selected, the elements within the image are handled as follows:

- Transparency will be maintained, although the file will need to be flattened before printing.

- Any clipping path will be respected, placed at the top of the stack of objects and all objects outside of the clipping path will be invisible.

- Layers with Vector masks applied are approximated in the Illustrator file by converting the Vector mask into a Clipping path.

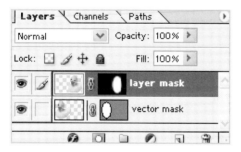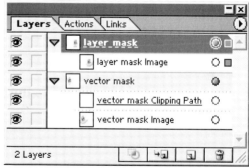

- Layer masks are retained, and the mask is accessible from within the Transparency palette. Although the mask itself cannot be actually edited as such because it is in bitmap format, it can be removed; additional elements either vector or bitmap can be added to it; and a limited number of the Photoshop filters can be run to manipulate it.

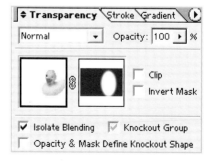

- Adjustment layers and layer effects are not supported, but the effects of these features, as applied in Photoshop, are maintained visually.

- Text is rasterized and thus not editable.

- Unfilled, unstroked paths on the Paths palette are discarded.

- Shape layers are converted into normal layers, with the shape often becoming a compound shape. It is fully editable using the Direct Selection tools, Vector filters, and Effects, and different fills can be applied in exactly the same way as a native Illustrator object.

- Any layer styles used in the original Photoshop image will be maintained, but they will no longer be editable. If a layer style has been applied to a Shape layer, the entire layer will be rasterised and therefore it will no longer be editable as a shape.

- Layer blending modes will be maintained and are editable from the Transparency palette.

- Spot color channels are not retained.

Opening a Photoshop generated EPS from within Illustrator

When saving as an EPS from Photoshop, the option to Include Vector Data will affect how the file opens within Illustrator.

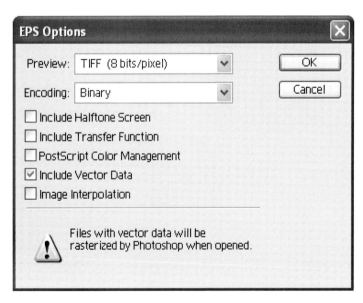

- If **Include Vector Data** is not checked, the Photoshop EPS will open as a single flattened image within Illustrator.

- If checked, the image section of the file will be a flat, non-transparent image, placed at the lowest level of the layer.

  - Layer masks, Vector masks, and Shape layers will be visually maintained through the creation of Clipping paths controlling the appearance of those components.

  - Type – whether a Type layer or converted to a shape in Photoshop – is handled by the creation of complex compound Clipping paths in Illustrator.

- Spot color channels are not supported in the basic EPS format; and DCS files cannot be opened in Illustrator.

- Unfilled, unstroked paths on the Paths palette are not retained.

If editability is the primary concern when opening the Photoshop image in Illustrator, the EPS format is fairly limited and thus would not be a good option.

Opening a Photoshop generated PDF from within Illustrator

The improved security options introduced to Photoshop 7 makes the PDF format even more attractive as a distribution option, but how it maintains information when opened in Illustrator is our primary concern here.

When saving as a Photoshop PDF, you have a number of options to consider in the Save As dialog box:

- The **Save Transparency** option will retain transparency when the file is opened in Illustrator. Note that if you have used a spot color in your Photoshop image, this option will not be available. If Save Transparency was not checked at time of saving, the bounds of the image will have a solid opaque background.

☑ Include Vector Data
☐ Embed Fonts
☐ Use Outlines for Text

- If **Include Vector Data** is not checked, the file will open in Illustrator as a single image, with transparency maintained if that option had been checked. If checked, simple image components – those without any Layer masks, Shape layers, or Vector masks – will be displayed at the base of the layer. Components which had masks applied will be displayed correctly, controlled by Clipping paths.

- Text converted to a shape within Photoshop will display correctly with the use of compound Clipping paths.

- Even if **Embed Fonts** were checked, you are likely to be presented with this dialog box, and the text will not display even though it appears as such in the Layers palette.

There is a way around this. The text is a group of individual text characters and do exist but are functioning as a Clipping path with no fill and no outline. To release the text shapes, the objects need to be selected and then choose Object > Clipping Mask > Release; *or use the* **Make/Release Clipping Mask** *icon at the base of the Layers palette. You may need to choose a fill color for the text to become visible.*

- Choosing **Outlines for Text** will convert all text to shapes and it will display correctly in Illustrator in that a compound Clipping path will clip the image.

- Unfilled, unstroked paths on the Paths palette are discarded.

- Avoid the use of spot color channels if you wish to open the file in Illustrator

Once again, although the PDF format offers some editability it does not retain the true vector shapes and if this were important, you'd be better to use the native PSD Photoshop format.

Drag and drop method

As with dragging Illustrator objects into Photoshop, it is just as easy to drag components from your Photoshop file into Illustrator, bearing in mind the following considerations:

- All dragged images will be embedded in the Illustrator file.

- The components will appear flattened, and in a rectangular shape even if they were on their own layer in the Photoshop file and the rest of that layer was transparent.

- Any Layer masks and Vector masks will be applied and then discarded, they will not become Opacity masks in Illustrator.

- Shape layers will be applied, and the resultant shape in Illustrator will be rasterized and anti-aliased.

- Text is no longer editable, as with Shape layers, it will be rasterized and anti-aliased.

- Layer styles will be applied and are no longer editable.

- Paths need to be selected with the Path Selection tool (A) and dragged across into the Illustrator file.

Copying and pasting a Photoshop file into Illustrator

A similar approach is to copy and paste the artwork from Photoshop into Illustrator, but this method also has some limitations that need to be considered:

- All pasted images will be embedded in the Illustrator file.

- The components will be flattened and transparency is discarded.

- On a Shape layer or a layer with a Vector mask, copying and pasting with the layer targeted and selected, will create a copy of all the layer content and ignore the mask shape.

- To copy the Vector mask shape or a path, it must be selected with the Path Selection tool (A) and then copied and pasted – the pasted path will have neither a fill nor a stroke. As these are vector paths, they will remain fully editable in Illustrator.

- When copying information from layers with Layer masks, the mask is ignored when the layer is targeted and selected, and thus the entire contents will be pasted. To copy and paste the Layer mask shape as a bitmap image, the mask icon must be targeted on the Layers palette.

- Text is anti-aliased and rasterized and is thus no longer editable.

- Paths selected with the Path Selection tool can be copied and pasted.

Exporting Photoshop paths for use in Illustrator

Previously it was mentioned that unstroked, unfilled paths were not retained if the file, PSD, EPS, or PDF, was opened in Illustrator. Yet there may well be instances in which you wish to use those paths without copying and pasting the path or using the drag and drop method.

This is achieved by using the File > Export Paths to Illustrator menu command, with the following considerations:

- The file that is saved is a native AI file.

- All simple paths contained in the Paths palette will be exported.

- If a Vector mask path is selected – by activating the layer – the path will appear in the Paths palette and will be exported.

- Similarly, if a Shape layer is selected, that path will be exported.

- When the file is opened in Illustrator all that will be visible are crop marks indicating the dimensions of the original Photoshop file. As the paths are both unstroked and unfilled, switching to Outline View (CMD/CTRL+Y) will show the paths which are then fully editable.

Placing a Photoshop file in an Illustrator graphic

Very often you may find yourself creating a design where the bitmap images are developed in Photoshop and then placed into an existing Illustrator document for further refinements in layout and design.

When files are placed, your initial choice after choosing the File > Place command and selecting the target file is to decide whether to embed the actual file so that it becomes part of the Illustrator file, or to link to the external file. The option is located in the lower left area of the Place dialog box; and when the Link option remains unchecked, the image is embedded in the file.

Whether or not you choose to embed or link the file is important because it will affect the editability of the file within Illustrator.

- If the file is **Linked**, you can return to Photoshop and edit the original file from within that application and then update the link.

- If the file is **Embedded**, dependent on the format of the file, many of the shapes and components will be editable.

When you place a Photoshop generated EPS or PDF in Illustrator then you will be faced with similar options and limitations as when you open these types of file in Illustrator, so refer to the section above for more information on this.

From the preceding discussion, it should seem apparent that if you wish to manipulate your original Photoshop file within Illustrator, your best option is to save the Photoshop file as a native PSD in order to retain as much of that vector information and editability as possible. Failing that, an option is to link the Photoshop file and then edit the original PSD file in Photoshop as needed.

Which program to use

Although not intended to be a prescriptive list for use of the applications as there will always be situations in your particular workflow where different options and approaches will be more suitable, the table below is intended as a general suggestion for uses of the applications.

Simple vector graphics

Previously considered the sole domain of Illustrator, the introduction of **Shape Layers** into Photoshop 6, clouds this area a little. Illustrator's strength in creating simple graphics including the creation of star and polygon shapes lies in the accuracy with which such shapes can be created initially by specifying its measurements.

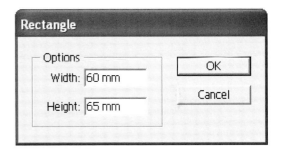

This does not necessarily mean that the vectors should be created in Illustrator as it is very much dependent on the job in hand. If the project is predominantly image-based, with the addition of some simple vector shapes, the entire project could be created within Photoshop. Questions of retaining the sharpness of the vector shape in final print output may present some concern, but this is easily overcome by specifying that vector data is included at time of printing. This is achieved by checking the option at the base of the dialog box accessed through File > Print with Preview (CMD/CTRL+P).

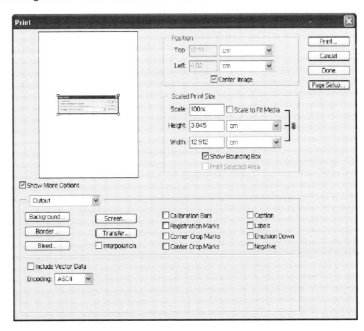

Using these options allows Photoshop to send the vector data from vector shapes and type to a Postscript printer. If the dialog box shows only details on the image position and print size, checking the Show More Options checkbox will display the additional features.

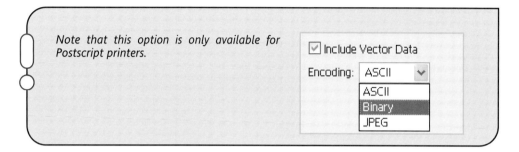

Note that this option is only available for Postscript printers.

Complex vector graphics and illustrations

As mentioned previously Illustrator's primary function is as an illustration application, and consequently it boasts some very powerful creation tools, including the Bezier pen.

Tools, which become so important for further transforming the illustration, include the various Compound shapes, Pathfinder filters, the versatility of the Transform tools, Blend options, Gradient Mesh, and more, allow for the effective development of the graphic at this stage. The Liquify tools and the Envelope distortions also facilitate the transformation and refinement of these components. If desired, the graphic can then be exported into Photoshop for further shading and manipulation.

Furthermore the creation of complex illustrations has been enhanced by the introduction of symbols and the various Symbolism tools in Illustrator 10. There is no comparable feature in Photoshop.

Graphs and charts

The existence of a Graphing tool and the accuracy with which initial shapes can be created in Illustrator makes it the application of choice for this type of illustration. However, once again, further embellishments in Photoshop can enhance what could be pretty dry information. Furthermore support for SVG interactivity enables the creation of dynamic charts and graphs for the web.

Maps and technical drawing

Illustrator has the strength here with its support for accurately created components and Smart Guides and conversion to a scalable PDF format for fine detailed work with high compression ability. Once the file has been created, however, additional features or textures can be added in Photoshop. If the graphic is designed for use on the web, Illustrator has additional support with the advantage of SVG support, and also Illustrator has the ability to compress detailed work into scalable PDF's.

Painting

Painting features are strong in both applications and much is dependent on the content and final result intended. The Artistic Brushes introduced in previous versions of Illustrator enabled the creation of illustrations, which in many instances resembled paintings. The ease of use in editing or redrawing the strokes made it a popular function. The use of global Process colors within Illustrator can also be a boon for added productivity when painting.

However, the new Painting engine introduced in Photoshop 7 firmly restores Photoshop as a medium for creating illustrations that look like real media paintings. The use of dual brushes and textures in brushes, the control over painting blending modes, fill, and opacity values, and the ability to make and save these brush presets makes the feature very powerful. Furthermore the Eraser, Smudge, and Blur tools add increased functionality for creating those 'paintings'.

Type

All applications have strong support for handling type, thus once again, using the application for type is not as dependent on the functionality of the application but rather the final destination of the product under development.

All design applications have multi-lingual support, but only Photoshop and Illustrator have the ability to check spelling.

- Support for paragraph formatting with justification, hyphenation, and word and letter spacing controls are present in all.

- Vertical type is a feature of all applications.

- Type layers in Photoshop and ImageReady allow for the creation of editable text, this is not necessary in Illustrator. Illustrator and Photoshop have the functionality that allows for the printing of vector-based type.

- Illustrator would tend to be the tool of choice for longer type because of its support for linked Type blocks and semi-automatic wraps around graphics. Furthermore only Illustrator can place type along a path or in an irregularly shaped container, which is a crucial factor in many advertising styles.

- All contain support for warped text, although Illustrator's additional Mesh Envelope distortions may yet prove popular for distorting type.

- Photoshop and ImageReady have greater support for controlling how type will display on web pages.

Web page design

Both applications have strong support for the design and selective optimization of web page designs. There is also support for the generation of valid HTML, CSS, image maps, and slices. Consequently, the application from within which the design is generated will depend on the content and if the media has been repurposed from print, the original application in use.

Web graphic design

Similar to the comment above, all applications have the functionality to create and generate web graphics with controls to selectively optimize areas of the graphic being generated. Although, with the exception of SVG graphics and graphics prepared for Flash animations created in Illustrator, the remaining formats for web design are pixel-based images, thus the application of choice may well depend entirely on where the graphic was originally generated. New support for Dithered Transparency in Photoshop and ImageReady add to the ease with which web graphics can be created in these two applications.

Rollovers

ImageReady offers direct support for the creation of interactive rollovers, especially with the introduction of the new states and new Rollovers palette. In Illustrator, the use of SVG graphics and the SVG Interactivity palette makes the creation of rollovers possible by creating events that trigger JavaScript commands, although knowledge of basic JavaScript syntax is required to use this functionality.

SVG graphics

Presently only Illustrator provides support for the creation of SVG graphics, which is understandable because the SVG format is a vector format. SVG graphics retain the crispness of vectors when displayed on the web, and have the added functionality of interactivity, however, these graphics can only be viewed if the required SVG Viewer plug-in is pre-installed on the machine of the individual viewing the web site. Saturation of the plug-in is not that heavy and thus this format still has a limited audience.

Animation

Each application has its own particular strengths in this field and it is dependent on where your animation will be viewed or developed which will determine which application you'll use at which stage.

- If your aim is to create the vector shapes and components required for use in Macromedia Flash, creating the file in Illustrator and then exporting it as an SWF is your best option. This approach will give you the cleanest, smallest files. However, the Flash format also supports the import of a number of other bitmap formats as well.

- Photoshop, ImageReady, and Illustrator provide support for importing and exporting files in a format suitable for use in Adobe Premiere.

- ImageReady has support for creating animated GIFs for publication in web pages.

- Illustrator has support for creating animations in SVG graphics.

With the exception of the animated GIFs in ImageReady and SVG graphics in Illustrator, the applications do not directly support the creation of animations. Images created in any of them can be used effectively for creating animations in other applications. The major concern would be the content of the illustration and whether the animation needed to be vector or bitmap-based.

Data-driven graphics

Both ImageReady and Illustrator support the use of variables and data sets for automating repetitive production issues. Whilst ImageReady's use of data-driven graphic support is used for web design, Illustrator can support both web design concepts and the automation of print production tasks.

Mixed formats – vectors and pixels

Both Illustrator and Photoshop have strong support for mixed format publications, and thus it is very much dependent on the content ratio whether you choose to complete the design in either Photoshop or Illustrator.

Blending components and images

This feature was previously the sole domain of Photoshop until Illustrator supported Transparency and Blending modes with the introduction of the Transparency palette. Again, use is very much dependent on content and the final desired result.

- If the desired result is a gradual transition between two relatively complex vector shapes, a subtle transition can be applied by creating an Opacity mask in Illustrator with a graduated fill for the mask. Whereas if two pixel-based photographs are to be blended, then a Layer mask in Photoshop is the best option.

- For sharp clipping of vector shapes, Clipping masks in Illustrator provide powerful support; and Vector masks in Photoshop can be used to create the same effect on pixel-based images.

- If a hand-painted, subtle mask is required, working with the Paintbrush, Airbrush, and Eraser in Photoshop allows for greater flexibility than attempting creating the same result in Illustrator.

- When the content is a combination of both pixel and vector-based shapes, the content and final desired transition result would determine, to a large extent, which application is used.

Although familiarity with the Photoshop method may often suggest that Photoshop is used to create these blends, the effect on file size and possible loss of resolution-independence must be considered as well.

Scanning images

Illustrator does not support the direct import of a scanned image, in that the pixel-based file must be saved in a format suitable for Illustrator before it can be opened or placed. Pixel-based components brought into a vector-based application still have the same restrictions on scaling and resolution (ppi) that were had in the component's application of origin. Pixel-based images will always suffer a loss of quality/clarity when scaled. Both ImageReady and Photoshop offer direct support for the option of scanning and importing in one command.

Pixel-based artwork

Whilst Illustrator offers some support for manipulating pixel-based images by use of filters, it cannot edit these images at a pixel-by-pixel level, consequently the tool of choice would be either Photoshop – for print and web – or ImageReady for pure web.

Image color correction

This is acceptably the domain of Photoshop. Illustrator does not support the correction of color casts within pixel images and ImageReady has some support which is often sufficient for manipulating images destined for the web. The true power lies in the industrial strength correction tools in Photoshop, which can handle the manipulation of images accurately for both print and web.

Image correction – removal of unwanted objects

Illustrator can be excluded from this part of the production process, as it does not have tools to support this function. ImageReady has the Clone Stamp tool, as does Photoshop; but the new Healing Brush and Patch tools offer unsurpassed strength for removing blemishes and unwanted objects from images.

Spot colors

The strength of the individual applications depends on how the spot color is to be created. Illustrator offers strong support for the use of flat spot colors in the use of logo and print design. Unlike Photoshop, it does not support Spot color channels and is therefore unable to subtly apply spot colors to areas of photographic images while retaining image detail.

Duotones and sepia tones

Only Photoshop offers functionality that enables the conversion of images to different color modes and then the additional application of duotone, tritone, and quadtone effects. Furthermore, the use of Adjustment layers also allows image enhancement not available elsewhere.

Summary

The suggestions contained in the table below are not meant to be prescriptive, as depending on your present knowledge of the applications and the design of your illustration you might find it easier to work in one application or the other.

Use	Application	Comments
Simple Vector Graphics	Illustrator Photoshop ImageReady	Both applications have the ability to create simple vector graphics, either by using the primitive tools in Illustrator, or Shape layers in Photoshop. Initial accuracy of creation may be the overriding factor in deciding which application to use, in combination with the final output destination.
Complex Vector Graphics	Illustrator	This is where Illustrator's real heart lies and whilst there is support for vectors in Photoshop, it does not have the power of Illustrator.
Graphs and Charts	Illustrator	Graph tool and primitive shape creation by dimension in Illustrator.
Maps and Technical Illustrations	Illustrator	Support for precise structure and placement makes Illustrator the preferred application.
Animation	Illustrator Photoshop ImageReady	Dependent on content of the final animation, graphics can be developed in any other applications. Illustrator offers direct support for Flash animations and animated SVG graphics whilst ImageReady can create simple animated gifs, which can also be saved as an HTML document.
Painting	Illustrator Photoshop	Both have support for painting, the choice of tool is dependent on approach and final content.
Type	Illustrator Photoshop ImageReady	The choice of tool is to some extent determined by the media for which the publication is being designed as all have type functionality.

Use	Application	Comments
Web Pages	Illustrator Photoshop ImageReady	All applications support strong functionality for the creation and optimization of web pages.
Web Graphics	Illustrator Photoshop ImageReady	The same functionality expressed above is relevant for web graphics.
Rollovers	Illustrator ImageReady	ImageReady has native support for the creation of rollovers, whilst Illustrator can add this functionality to SVG graphics.
SVG graphics	Illustrator	Illustrator is the only application supporting this format at present.
Data-driven graphics	Illustrator ImageReady	Illustrator and ImageReady both support data-driven graphics. Although ImageReady's support is limited to web production.
Mixed Formats – Pixels and vectors	Illustrator Photoshop	Both application support and maintain the editability of vectors and transparency of pixels. The final choice is largely dependent on content.
Blending Components and Images	Illustrator Photoshop	Use is dependent on the file contents and the type of transition required.
Scanning Images	Photoshop ImageReady	There is no support in Illustrator for the direct import of scanned images, the files must be saved first.
Pixel-based artwork	Photoshop ImageReady	Illustrator does not support pixel-by-pixel editing.
Image Color Correction	Photoshop ImageReady	Although ImageReady has limited support, Photoshop has the most powerful tools for fine-tuning color in images.
Image Correction	Photoshop ImageReady	Photoshop and to a lesser extent ImageReady have tools which can achieve this. If the purpose of the image is for both print and web, correction would logically be made in Photoshop.

Use	Application	Comments
Spot Colors	Illustrator Photoshop	The application used is dependent on how the spot color is to be applied – if to a vector, Illustrator is the choice product. If to a photographic image, Photoshop becomes the favorite.
Duotones/ Sepia Tones	Photoshop	The ability to change image color modes, create duotones, and adjustment layers give Photoshop the power to achieve these effects.

Conclusion

To start this book, we have looked at Photoshop and Illustrator as companion tools, including how to transfer data between the two. Also, we examined the different circumstances where the features of the applications are chosen individually to achieve a particular result with a minimum of fuss and greater productivity.

Throughout this chapter, you have been constantly reminded that each application has it's own strengths and weaknesses and only by knowing which tool is more suitable for the job in hand can you effectively integrate your usage of the applications. This theme is going to be maintained throughout the rest of the book with choices made between Photoshop and Illustrator depending on the most efficient way of producing the desired result.

2 Illustrator and Photoshop in Tandem

Photoshop and Illustrator have been engineered to allow a strong degree of cross-application integration, however, to get the best out of the two applications working together we need to set them up properly and select the most appropriate settings and preferences. In this chapter we will examine these preferences for both applications, choosing a common color management scheme across the applications. Also, we will consider how we can, within reason, anticipate the final appearance of our product – be that for print or web media.

Setting cross-application preferences

A major consideration when integrating Illustrator and Photoshop is maintaining cross-application file compatibility. It's all very well designing in both applications, but if the files have not been saved in a format that can be opened by the other, you're pretty much back at the starting gate. Granted, as mentioned in the previous chapter, dragging and dropping or copying and pasting components from one to the other is an option, but as we discussed previously this does have its own limitations.

Setting file saving options for native PSD files

Unlike previous versions, Photoshop 7 has the option to maximize backwards compatibility switched on as a default setting. One can change this by accessing the preference via Edit > Preferences > File Handling on either the Windows platform or Mac OS 9.x. On Mac OS X, choose Photoshop > Preferences > File Handling.

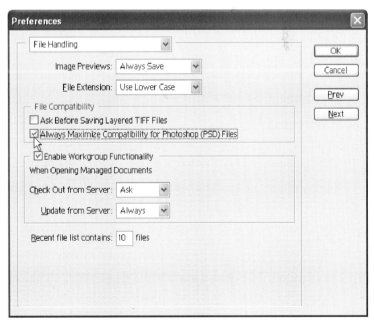

- When this option is enabled, Photoshop will always include a flattened composite image within the saved layered file.

- When this option is deselected, you will see an options dialog box enabling you to save with maximum compatibility on a file-by-file basis when you save as a PSD file.

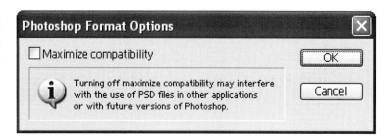

The downside of maximizing compatibility is the creation of large files, but the upside is being able to create files that are more compatible with other Adobe flagship applications. In practice, having this option enabled or disabled does not seem to adversely affect how PSD files are handled in Illustrator, but if you seem to be having problems, it might be worthwhile checking this option.

If it does not solve your problem – maybe Shape layers, Layer masks, or some other aspect of a PSD file should be editable in Illustrator but isn't – then you'd be well advised to take a look at the comments made in part 1 about *Opening Photoshop Files in Illustrator* as something else, for example Layer styles, might be causing the unexpected problem.

Setting file saving options for native AI files

Although not essentially a preference, an option chosen on a file-by-file basis is the choice for creating PDF compatible files when saving an Illustrator file. If you wish to open or place an AI file in Photoshop, it is imperative that you check this option.

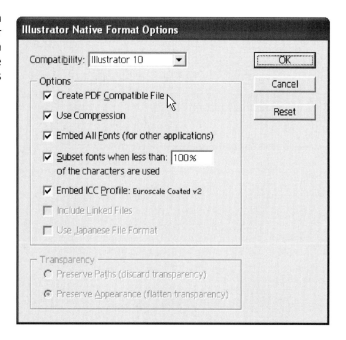

Once again, saving files with this option will create a larger file on disk, but deselecting the option will create files that cannot be placed in Photoshop. If you attempt to open or place such a file, the following is displayed in the Photoshop file window:

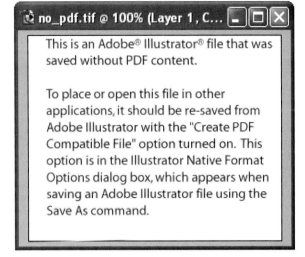

With these options set for saving both file formats, you should be able to swap information easily between the two, bearing in mind the limitations that were mentioned in the previously.

Managing color across the applications

Besides ensuring that files can easily be shared across applications, you also need to ensure that the color used in illustrations, images, and graphics is being managed in a way that makes the on-screen display as reliable as possible in both applications. Fortunately, because both are Adobe applications, the back-end functionality has already been put in place. The only thing that you, as the user needs to do is to ensure that your settings in each application handle color as you would expect it. Both Illustrator and Photoshop let you embed profiles into your graphics, and both applications will read profiles in opened or placed documents. By ensuring that the color settings in the applications are set together, you can predict that color will display consistently across the applications.

Why do we use Color Management?

In a nutshell, because we want to ensure that what we see on our screen is the way that the final publication will appear in print or on screen, to reduce color-matching headaches as we convert from scanner to monitor to print. If only it were that simple or that reliable.

Let's stop for a moment and consider what happens in a traditional development process. As is evident in the diagram below, our images may be coming from a multitude of different sources and in different color spaces. This is further complicated by the fact that each device, even if it is the same type of device, may interpret the RGB color space differently; and that some images we receive may have been tagged with embedded color profiles. In the previous chapter, we discussed the concept of resolution-dependent and resolution-independent images, there is a similar situation here; without an effective **CMS – Color Management System**, our color is in fact device-dependent, meaning that the color that we see is dependent on the device that is producing it.

Our scanner records an image with RGB values according to its particular specifications, which could be different from the specifications that determine how digital camera A records RGB, and different again for digital camera B.

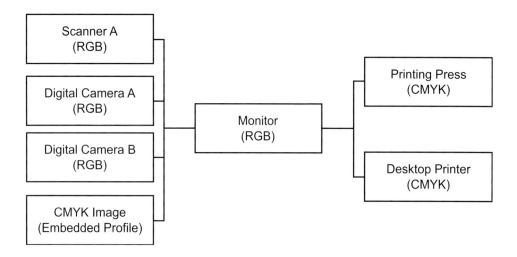

The next step is displaying these images reliably on our RGB monitors, which also displays colors according to its specifications, even if our images are destined for CMYK print output and possibly even for production in different countries on different presses with different inks and different specifications. As becomes evident, there are so many variables at play as we develop our publications that reliable, consistent color from one step to the next is difficult to predict. We could go on to mention how ageing monitors and scanners, the differing color gamut of paper sources, the way different applications display color differently, and even how the lighting in your room or the color of the walls will affect the display of color, and it becomes a veritable minefield.

This is where color management comes in, by using profiles that describe the color spaces of our various input and output devices we aim to create device-independent color. The intended result is that colors displayed on our monitors accurately reflect the final output colors of the publication. Using a CMS accurately should also ensure that the colors are consistently displayed in different applications and on different operating systems.

How does a Color Management System work?

A useful analogy when understanding what happens in a CMS is to view the different input and output devices as speaking different languages. What is needed for them to understand each other, and consequently deliver consistent reliable color, is some form of central interpreter or translator that is capable of speaking all their languages and thus making sense of it all. This exists in the form of the **CIE** (*Comission Internationale de l'Eclairage)* color model, a master color space.

Because the color spaces (CIELAB and CIEXYZ) are extensive enough to be able to reproduce all the colors that can be perceived by the human eye, they include all the colors of all the other color models and as such it can exist independently of any single device, be it a monitor, a scanner, or a printer - **device independent**. The CMS takes advantage of this independence and uses the color model as a reference color space, mapping the device-specific colors into a color space where color can be defined objectively. Returning to our analogy, using the device-independent color space to map the colors of the other devices means that they are, to an extent, speaking the same language even if their vocabulary does not necessarily overlap.

In order to be able to translate the color spaces of individual devices, the CMS needs to know the characteristics of each of the devices in use. It needs to know their specific color gamut, which is the total range of colors produced by a device, and the way they handle color. This information is gained from device profiles that can be included as part of the CMS, provided by the manufacturer of the particular device, or by using third-party software to generate profiles. Once it has this information, the CMM (Color Management Module) or Color Engine of the CMS uses these profiles to convert the device-dependent color space into the device-independent space and then into the second device-dependent space. For example, if you have a scanned image that you wish to display on your monitor, the CMS will look at the embedded profile in the scanned image, convert those values into either the CIELAB or CIEXYZ color space, and then using the monitor profile, convert those values again into RGB so that the image displays more accurately on your monitor.

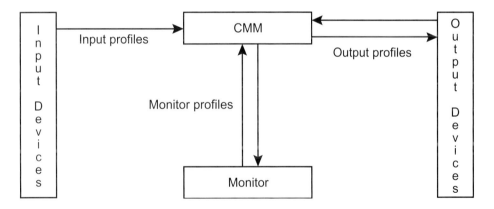

Consequently, our traditional development process has changed slightly with the use of profiles from all the input, output, and display devices being translated by the CMM.

Consistent color between Illustrator and Photoshop

In order to have color images and graphics display consistently in both Illustrator and Photoshop, we need to ensure that both applications are handling color and possibly embedded profiles in exactly the same manner. To do this, we would follow three steps:

- **Assemble accurate profiles** for all aspects of the production process – including profiles for input, output, and display devices. As mentioned before, many distributors provide such profiles, some may be supplied by your CMS and you can use third-party software and hardware to generate your own. You might also find that your service bureau will provide you with profiles for their particular output devices. Often the supplied profiles are not exactly suited to your environment, but they can provide a good starting point from which you can generate custom profiles to suit your environment. Such an example is the default ICC profiles supplied with the Adobe Gamma application used to **calibrate your monitor** and create an ICC profile that describes your particular environment.

- Choose your **Color Settings in Photoshop**, select the workspace and workflow options you require.

- Ensure that these Color Settings are duplicated in Illustrator.

The last two steps will take a fair amount of time and consideration, but we'll go through the options giving you as much information as possible so that you are in a position to make a decision that is useful for your environment.

> *Using a color management system does not guarantee that your graphics will print as they display on the monitor, but they should bring you closer to the desired result.*

Calibrating your monitor

The first place to start when adopting a CMS is to ensure, as far as possible, that your monitor is displaying colors accurately. This can be done using a supplied profile, or one of the many hardware and software solutions available on the commercial market, or by using the Adobe Gamma application installed with Photoshop.

What you are doing when you calibrate your monitor is characterizing how it displays color, and then saving that as an ICC profile. You might wonder about the need to calibrate your monitor, especially if you have been supplied with a manufacturers monitor profile. Although the supplied profile would be a good starting point, you would still want to characterize your monitor to take into account the variations you can get between two different monitors, both the same make and model. Furthermore, you'll need to consider your personal lighting environment and that the way in which the monitor displays colors may change as the monitor ages.

Bear in mind that if you are using Adobe Gamma or a similar software application, some of the settings and responses will be your own personal interpretation of what you are seeing on screen. Thus, you may find it useful to run through this setup a few times until you are familiar with the steps and satisfied with the results. Also, as you proceed through the calibration setup, you will be prompted to give information about your monitor including its color temperature, phosphors, and gamma. If you have a high-end monitor, it is possible that much of this information has been supplied in the accompanying documentation; otherwise you may have to contact the manufacturer and ask them for the values. If you are unsuccessful in locating the information, do not decide that calibrating your monitor is a waste of time, it's just more reliable if you have the information to hand.

The Adobe Gamma application is designed for use with a CRT (Cathode Ray Tube) monitor – in other words the standard large monitor still found today on many desktops. If you are using an LCD (flat screen) monitor, you'll need to use either the CMS supplied with your monitor or one designed specifically for LCD monitors. Having said that, you'll find that LCD monitors tend to be less prone to displaying colors incorrectly.

1. The first thing you'll need to do is to switch your monitor on, and leave it on for at least 30 minutes before you start to calibrate it. This gives the monitor a chance to warm up properly and will result in a more reliable color reading. Try and make your environment as neutral as possible by removing any bright distracting backgrounds or wallpapers from your desktop as these could influence your perception of color. Pay attention to the lighting as well as you'll be looking to create an environment, which at best duplicates the norm for your working situation.

2. The Adobe Gamma application is located within the Control Panel on both the Mac and the PC. Double-click the application icon to launch it, and the following dialog box will be displayed:

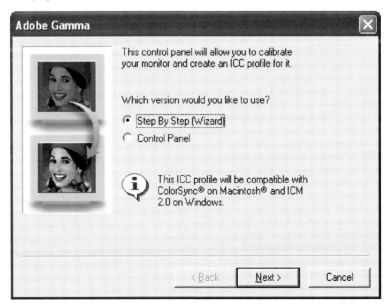

3. Choose the step-by-step approach if you are new to the process, as the Wizard will guide you through each step in the calibration process. If you are re-calibrating your monitor and know the procedure, you might opt for the Control Panel approach where all the options are available from one panel.

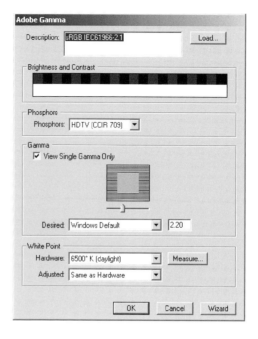

The instructions below presume that you have opted for the step-by-step method.

4. Click the **Next** button to proceed to the next screen.

5. If you have a default profile for your monitor, click **Load** to load it as a starting point for your calibration. In the space provided, type a descriptive name, which will help you identify this profile in future. Click **Next** to move to the following dialog box. If you do not have a specific profile, starting with the Adobe Default Monitor profile is a fair place to start.

6. The next dialog box marks the first of the steps you'll take to actually calibrate the screen. Using the controls on your monitor, adjust the brightness control so that the center gray square is as dark as possible, whilst still being visible from the black frame around it. You must also end up with an outer frame that is still a bright white. Note, this is the first of the subjective decisions you will need to make in performing this calibration

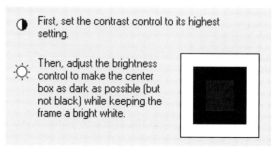

7. In the next screen, you'll be prompted to choose the phosphors for your monitor. If you were unable to locate information on your phosphors, then opt for the guess that the Gamma has made. If you do have values, choose **Custom...** from the drop-down list and enter the values in the dialog box that appears.

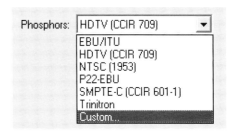

8. The next step will look at how your monitor displays mid tones. The first thing is to find the current gamma value. The slider alters the color of the central square. The object is to increase the slider value until the lines just become the same color as the square, at which point the box will appear to fade into the lines. The best way to achieve this is to sit a little way away from the monitor and blur your eyes. Once again this is a subjective judgment that you are making about the monitor.

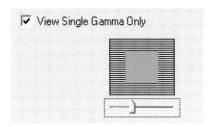

9. If your monitor seems to have a slight color cast to it, you might wish to adjust the red, green, and blue values independently. To do this, deselect **View Single Gamma Only,** and when you are shown the three striped squares adjust each one individually. Remember you are attempting to make your screen as neutral as possible.

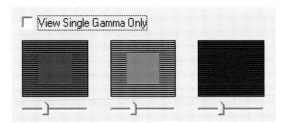

10. From the Gamma drop-down option at the base of the dialog box, choose the relevant gamma value. If you have obtained a different gamma value from your monitor manufacturer, enter this value by choosing the **Custom** option. Note that the gamma option may not be available on some operating systems.

11. After setting the gamma of the monitor, you'll attempt to remove any cast from the white point by setting the Hardware White Point. The white point is when white light is created from an equal mixing of red, green, and blue light. This can be done in a number of ways:

- If you have a value from the manufacturer, and it corresponds to one of the presets in the drop-down list, choose that option.

- If you have a colorimeter or spectrophotometer, use that to measure the monitor's white point and enter that value.

- If your value does not match any of the presets, enter the x and y values in the **Custom...** dialog box.

- Choose the **Measure** option to visually check for casts. It is often a good idea to do this check even if you have opted for one of the previous choices, so we'll discuss this in a little more detail.

12. If we accept that all light, unless your lighting is specifically daylight balanced, includes some color temperature that might interfere with our perception of color, then it's a good idea to follow the on-screen suggestion of ambient lighting before attempting to distinguish between the squares that appear.

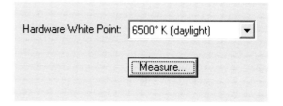

13. You will be presented with three gray squares, the aim is to make the central square as neutral as possible. If your square looks too warm, you click on the left-hand square to add more blue to it, and if it is too cool, click on the right-hand square as needed. When you are satisfied with your results, click the central square. As you do this, bear in mind your eyes' and brain's great capacity to filter out colorcasts.

14. The final screen before saving the profile, allows you to choose an alternate white point. If you have no need for this, remain with the **Same as Hardware** option. You would choose this option if you knew that your product would be viewed in a specific environment, for example Page White, which is 5000K. Dependent on your operating system and your video display adapter, this option may not be available.

15. Click on the **Before** and **After** buttons to check the difference between your non-calibrated and calibrated monitor display. If you are satisfied with your results, save the profile with a short descriptive name.

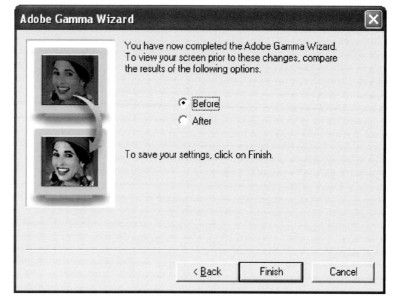

At this stage you would have successfully calibrated your monitor display, and created a profile that describes how your monitor displays color, for use in your color management workflow. However, a few points deserve to be mentioned:

- This calibration is based on your perception with a number of subjective observations determining the result. This is not to suggest that the profile is totally unreliable, but calibrating with more sophisticated hardware and software commercial options would certainly give you a more accurate and dependable profile.

- External influences such as ambient light, and the light coming through windows may have influenced your results.

- The calibration process should be repeated as monitors age and display light differently as time passes.

Choosing Photoshop color settings

Photoshop offers you a range of predefined color management settings, each geared to produce consistent color within a specific workflow scenario such as a print environment or output for the Web.

In addition to the predefined color management settings, **color management policies** provide a way to deal with the color in images that do not match the current color management workflow. These color management policies assist you in making decisions in how to deal with files whose color settings do not match the current intended workflow.

To access the Color Settings dialog box, choose Edit > Color Settings on the Windows and Mac OS 9.x systems. If you are using Mac OS X, choose Photoshop > Color Settings.

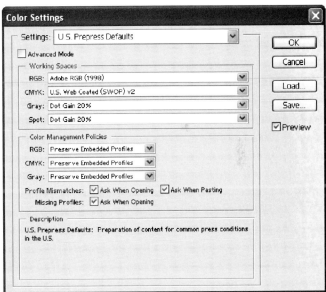

Notice that at the very top of the dialog box there is a drop-down box labeled **Settings**. This provides the range of predefined color management settings with the associated profiles and conversion options to generate consistent color within a given workflow situation. These settings will provide a level of color management suitable for the majority of cases, although as you become more experienced in color management, you will find yourself creating custom settings that are exactly tailored to your requirement.

If you work in a very loosely integrated system, you might find that you are being sent custom CSFs (Color Setting Files) from production houses, specifying exactly the press requirements for their particular system.

Click the Settings drop-down box to reveal the settings available. Choose the setting applicable to the kind of work you are doing, as summarized below:

- **Custom**: Allows you to specify your own set of options.

- **Color Management Off**: Best used to emulate how applications work that do not support color management. Good for files that will be used within video or other on-screen media.

- **Color Sync Workflow (Mac only)**: Color Sync is Apple's own Color Management System. This option uses Color Sync 3.0 CMS with the profiles chosen in the Color Sync control panel. This configuration is not recognized by Windows, or by earlier versions of Color Sync.

- **Emulate Acrobat 4**: Uses the color workflow as used by Adobe Acrobat version 4.0 and earlier.

- **Emulate Photoshop 4**: Uses the color workflow as used by Adobe Photoshop version 4.0 and earlier.

- **Europe Prepress Defaults**: Deals with color for work that will be printed under common press conditions in Europe.

- **Japan Prepress Defaults**: Deals with color for work that will be printed under common press conditions in Japan.

- **Photoshop 5 Default Spaces**: Uses the color workflow as used by Adobe Photoshop version 5.0.

- **U.S. Prepress Defaults**: Deals with color for work that will be printed under common press conditions in the U.S.

- **Web Graphics Defaults**: Deals with color for work that is intended for the Web.

When you select your desired option from the Settings drop-down box, you will see the Working Spaces section and the Color Management Policies section change accordingly to reflect your choice. Also notice that when you hover over a selected setting, the description box at the base of the dialog box displays a description of the setting. This is useful if you do create your own settings and save them, because you would be able to input a description to remind you of the uses for that particular setting.

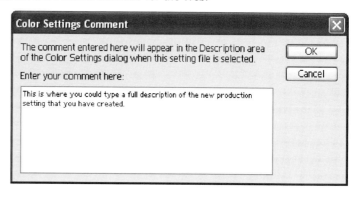

Understanding the Working Space profiles

The Working Spaces options specify the color profiles that will be associated with RGB, CMYK, and Grayscale color modes. They also specify how spot colors will be managed. If you have chosen US Prepress Defaults, then the Working Space options have changed to reflect the best profiles for each of these color models in this situation. If you select different descriptions from the Settings drop-down box you will see the other options change accordingly, in each case using the best profiles for that particular output.

A Working Space acts as the color profile for untagged documents – documents that do not have embedded profiles – and for newly created documents that use the associated color mode. For example, if **ColorMatch RGB** is the selected RGB working space, each new RGB document that you create will use colors within that color space. Working Spaces also define the destination color space of documents converted to RGB, CMYK, or Grayscale color mode.

To help you assess what each of the drop-down box options in the Working Spaces section does, you can hover the cursor over the drop-down box as in the screenshot below and a brief description appears at the bottom of the dialog box describing the nature of the option. In this example, Europe Prepress Defaults has been selected as the predefined Color Setting, and the CMYK profile has changed accordingly, with an explanation showing in the description area of the dialog box.

These presets are useful if you have to produce images for different worldwide settings. Having said that, they are designed to provide consistent color in a specific publishing workflow under usual conditions and you will achieve the most consistent color using ICC profiles created for your specific devices and workflows.

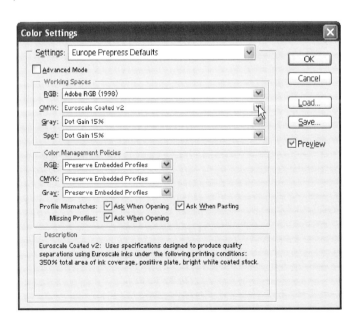

Choosing Color Management policies

Obviously all files that come onto your system will not be tagged with exactly the same profiles as you have allocated in your color management workflow. Policy options exist so that Photoshop knows what to do when you attempt to open or place components from a file that has a different profile embedded; or no profile embedded at all. The decision is based on comparing the profile or non-existent profile with the current working space. If there is a match between the profile and the current working space, the file is opened or imported as normal slotting into your selected working space profile. If there is no match, you will be alerted to the fact by a warning message and depending on the options you choose, the colors in the file will be treated in the manner you have specified.

For each of the color modes you have three options, which will dictate how the files and their profiles or lack thereof, will be handled:

- Choose **Off** if you do not want to color-manage any new, imported, or opened color data.

    - New documents and documents opened without profiles are saved without profiles.

    - Mismatched profiles are discarded and not saved with the document.

    - Matching profiles are preserved and saved with the document.

- Choose **Preserve Embedded Profiles** if you will be working with a mix of color-managed and non-color-managed documents, or with documents that use different profiles within the same color mode. This would be very pertinent if you were designing for differing print press or environments and would be choosing different profiles during the production process.

    - The chosen profile is saved with new documents.

    - Mismatched embedded profiles are preserved and saved with the document.

    - In documents without a profile, the working space is used for editing the document, but is not saved with the document.

- **Convert to Working Space** forces all documents to use the current working space.

  - Profile is saved with new documents.

  - Mismatched profiles are discarded and the document is converted to the current working space and saved with the document.

  - In documents without a profile, the working space is used for editing the document, but is not saved with the document.

Specifying how to be alerted to missing or mismatched profiles

Further below in the section on Color Management policies is an option to specify how Photoshop will let you know whether files you are opening or importing have missing or mismatching profiles. If an embedded profile is not the same as the one you are using and you open or paste a file, you can ask Photoshop to tell you and request that you make a decision on how to handle the file.

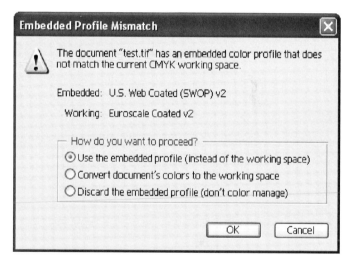

Similarly, if you open a file without an embedded profile, and you are working with Color Management on, you'll be faced with the following dialog box:

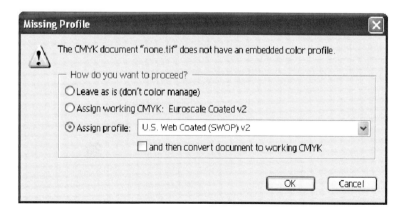

Of course you could deselect the options to ask on mismatches and missing profiles, especially as they can become a little tiresome. You'd be well advised to keep them on so that you have a handle on what is going on in the background, and thus eliminate the possibility of some very ugly surprises on the printing press.

In previous versions of Photoshop, if you chose to discard or ignore embedded color profiles when opening a file, and then closed the file without making any further changes to the file, the file would close without a Save prompt. However, options have changed in this version. If you discard the embedded profile, even if you make no material changes to the file, Photoshop views this action as a change to the file and will always display the following prompt when you go to close the file. This could be annoying if you just wish to open a few hundred files to have a quick look at them and do not wish to make any changes, including managing color.

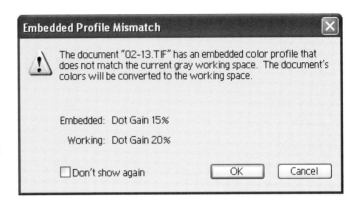

Even if you do deselect those 'Ask when...' options, you'll be faced with the above dialog box each time you open a file with a missing or mismatched profile. Once again, you could check that **Don't show again** option, but possibly the fact that Photoshop has built in this second warning should suggest how important it is to be aware of when and what profiles are being embedded, converted, or discarded.

Managing conversion options

Management conversion options are not ordinarily visible, and you'll need to check the Advanced Options checkbox at the top of the Color Settings dialog box to display them.

The Adobe Color Engine (ACE) is the default option for managing color in the Adobe applications and is recommended for use. However, if you have any other color engines installed on your machine and wish to use them, they should be displayed in this drop-down menu.

Understanding the rendering intent options

Whenever we convert colors from one color space to another, **gamut mapping** is performed. It is necessary for colors in the image that fall outside of the new color space to be adjusted so that they fall within the gamut of the chosen destination color space. These translation methods – or **rendering intents** as they are known – have been optimized for different types of graphics.

Perceptual
Saturation
Relative Colorimetric
Absolute Colorimetric

Perceptual

Perceptual tends to be the option used for mapping photographic images into another color space. In an attempt to preserve the visual relative differences between colors in an image, even those colors falling within the gamut of the chosen destination space may be remapped. This is because it is more important visually to keep the relative color differences rather than the absolute colors.

Saturation

Saturation tends to be used for images containing business-type graphics, for example graphs and charts. This is because the actual hue of the colors within the image is not that important, but maintaining the vividness or saturation of the color is. Consequently, when images are mapped to a smaller color space, the actual hues used may shift because the relationship between colors is not the primary concern.

Absolute Colorimetric

Absolute and Relative Colorimetric (discussed below) are used as rendering intents for company logos, where maintaining the actual colors in the image is deemed to be more important than preserving the relationship between colors in the original color space. With both colorimetric options, colors falling within the destination gamut are not remapped, whereas for those colors that have no match within the smaller gamut, a closest possible match is the option, with the result that two colors that were distinct in the original color space may, with this conversion, be mapped to identical color values.

Relative Colorimetric

This rendering intent is identical to Absolute Colorimetric except that the white point in the original source color space is mapped to that of the destination and all other colors are shifted accordingly to that change. This option is also used for mapping logos and increasingly for images if **Use Black Point Compensation** is checked in the Advanced Options as well. Using this option can give better results in photographic images because it preserves both the relationships between colors, which is important visually, without sacrificing color accuracy in the image. Relative colorimetric is the default rendering intent used in all the preset configurations available from the Settings drop-down menu.

Using Black Point Compensation when converting images

Black Point Compensation adjusts for differences in black points when colors are converted between color spaces where the darkest neutrals from the source color space are mapped to the darkest neutrals in the destination color space.

When this option is selected, the full dynamic range of the source space is mapped into the full dynamic range of the destination space. When deselected, the dynamic range of the source space is simulated in the destination space and can result in blocked or gray shadows. Deselecting Black Point Compensation can be useful if the black point of the source space is darker than that of the destination space.

Saving files with embedded profiles

By default, the option to save the embedded profile with the file is checked, and consequently the profile is automatically saved with the file when the file is saved.

If you wish to save the file without the embedded profile, this option should be deselected when it is displayed with File > Save As... (CMD/CTRL+SHIFT+S).

Converting and assigning profiles

There will be occasions where you wish to make changes to the embedded profile within an image. For instance, your specified workflow may have changed, or you need to repurpose the image for a different regional printing press or different media. Photoshop has options enabling you to do this – the Assign Profile and Convert to Profile options.

Viewing the embedded profile

Before you can determine whether or not you need to change the profile within an image, you'll need to know which profile is presently embedded. This is displayed by choosing the Document Profile option displayed on the pop-up menu on the status bar. To display the menu, click on the small triangle arrow as shown in the screenshot below.

If the Status Bar is not visible, choose Window > Status Bar.

Also, if an image is in a space other than the working space, the color mode in the image's title bar is displayed with an asterisk (*).

If an image is untagged, the title bar displays the color mode with a number (#) sign.

Using the Assign Profile command

With this command you may see a shift in color appearance as the color numbers are mapped directly to the new profile color space as you reassign or discard the embedded profile.

When you select Image > Mode > Assign Profile, the **Assign Profile** dialog box is displayed, providing you with the following options:

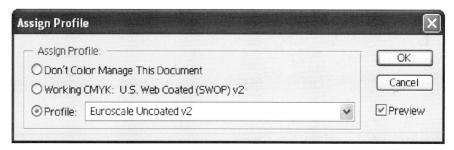

- **Don't Color Manage This Document**: This option removes the profile from a tagged document, and the document becomes untagged. Notice that if you do this, the number (#) sign appears after the color mode indicating that the document is now untagged.

- **Working (color mode)**: A file that was opened in a different color space, which would be indicated by an asterisk (*) after the color mode, is tagged with the current working space profile, and the asterisk is removed.

- **Profile**: Choose the profile from the drop-down menu to reassign a different profile to a tagged document. The document is tagged with the new profile mapping the color numbers directly to the new space. This may dramatically change the appearance of the colors as displayed on your monitor.

- **Preview**: Check this option to see how the changed profile will affect the appearance of the image.

Using the Convert Profile command

With the Convert Profile command changes in color appearance should not be a radical as the color numbers are shifted before they are mapped to the new profile space.

This command offers a fair amount of flexibility when choosing a destination space and rendering intent, especially with the Preview button allowing you to assess the impact of the changes before you commit to them. You may remember earlier how we discussed the Perceptual and Relative Colorimetric rendering intentions in relation to photographic images and also how the use of Black Point compensation affects images. If you wish to assess the impact of the differing rendering intentions on a particular image, you could do that here.

To display the **Convert to Profile** dialog box, choose Image > Mode > Convert to Profile.

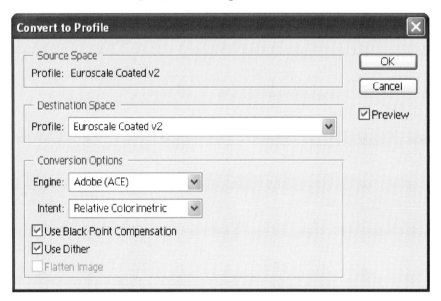

- The **Source Space** refers to the present working space of the document, and is displayed at the top of the dialog box.

- From the **Destination Space** drop-down menu, choose the new destination color profile for the document. The document's colors will be converted to this working space, and the file is tagged with this new profile.

- Under **Conversion Options**, choose a color management engine if you wish to change this, a rendering intent, use black point, and dither options.

    - For instance, presume you have a document that is in the correct working space, but you wish to check the impact that changing the rendering intention would have on the image. In this case, the embedded profile would be retained, but you could change the rendering intention and preview it before you accepted or discarded the change.

    - The **Flatten Image** option will flatten the file when the file is converted. If this option is selected when you preview the image, the preview will be more accurate. If you wish to preview accurately, and then convert the file without flattening it, deselect the Flatten Image option before you press OK.

Although there are further color management options that can be set in Photoshop, this chapter is essentially about getting the two applications to work with each other. Now, we'll compare how color management differs in Illustrator, and then how to save a custom setting so that it is available for use in both Illustrator and Photoshop. This has been our aim all along, to set up the applications so that they work together and that we can reliably expect a consistent handling of color between them.

Choosing Illustrator color settings

As many of the options available in Illustrator are identical to those available for managing color in Photoshop, you should feel familiar as we run through the settings. To access the Color Settings dialog box, choose Edit > Color Settings on both platforms.

At first glance, you'll notice that the dialog box is very similar to that you encountered in Photoshop, with a few minor exceptions – the lack of working spaces for Grayscale and Spot Color. This is because Illustrator only supports color management for RGB and CMYK color models. Grayscale color model files or files with Spot Colors will not be color managed. You'll also notice that the majority of the pre-defined settings are identical to those available for Photoshop as well. This is where the ability to create custom settings once in Photoshop, and then use those settings again in Illustrator to ensure consistent handling of color across the applications becomes very important.

Notice again that the options for Color Management policies follow the Photoshop example, with the omission for handling Grayscale working space. If a file containing grayscale objects is opened or placed in Illustrator, the objects will keep their grayscale qualities but will not be color-managed.

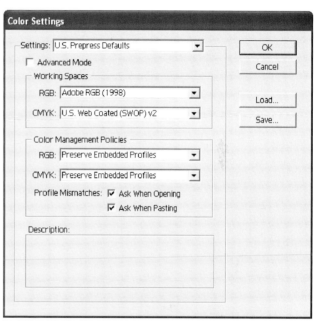
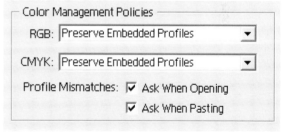
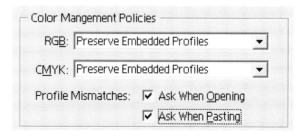

Note also there is no explicit option for handling missing profiles, but if you are using color management and a file without an embedded profile is opened, the following dialog box will display if you have checked for Illustrator to ask you how to handle profile mismatches.

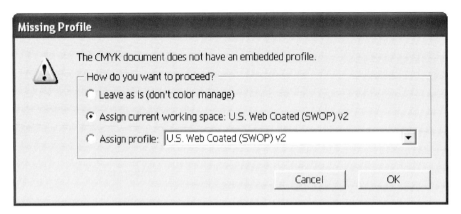

As with Photoshop, if the Profile Mismatch options have been deselected, and a file with an embedded profile different from the current working space is opened, Illustrator will display a warning dialog box, which can be disabled. Once again, it is suggested that you do not deselect the Profile mismatch options so that you can be aware of when files without profiles or files differing from the current workspace are placed. If you do opt to do this, then the second warning box should always display as an additional safety guard, thus checking the **Don't Show Again** option is not advised.

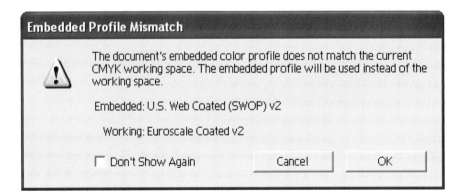

Changing profiles in Illustrator

Unlike Photoshop, you do not have extensive options to either assign or convert en embedded profile. If you need to change the color profile of an Illustrator document, choose Edit > Assign Profile and the following dialog box is displayed. Although the dialog box options are identical to those offered in Photoshop, note that you do not have a chance to preview the document before you assign a new profile, and the asterisk (*)

and hash (#) signs do not appear in the title bar.

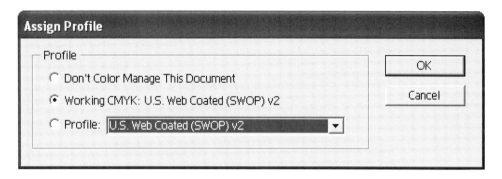

- **Don't Color Manage This Document**: This option removes the profile from a tagged document, and the document becomes untagged.

- **Working color mode**: With this option a file that was opened in a different color space is tagged with the current working space profile.

- **Profile**: Choose the profile from the drop-down menu to reassign a different profile to a tagged document.

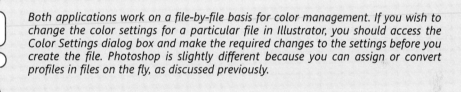

Both applications work on a file-by-file basis for color management. If you wish to change the color settings for a particular file in Illustrator, you should access the Color Settings dialog box and make the required changes to the settings before you create the file. Photoshop is slightly different because you can assign or convert profiles in files on the fly, as discussed previously.

The remainder of the options as discussed in the section on managing color in Photoshop are exactly the same as Illustrator, and thus it seems pointless to repeat them here. But what is important is how we can get these two applications to work together perfectly.

Saving custom Color Management Settings

Imagine for a moment that you have been given a complete list of how to set your color management settings for a specific workflow. To ensure that both applications are using the same settings, you have two options:

- You could set the options in Photoshop, and then open Illustrator and repeat all the new options that you set. This is both time-consuming and open to error.

- You could create a custom Color Setting and save it in a folder that would be accessed by both applications.

Returning to our previous discussion about rendering intents, assume for a moment that you wish to save a custom color setting, which retains all the default U.S. Prepress Defaults except you wish to change the rendering intent from Relative Colorimetric to Perceptual in both Illustrator and Photoshop.

1.   Display the Color Settings dialog box in Photoshop by choosing Edit > Color Settings (CMD/CTRL+SHIFT+K).

2.   Ensure that Rendering Intents display by checking the **Advanced Mode** option.

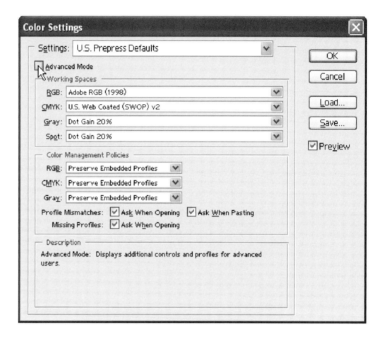

3.   Choose Perceptual from the drop-down menu that appears next to Intent in the Conversion Options area of the dialog box. Note that immediately as you make this change, the Color Settings name has changed to Custom.

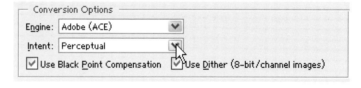

4.   Click the Save button and give the new CSF (Color Settings file) a descriptive name. In this example, I'll name mine FoED Default. Where the file is saved is the really important bit – as you want both applications to access it, consequently it must be saved in System Folder: Application Support: Adobe: Color: Settings folder on the Mac, and in Program Files/Common Files/Adobe/Color/Settings folder on the PC.

An additional option is to enter a full descriptive explanation in the dialog box that appears after you have named and saved the new CSF. Completing this information as fully as possible will remind you what this particular color setting was created to manage.

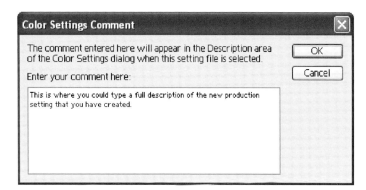

5. Switch to Illustrator and display the Color Settings dialog box You should notice from the drop-down Settings menu that the Color Setting created and saved in Photoshop, is now displayed as one of the options in the Settings drop-down menu. Choosing this option from within Illustrator will ensure that the same settings are used in both applications with a minimum of fuss, and reducing the chance of errors.

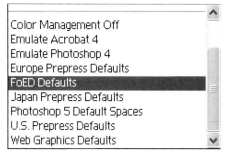

Furthermore, saving these custom CSF files and then distributing them to others involved in your workflow is a pretty neat way of ensuring some form of consistency in the production process. The important thing is to ensure that they are saved into the specified folders mentioned above – it just makes life so much easier.

It is a good idea to have backup in a folder outside of Adobe, perhaps on a CD in case you have a major computer trauma. That way, if you have a regular client with established, frequently requested items (base images, contours, brushes, styles, or colors) you can reload them easily.

To Color Manage or not, that is the question...

The preceding pages have covered a fair amount of detail concerning how to implement a Color Management System in your workflow and across applications, but using such a system does not necessarily mean that you will never be met by those horrid color surprises. The system is both powerful and complex and needs to be tested and tested again before you can be sure that you have chosen the correct options for your particular workflow. Having said that, it is worth the effort if you put all the pieces in place.

Soft proofing your colors

Now that you are more familiar with the concept of using a Color Management System to embed profiles and ensure a more consistent final printing result, the next question is 'How can you preview how images will print in both Illustrator and Photoshop?' Obviously having a strong, reliable CMS in place is a great advantage, but from that point onwards you can ask both applications to simulate different press conditions on screen with relative accuracy.

CMYK vs RGB: Viewing print simulations

You are no doubt familiar with the problem that what you see on screen is always displayed in RGB mode, yet what you print is more often than not in CMYK. Of course, there are exceptions as there are to most things, but the bottom line is that what you see on the screen is always going to look brighter and more saturated than the final print product, and this is because of the narrower CMYK printing gamut.

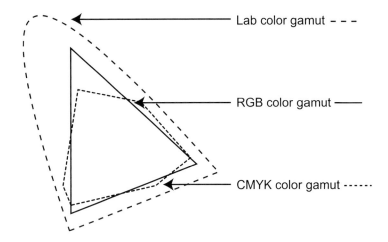

Thus the inherent problem is how to emulate on screen – in an RGB environment – how CYMK images will print. Both Illustrator and Photoshop provide support for just such the situation with the on-screen proofing options. Of course, as with all options with color printing, we cannot rely totally on the proofing preview, as this is dependent on the quality of the monitor, the reliability of the display and output profiles, and the lighting conditions in the studio. But rather than discounting it out-of-hand as a totally unreliable option, using soft-proofing will alert you to serious problems in the proposed production of your print.

Mac vs Windows: Viewing web simulations

However, soft proofing is not only useful for your print materials. Many of your materials will be repurposed for web pages and having the options to simulate how your image will look on another platform when viewed as a web image is also very useful.

Granted, it is even more difficult to accurately predict how your image will display when viewed on the web because you have no control over the viewer's environment. You may have carefully calibrated your on-screen display, removed any influencing factors such as colored lighting and yet your image appears washed out, too dark or with a color cast when viewed by someone else in their living room. It is not a good practice to completely disregard how your image might display because you have no absolute control over the final output, rather put in place the fundamentals ensuring that your image has a good chance of being viewed predictably.

Ignoring individual monitors' brightness, color, and contrast levels, there are two other factors that influence how your image will display on different machines and different operating systems:

- The capability of the video display adaptor on the host machine.

- Differing gammas (screen brightness) on the Mac and Window platforms.

In the earlier days of the web, monitors were not capable of displaying the wide range of colors available to them today. Consequently, of the 256 colors available, the overlap between Mac and PC platforms was limited to 216 colors – web safe colors – also known as hexadecimal colors. These colors, which are normally displayed in the following format #3366FF, allowed the designer a limited degree of predictability in how colors would display across platforms.

Recently, with the rapid advances in computer technology, monitors are capable of displaying so many more colors. Coupled with increasing sophistication in web page design, this has led to a major change in attitude concerning the use of color being restricted to the base 216 colors especially if components on monitors need to match corporate logo colors.

The second issue that needs to be considered is the differing gamma across platforms. The default gamma on a Mac screen is 1.8, whilst the gamma on a PC is 2.2. The result of this difference is that images designed to look good on the PC will look washed out on a Mac; and images designed to look good on the Mac will look dark on a PC.

Soft proofing options to gauge how your images will display on these differing platforms are also provided in the Proof Setup menu.

Displaying soft proofs in Photoshop

With color management in place and an understanding of your proposed output environment, it is possible to get a fairly accurate on screen simulation of how your image will print to various commercial and in-house output devices, and how it will display across platforms.

Choose View > Proof Setup to display the soft proofing options menu. Notice that in addition to the **Custom...** option, which we'll discuss in detail a little later on, you have the choice of a number of other soft-proofing options.

- **Working CMYK** will provide a preview using the current CMYK working space previously defined in the Color Settings dialog box.

- **Working Cyan Plate, Working Magenta Plate, Working Yellow Plate, Working Black Plate**, or **Working CMY Plates** will display an on screen simulation of the specified CMYK ink colors once again using the current CMYK working space. This option can be very useful if you are looking to see how the image should separate to different plates on the press.

- **Simulate Paper White** will preview the specific shade of white that will be exhibited by the print medium as specified by the embedded profile. If this option is not checked, the paper white is mapped to monitor white when creating the preview.

- Similarly, **Simulate Ink Black** previews the actual output black on the monitor as defined by the embedded profile. This is useful if you want to simulate press conditions which produce a lighter black ink such as newsprint.

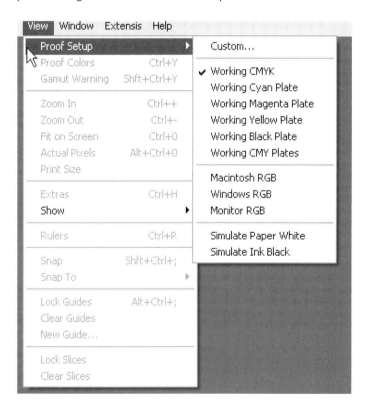

All the options mentioned above detail simulating press conditions, but there are the three monitor previews that are also important if you are designing for the web and print. These options are not available for LAB and CMYK documents.

- **Macintosh RGB** simulates the screen colors in an image using the standard Mac profiles as the proof profile color space. This is useful if you are designing for the web on a PC, and wish to preview how your image may appear on a Mac monitor.

- Similarly, if you are designing on a Mac, using the **Windows RGB** will provide an impression of how your image will display on the Windows platform, using the standard Windows monitor as the proof profile space to simulate.

- **Monitor RGB** simulates colors in an RGB document using the current monitor color space as the proof profile space.

Once you have selected a Proof Setup, choose View > Proof Colors to toggle the soft proof display. When soft proofing is on:

- A check mark appears next to the Proof Colors command.

- The name of the current proof profile appears next to the color mode in the document's title bar.

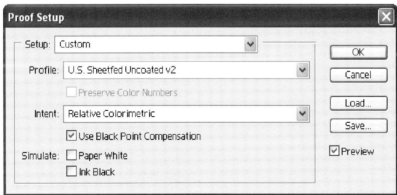

Creating a custom soft proof setup in Photoshop

In addition to soft proofing your image based on the color settings previously determined for the document, you could also create a custom setup enabling you to soft proof for specific output options differing from settings chosen in the Color Settings dialog box. The Custom soft proof dialog box is displayed by choosing View > Proof Setup > Custom..

- If you wish to use one of the presets as a starting point for your custom proofing setup, choose the option from the drop-down menu in the **Setup** field.

- The **Profile** pop-up menu lets you choose the profile for the output device that you want to simulate on-screen.

- When checked, the **Preserve Color Numbers** check box lets you see what would happen if you simply sent the file to the output device without converting colors from the document space to the proof profile space. This is useful for previewing how your image would preview on presses and stock that differ from the settings chosen in the Color Settings dialog box. It will display any color shifts that may occur when the document's color values are interpreted using the proof profile instead of the document profile. When unchecked, the preview will simulate how the document will display if the colors are converted from the document space to their nearest equivalents in the proof profile space.

- The **Intent** pop-up menu lets you control the conversion from the source space to the output space. Once again, making the decision between a Perceptual or Relative Colorimetric render intent could be previewed here.

- The **Simulate** check boxes let you control the conversion from the output space to the monitor. The default for both controls is off, which means that Photoshop maps the paper white in the output space to your monitor's white, and the output black to your monitor's black.

  - Checking the **Paper White** box simulates both the paper white and the ink black on your monitor, which with a good monitor profile will give you an accurate preview of the image.

  - Checking the **Ink Black** box makes Photoshop display the actual output black on your monitor. It's mostly useful for output processes that produce a relatively light black, such as newsprint, or fine-art inkjet on watercolor.

- Choose **Preview** to display a live preview of the proof settings in the document while the Proof Setup dialog box is open.

Custom proof setups can be saved as one of the presets that appear in the drop-down menu if the preset is saved in one of the following folders dependent on your operating system and platform:

- Mac OS 9.x: System Folder/Application Support/Adobe/ Color/Proofing folder

- Mac OS X: Library/Application Support/Adobe/Color/ Proofing folder

- Windows: Program Files/Common Files/Adobe/Color/Proofing folder

If you want the custom proof setup to be the default proof setup for documents, close all document windows before choosing the View > Proof Setup > Custom *command.*

Displaying soft proofs in Illustrator

Once again, it's all very well being able to achieve something in Photoshop, but what about Illustrator? Does it offer the same support for soft proofing our images and graphics? Will images created and soft proofed in Photoshop display consistently when placed in an Illustrator document? The answer is yes, once again illustrating very clearly how the two applications can be used in tandem to create reliable color output, although as with the Color Management settings there are some differences.

As with Photoshop, the Proof Setup options are displayed by choosing View > Proof Setup.

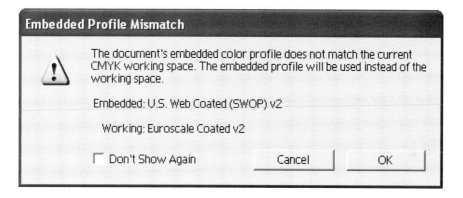

At first glance you should notice that the menu is rather more limited than the options you saw in Photoshop – there is no support for displaying individual or combined CMYK plates. If you wish to preview how the image will print on a specific output device, you must choose the **Custom...** option. You may also notice that the RGB options are grayed out, this is dependent on the **Document Color Mode** selected on the File menu. If your file is in CMYK, the RGB options will not be available to you. This is a little disconcerting if you are designing for print, but wish to preview how the image will display on the web, and means that you will either have to switch color modes or create a duplicate file in another color mode.

As with Photoshop, you choose Macintosh RGB or Windows RGB to simulate how the image will display on the platform using a standard monitor profile. Choose Monitor RGB to soft proof colors using your current monitor color space as the proof profile space.

Choose View > Proof Colors to switch the soft proof display on and off. When soft proofing is on:

- A check mark appears next to the Proof Colors command.

- The name of the current proof profile appears next to the color mode in the document's title bar.

Creating a custom soft proof setup in Illustrator

In order to preview your graphic for a specific output device, you'll need to specify a custom soft proofing setup.

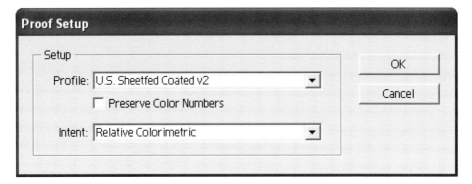

Once again you'll notice that the options in the Proof Setup dialog box are more limited than those available in Photoshop, however the options that are included operate in exactly the same way as they do in Photoshop.

If you have chosen Emulate Adobe Illustrator 6.0 setting in the Color Settings dialog box, the soft proofing commands are not available.

Conclusion

Like any piece of software we can fine tune the performance of Photoshop and Illustrator by selecting the most appropriate settings for our needs. Throughout this chapter we have looked at the best ways to prepare the two applications to work efficiently with the other, focusing on establishing a successful color management scheme across the two applications to ensure a satisfying output for both web and print based projects.

In the next chapter we will round off the theoretical part of the book by looking at the essential functions of both Photoshop and Illustrator, to investigate their shared features and inherent distinctions.

3 The Building Blocks

When we compare Photoshop and Illustrator, there are a number of tools and functions that are similar. For example, both applications use layers, offer masking options, use type, and allow for custom brushes and styles. With all these similarities, it can be a challenge to decide which program to use. Actually the more important question really is which program should you start with. When you start a project in Photoshop you must choose both the physical size and the resolution of the document. This decision is crucial since you are, in effect, determining the ceiling – a quality setting you can't easily increase later. So, if we create a new document (or scan an image) that is 4 x 5 inches at 140 ppi, we cannot simply increase the resolution later if we realize we need 300 ppi. Starting an image in Illustrator on the other hand, offers much more flexibility since by nature, vector images are more scalable. So, two factors to use when determining which program to start with are: what is the final output of the artwork and is there a chance of the size and/or resolution changing.

You may well end up in the other program, but where you start has a major influence on what you can or cannot do later. If you start in Photoshop – a raster image – and move into Illustrator later, the graphic does not become vectorized, but remains a raster graphic in a vector program. This means we still face limitations in how much we can scale the image. If we start a design in Illustrator and then bring that into Photoshop, the artwork will be rasterized – converted to pixel-based information – and will be limited just as if we started in Photoshop. However, if we have kept the vector original and imported a copy into Photoshop, we'll at least have a vector version to go back to that can be scaled and edited.

Here's my personal philosophy: if there's even the remotest possibility of a design having to be output at a larger size somewhere down the road (or changing shape or color) then I'll start in Illustrator so I can use vectors. If I need to work with the design in Photoshop (and more often than not, the need is there) then I keep my original vector art and bring a copy into Photoshop. The best of both worlds I suppose.

This is not to suggest that we would always be able – or should – start in Illustrator. If we start with a scan or a digital image, then of course, we'll begin in Photoshop. Or, if you know you need to create buttons for a web site, then the possibility of scaling the graphics to a larger size is pretty much slim to none, so again, Photoshop is the tool of choice.

Also, what about type? Is there any text in your artwork, or is there lots of type? This could influence your decision too. Although both programs offer the ability to resize type, without loss of quality, Illustrator does handle type better.

Layers

Photoshop layers

By nature, working on scanned images is very much like painting – rather than working with separate objects, we work with, in effect, paint on a canvas. Rather than being able to pick something up and move it – as we could in Illustrator – we have to cover things up as if we were painting. For example, if the position of a hot air balloon is not in the right place, you can't just move it. Instead, you would have to select the balloon using one of the selection tools, copy it to a new layer, move that layer, and then cover up the original balloon with some of the sky.

Unless you have combined, or merged, the layers in the original image, each layer remains independent of the others and hence gives the freedom of making any changes. You can take advantage of techniques such as blending modes, layer sets, layer masks, and clipping groups to provide the utmost in flexibility. I guess you could say, if you're afraid of commitment, use layers!

Structuring a document

If you plan from the ground up to create a flexible document, it can be relatively easy to end up with a layered document, full of components that can be combined into a composite image. Ideally, use methods that are non-destructive – create the illusion of the result you want rather than altering the pixels themselves. For example, to alter a photographic image, duplicate the Background layer and work on the copy. That way, you have a back-up version just in case you change your mind (or someone else changes your mind for you). Rather than deleting pixels from a layer, use a mask to hide them – this allows you to show them again should something change.

Two essential keyboard shortcuts when working with layers are CMD/CTRL+J (New Layer via Copy) and CMD/CTRL+SHIFT+J (New Layer via Cut). If you have nothing selected, the entire layer is duplicated, whereas if you have a selection, only the selected pixels are duplicated onto a new layer. So, to quickly duplicate the Background layer to work on a copy, press CMD/CTRL+J

Let's look at a simple example of the power of this shortcut. I opened an image and duplicated (CMD/CTRL+J) the Background layer. I then double-clicked on the layer name to change the name to train copy (another important aspect of layer structure is creating a naming system to help keep track of your layers). I selected just the man and pressed CMD/CTRL+J again to copy that selection onto a new layer. The resulting image doesn't look any different from the original, but take a look at the Layers palette: I have the original Background layer (my back-up layer), the copied background I can work on, and the man on a separate layer, ready to work with.

Now many design possibilities exist with the structure I've created. I could apply a filter such as a Motion Blur to the copied background.

Or, I could use Levels to lighten the man only layer with the blurred background visible.

(I could also hide the blurred layer so the lightened man showed on the original image, I haven't shown this here, but you get the idea.)

Here I've hidden the other two layers to work with just the man only layer.

Also, I always have the option of going back to the original image by hiding (or deleting) the additional layers that I created.

In contrast, the other way I could have worked with this same image was to select the man, inverse the selection (CMD/CTRL+SHIFT+I), and apply the Motion Blur. Similar end result to that shown above with one vital exception: after saving and closing this document, I have absolutely no option to change my mind.

One layer, no options!

As we're talking about structure, it's worth noting that functions, such as Layer Masks, add a great deal of flexibility to our layer structure (we'll look at Layer Masks in more detail a little later). In this example, I made a feathered selection around the large clock and dragged and dropped it into the forest image. Note that, although a new layer was created, I'm pretty limited in my ability to change anything.

If, for example, someone asked me to show more of all three clocks, I'd have to start again with the original image and a new selection, since I only brought over a small portion of the pixels.

In contrast, this time I selected and dragged over more than I needed and added a Layer Mask to hide portions of the layer.

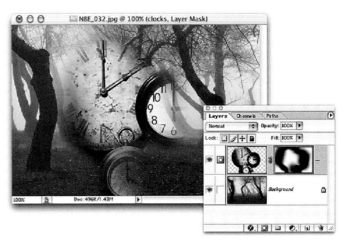

If I need to change the appearance of the layer, I simply work with the Layer Mask to hide or show portions of the layer.

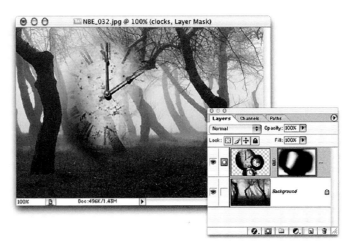

As you create layers, think of both the end result you're aiming for, and ways to allow yourself opportunities for change, experimentation, and variations. Here's a simple structure for a button for a web site that offers a lot of possibilities. The document was built using a shape layer, several layers on a clipping group, a layer mask, an adjustment layer, and type layers.

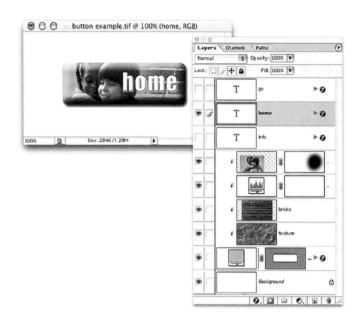

Now, by showing and hiding different layer combinations, we can create many different looks for our buttons – find the look you like and Save for Web (keeping the multi-layered Photoshop original). Here are two more examples where different layers were shown and the shape of the button was altered:

You can build on the inherent flexibility of layers to create pieces that come together to make finished designs (by saving a flattened copy of your layered original).

Layer blending modes

Another technique to add many options to a layered document is through the use of **Blending Modes**. These modes, with names like Multiply, Overlay, Soft Light, and Difference, change the way that layers interact with each other, by comparing the pixels on each layer. By default, when a new layer is created, its mode is Normal – the pixels on the layer have no interaction with the layers below. Change the blending mode from

Normal to some other choice, and suddenly the rules change: the pixels on the layer will be compared (blended) with the layers below, based on a form of mathemetics, but I wouldn't worry too much about how they work, just understand which modes work best in which situations.

Let's look at using Opacity versus blending modes. I dragged one image on top of another, which created a new layer with the mode Normal.

Compare the results between lowering the Opacity to 70%:

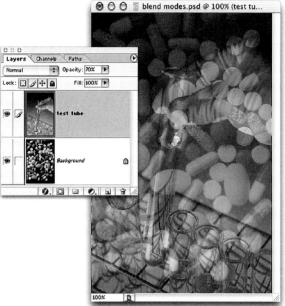

...changing the mode to Lighten...

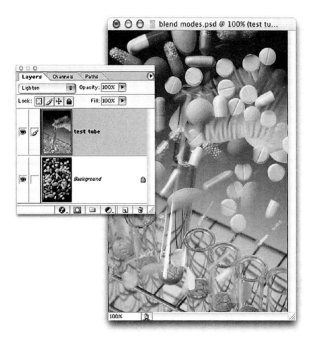

...and finally changing the mode to Luminosity:

Now I doubt that anyone has ever done scientific research into use of blending modes, but if they had, I'd suggest that the most commonly used blending modes would include: Multiply; Screen; Overlay; Soft; Light; Hard; Light; Darken; Lighten; and Color.

Moveable filters

As amazing as filters can be, some can also be somewhat limited. The Lens Flare filter for example, adds a great effect, but one that is in a fixed position. Here's how to change that.

1. Open the Palm Tree image found in the Samples folder that is installed with Photoshop.

2. Add a new layer and fill with black. For added flexibility move the layer to the side and fill again, then repeat this operation. This will create a black layer that is larger than the photo itself.

3. On the black layer, run the Lens Flare filter (Filter > Render > Lens Flare). At first, the black layer will continue to cover up the Background layer.

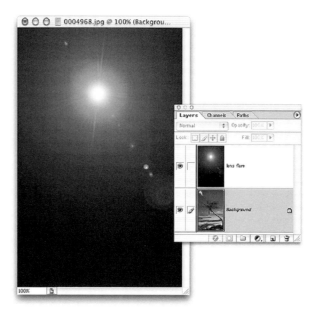

4. Change the blending mode to Lighten, and the black will all but disappear, leaving the Lens Flare still visible.

5. Use the Move tool (V) to move the Lens Flare layer and experiment with various positions.

By the way, Multiply mode would have a very similar effect, except it would enhance the shaded areas covered by sections of the lens flare, while other modes would (of course) offer other possibilities.

Layer clipping groups

Don't let the name of the function 'Layer Clipping Group', or the command – Group with Previous (CMD/CTRL+G) – fool you. This grouping function is unlike any other application. Rather than grouping objects together so they act as one object, Group with Previous creates a special combination of layers, where the pixels on one layer are clipped by the layer immediately below. We can use this in many different ways, sometimes offering a level of flexibility that would be hard to create otherwise.

The procedure is quite simple (but incredibly powerful).

1. Create a new document and type in some text.

2. Then, open a photo and drag and drop it onto the original document. This is one of those techniques where you'll know you're doing it correctly if it looks wrong at this point! Avoid the temptation to change the order of the layers – your photo layer should cover up the type layer.

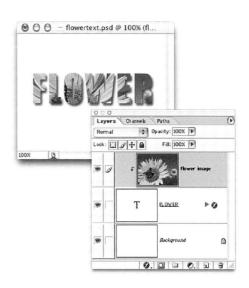

3. With the image layer active, go to Layer > Group with Previous (CMD/CTRL+G). The pixels on the bottom layer (the text) will clip the image layer so that the image is only visible inside the type.

4. The two layers remain completely separate and editable – use the Move tool (V) to move the image, or the Type tool (T) to edit the text. Here a drop shadow was added to the type layer.

It is also possible to add multiple layers to the clipping group. Here a second image layer was added to the document and added to the clipping group:

Clipping groups can also provide flexible solutions to a potential problem such as applying filters to text. If you attempt to apply a filter to a type layer, you'll get a dialog box prompting you to Rasterize the type?

Click Cancel! Avoid this step if you can – rasterized type cannot be edited as it is turned into pixels.

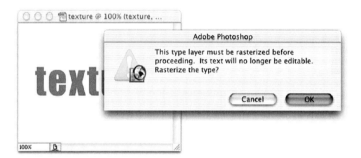

Here's a way around rasterizing the type layer. Add a new layer above the type layer and fill it with a color. Apply a filter such as Texturizer (Filter > Texture > Texturizer) to the solid color layer, and then press CMD/CTRL+G to create the clipping group. The result? The text looks like it has a texture in it, but the text didn't have to be rasterized.

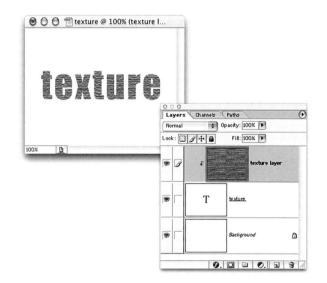

You can still edit the text and edit the texture layer.

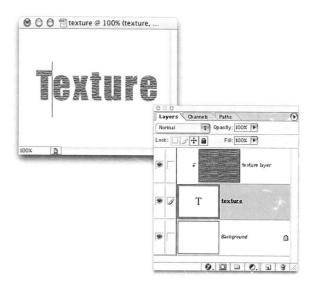

This is also very useful when creating web buttons, particularly when you want a number of options. Simply create a layer with the button shape, position various layers above that shape layer (photos, textures, solid colors...) and then create a clipping group. You can hide layers to create various buttons within the same document.

Complex layer combinations

Without too much effort, it's quite possible to experiment with these Photoshop layer functions and come up with some pretty complex documents. This document – a result of about 20 minutes of creative playing – has a structure to it that allows a lot of latitude to experiment later. Here's the original version with 14 layers and various layer masks, clipping groups, and blending modes:

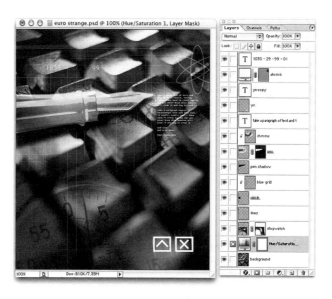

Here's the same document after making only a few minor changes: altering the Hue/Saturation Adjustment layer, adding a Layer Effect, rotating a layer, and changing a couple of blending modes. The end result is a similar document with some key visual differences. Once again this is possible by creating a complex document with a flexible structure (Also note the attempt to give my layers logical names so I didn't end up with many un-named layers).

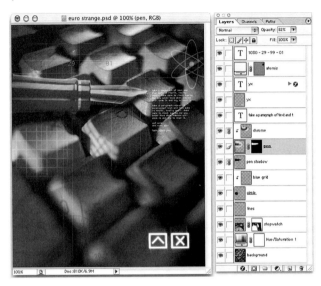

Illustrator layers

Layers are a vital part of Photoshop, however, in Illustrator they are useful but are by no means necessary. In fact, you may create many pieces of artwork in Illustrator before ever using layers. So when are layers used in Illustrator? Well, layers can be a very effective tool to organize a complex piece of artwork, since you can help keep track of objects by putting them on named layers, similar to layer sets in Photoshop. Plus you can show and hide layers to generate different looks. Illustrator offers a unique feature (as compared to Photoshop) since you can work with sub-layers in addition to the overall layers.

Let's look at a basic example. Here I created a simple 'no smoking' sign using seven objects stacked on top of each other. All objects are on the same layer, so it's the order of the objects on that layer that determines the look of the artwork.

I drew the big red circle, then the smaller white circle, the cigarette, the filter, the glowing end, the smoke, and put the slash on top. If I had not created the objects in this specific order, I would have had to re-arrange objects using the Arrange commands: Bring Forward, Bring to Front, Send Backward, Send to Back.

If I click on the triangle beside Layer 1 to expand the layer display, I can see all seven objects listed (shown as Paths).

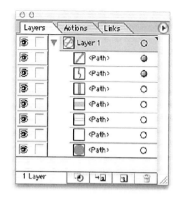

That way I could hide these objects individually to work with or edit objects. Or, if objects are in the wrong order, I can drag the sub-layer up or down in the Layers palette to change the order – the end result is the same as the Arrange commands. In order to get a little more control, I want to add a separate layer to put all the objects that make up the cigarette. From the Layers palette pop up menu I created a new layer and called it cigarette. Then, one at a time, I selected each object for the cigarette and moved them onto the new layer. (This is done by selecting the object, then in the Layers palette, moving the small square beside the path, and dragging that square onto the new layer).

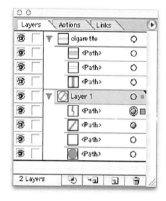

We now have a slight problem though. By creating this new layer on top of the original layer (which we need to do so the cigarette appears above the circles), the slash is in the wrong position.

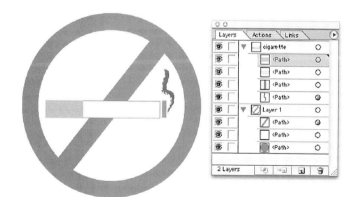

Unfortunately, the Arrange > Bring to Front command won't help, since it will only move an object to the front of its layer, not the entire document. In order for the slash to appear on the very top, we must move it onto the cigarette layer and make sure it's on the very top of that layer, or create another layer with just the slash on it above the cigarette layer.

That is one of the potential drawbacks to using layers: the Arrange commands do not work the way you are used to.

Layer blending modes

Much like Photoshop, Illustrator also has blending modes – although you do not have to be working with layers for these modes to work. Simply select an object and then in the Opacity palette pick the blending mode.

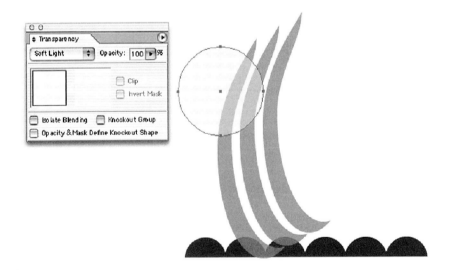

The modes work in the same way as the Photoshop blending modes (they're the same functions) with one very important difference. By nature, vector objects do not really allow transparency and blending modes, so, in essence, Illustrator is faking it. The implication for us comes when it's time to print. This simulated transparency could possibly cause printing problems.

Does that mean we shouldn't use these effects? Not necessarily, but it does need to be considered. I would check with my service bureau or print shop to get their advice. In addition, I would take advantage of an Illustrator command that lets me deal with issues of transparency and prepare the file for printing. This is the Object > Flatten Transparency command and works with whatever objects you've selected. Here I've selected a number of objects, some of which contain transparency or blending modes (both potential printing issues). In order to see the effects of the Flatten Transparency command, I can take advantage of the Preview function (be prepared, with complex artwork, even the preview could take a while).

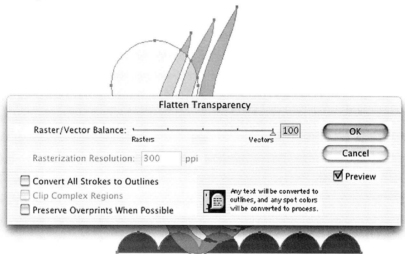

As long as nothing jumps out as looking very different, or unexpected, I can click OK. This will convert my artwork into a series of objects that will simulate the transparent and blended areas. In this close up, the artwork does not appear any differently than in the original.

Here, I've pulled the artwork apart to show that separate objects were created to simulate the transparency.

This is really the key: the artwork is basically destroyed to simulate transparency for printing. So, it is most strongly recommended to save one original with transparency, and then make a copy before Flattening Transparency.

> *This also applies to Effects such as Drop Shadow, Blur, Glow, etc. (any Effect that has a soft, Photoshop look to it). It could also apply to some Styles, since they might contain some of these Effects.*

Layer Clipping Masks

Illustrator has a layer function to create Clipping Masks. A Clipping Mask is an object or group of objects whose shape masks artwork below it so that only artwork within the shape is visible. These work in a similar manner to Photoshop's layer clipping groups – once again with some important differences. There are some points to be kept in mind when using Clipping Masks:

- A Clipping Mask and the objects to be masked must be in the same layer or group in the Layers palette.

- The Clipping Mask is always at the top of the clipping set.

- Objects in the Clipping path are indicated with a dotted line in the Layers palette.

- A top-level layer cannot be a Clipping Mask.

Now, let's try a basic example of using Clipping Masks:

1. Create a series of objects all on the same layer.

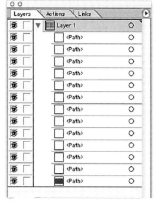 

2. On the very top of the layer, draw the object that will act as the mask.

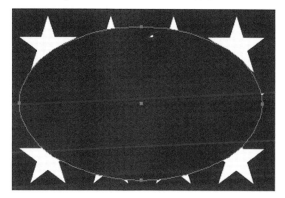

3. From the Layers palette pop up menu, choose **Make Clipping Mask**. All objects will then be masked by this top object.

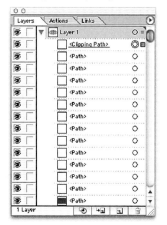 

This function has some great advantages, and at least one potential drawback. When you create a Clipping Mask, all objects affected by the mask are still completely editable – you do not need to release the mask to be able to work with the individual objects.

This has many possible uses – any time you want objects to appear inside another object. For example, a paragraph of text on a layer with one large letter converted to outlines and acting as a Clipping Mask:

... or a series of lines masked inside a star shape:

You can also use the Object > Make Clipping Mask, which we'll discuss in more detail later. One of the potential drawbacks to using a layer Clipping Mask is the way it affects the layer it is on. Once you've created a Clipping Mask, the mask will affect any object you add to that layer even if you move the object above the mask in the Layers palette. The only way to get this object to show is to move it to a different layer. This aside, layer Clipping Masks are indeed a powerful technique, well worth exploring.

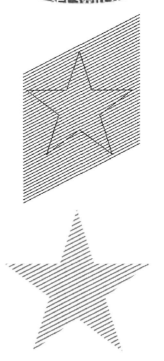

Masks

You want the ultimate in flexibility? Use masks! The masking functions in Photoshop and Illustrator really are about the most flexible techniques you can use for one simple reason: masking hides objects rather than deleting them. Masks let you isolate and protect areas of an image while editing the complete image.

There are a couple of minor drawbacks that we need to be aware of, but these are greatly outweighed by the advantages of masks. One of the drawbacks (particularly in Photoshop) is an increase in file size. This of course, is not as big a problem today as it was when a 40MB hard disk was considered huge. Still, it is something to be aware of. Perhaps the greater issue is that masks can add to the complexity of a document – masks add one more thing to worry about as you are working with the document.

Photoshop Layer Masks

Any time you delete pixels, not only are you throwing away information, you are also giving away a chance to change your mind. Here's a simple example that clearly shows the advantage of a Layer Mask. First, the wrong way…

A selection has been made and feathering added. Notice how only a portion of the image is selected.

That selection was dragged and dropped onto a second image, which creates a new layer.

There is nothing really wrong with this technique on the surface, unless you decide (or someone asks you) to show more of the original image. The only way to see more of the image would be to throw away the layer, go back to the original image, make a larger selection, and drag and drop again. This of course assumes that you still have the original image!

Now, we'll use Layer Masks to get the same end result – a portion of the original image on the new background – but with a much greater degree of flexibility. Rather than selecting a portion of the image, just drag and drop the entire image onto the second document. Then, click on the Add layer mask button. Now, anywhere you want to hide pixels, paint with black (with the Brush, or select and fill an area with black).

The result (visually) is the same as the first method, but with one important difference: now if you want to reveal more of the layer, simply paint with white. That's the essential rule of masking you need to remember: Black = mask (hide), white = show (we'll add gray into the equation shortly).

I mentioned previously the added complexity of Layer Masks – here's what I mean. When you have a document with lots of layers, you've got to ensure that you click on the correct layer before you start working on it. With the addition of Layer Masks, now you've got to worry about not only choosing the right layer, but also choosing between the layer itself and its mask. Make a poor choice and you'll get yourself into hot water: if you think you're painting on the mask but you see black paint on your layer, then you clicked on the wrong layer thumbnail. Here's the visual clue: when you're working on the layer, you'll see the paintbrush icon in the Layers palette:

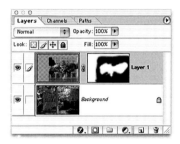

... when you're working on the Layer mask, you'll see this icon:

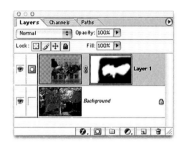

We're going to quickly look at an example of what I would consider a classic technique – a very easy yet effective use of Layer Masks.

Start with an image and press CMD/CTRL+J to duplicate the Background layer. Then, make some obvious change to the copied layer (apply a filter, desaturate, lighten...) – here I applied a Motion Blur filter.

Add a Layer Mask and paint with black to hide the altered layer so the original shows – in this case I've hidden the blurry layer to let the sharp original show though.

This simple technique opens up a world of possibilities.

One last Layer Mask technique to talk about, that is created slightly differently, but is also very powerful. The goal is to take a photo of a person and make it look like they are standing slightly behind someone in another image. I could drag and drop the second person and then spend a lot of time painting with black, but it might be easier to use a command called **Paste Into**. Here's how it works:

1.	Open an image with a person in it (I used SFB02 from the Stock Photography 2 folder that is supplied with Illustrator 10).

2.	Select the person using the selection tools and then Copy (CMD/CTRL+C).

3. Open another image (image SFB07) and select the area into which you want to paste, making sure to carefully select along the edge of the other person. I would suggest using the Magnetic Lasso tool, which is very useful on this kind of extraction (or the Extract Tool).

4. From the Edit menu, choose Paste Into (CMD/CTRL+SHIFT+V).

A Layer Mask is automatically created.

5. If necessary, move/transform the new layer (here I flipped, scaled, and rotated the layer).

When you add a Layer Mask, the layer and its mask are linked together by default. That is, if you move the layer, the mask moves with it. Most of the time (as in our real estate example), this makes sense – if you move the layer you want the mask to continue to affect the layer. When you create a mask through the Paste Into command, the mask is not linked with the layer, allowing you to move the layer independently of the mask. In these cases this also makes sense – move the person you've pasted while the mask stays put to continue to create the illusion you want. You can always change the setting by clicking on the chain symbol to unlink the mask (or vice versa).

Using Layer Masks with gray

Now, we've covered the use of black and white on a mask, but what about gray? In the world of masks, gray provides a very interesting function. While black hides pixels and white shows pixels, gray is somewhere in the middle. So, if you want portions of a layer to be somewhat transparent, paint with gray on the Layer Mask. Here's the difference between changing the layer Opacity versus paint with gray on the Layer Mask.

In this first image, the Opacity of the layer has been lowered – an interesting effect, but you can see through the entire layer.

What if we want only a portion of the layer to be transparent?

Now the Opacity has been put back up to 100%, a Layer Mask added, and painted with different percentages of black (gray) to selectively change the opacity.

In this final example, a radial gradient was painted on the mask, creating gradual shades of gray and a gradual fade.

> You can make working with Layer Masks even better with a few key shortcuts: press X to switch between black and white. Press 1 – 9 to change the Opacity of the Brush tool (and therefore the shade of gray). Make the brush size bigger by pressing [, and smaller by pressing].

Of all Photoshop functions, Layer Masks rank right up there with the most powerful and flexible functions available. Given the choice between using Layer Masks or not – well there really isn't a choice, is there?

Illustrator Opacity Masks

This is a somewhat complex technique, but one that opens up possibilities that were previously impossible in vector software. An Opacity Mask will temporarily hide portions of vector objects – including partial opacity – using the mask's luminosity. What makes this a complex technique is the potentially confusing visual aspect of work with these masks. Here's how it works (and an example of the possible confusion).

1. Create a filled object and show the Transparency palette.

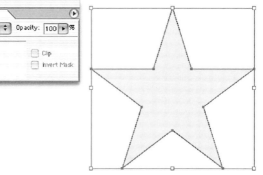

2. From the pop up menu choose Make Opacity Mask – the fill will disappear.

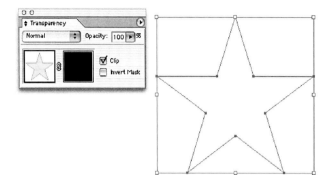

3. Click on the mask thumbnail in the Transparency palette – the object will disappear (in this example I switched to Outline view – CMD/CTRL+Y – to help see what's happening).

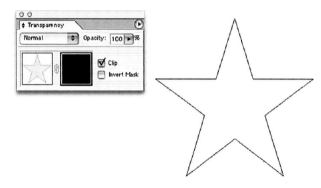

4. Draw a rectangle slightly larger than the object and change the fill to a black and white gradient. Back in Preview, the object gradually fades out.

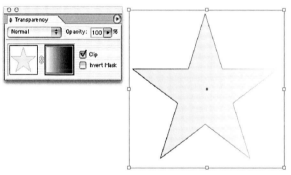

Here I changed the gradient in the masking object to a Radial gradient.

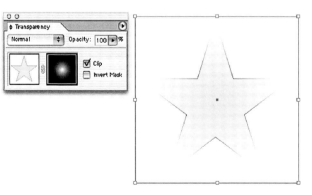

5. To remove the effect, choose Release Opacity Mask. Both objects will be visible – delete the gradient shape to end up back where you started.

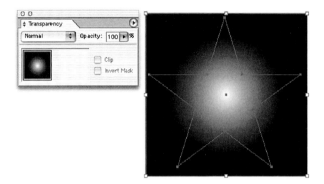

The possible confusion with this technique comes from the interaction with the Transparency palette and the difference between Illustrator and Photoshop masks. Make sure you click on the mask thumbnail to work on the mask, or the object thumbnail to edit the object itself. (Seems pretty obvious, but it can be easy to overlook this step and get very frustrated with Opacity Masks).

In Photoshop, you add a Layer Mask and paint directly on the mask with shades of gray. In Illustrator, you add an Opacity Mask and then create an object on the mask – the object is filled with shades of gray. The similarity between using masks in both programs is very clear – they're both incredible, everyday practical techniques.

Illustrator Clipping masks

Earlier we looked at Layer Clipping Groups when working with layers in Illustrator. Let's see how that method compares with a Clipping Mask. On the surface, the net result is very much the same – hiding a portion of one or more shapes with a masking shape. The key differences are as follows:

- You do not need to use layers (in fact, better to not use layers for this function).

- The objects must be selected and the clipping object must be on top (and selected).

- The objects are automatically grouped for moving (objects within a Layer Clipping Group remain ungrouped).

- The clipping mask only affects the selected objects (unlike a Layer Clipping Group that affects any object that's added to the layer).

Clipping masks are based on the shape of the top object, whereas an Opacity Mask is based both on the shape of the masking object, and the shade of gray of the fill of the object.

The process is very simple.

1. Create a series of objects to be masked and draw the masking object on top (don't worry about the fill or stroke – it will disappear when you make it into the mask).

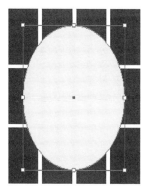

2. Select all of the objects.

3. From the Object menu, choose Clipping Mask > Make (CMD/CTRL+7).

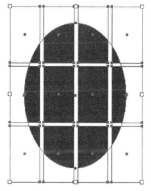

Here's the result once all the objects are deselected:

To move the group of objects that's created by this function, use the Selection tool (V) and click and drag. To edit the position, shape, or color of the any of the objects, use the Direct Selection tool (A). To remove the effects of the Clipping Mask, select the group with the Selection tool and choose Object > Clipping Mask > Release.

The power of vectors

Vectors and Photoshop

Up until the release of Photoshop 6, the discussion of using vectors in Photoshop was pretty short and sweet – you can't! Now vectors play an important role in Photoshop – with some important restrictions. Before we go too far in discussing vectors, we need to address a very important issue: getting the vectors to **output** as vectors. One of the most important advantages of vectors is their high quality (sharp) edges and their scalability. The ability to work with vector objects within a pixel-based program is very useful, however, it means a lot less if these objects do not output as vectors. In order to preserve vectors you must save your document in either Photoshop format (PSD) or as a PDF file. As soon as you save in any other format, the vector objects are rasterized to the resolution of the document. The challenge of course is in finding other applications that can work with (import) either PSD or PDF files. (It should be no surprise that the Adobe software collection will be your best choice!)

It also important to note that even if you cannot save in either vector format, there are still advantages to using vectors within Photoshop. Assuming that you will work on your artwork in Photoshop and then Save As a raster format – and you definitely should – you'll still have more control and options in Photoshop by using vectors.

The artwork in the following images looks the same but actually the first one was created using raster graphics (even the text was rasterized):

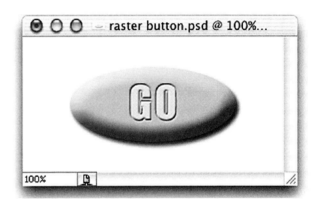

... and this image was created using vector shapes:

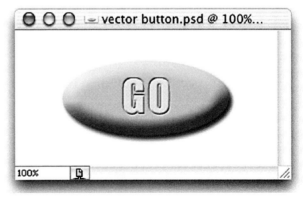

At first there is no apparent difference (at the original size of each graphic). Compare the difference when we use the Image Size command (Image > Image Size) to increase the resolution from 72 to 300 ppi.

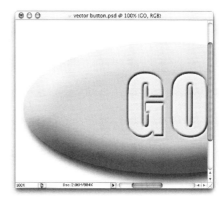

The raster image has to invent pixels to increase the resolution, resulting in blurry edges and soft focus quality. In contrast, the version that uses a shape layer and vector type is actually scaled upwards, with no loss in quality. Needless to say, the option to increase the resolution after the fact can be a real advantage, and should not even be considered unless the document contains only vector objects.

Layer Effects, although not vector based, are also scaleable. That's why, in this comparison, the beveled edge and drop shadow looked quite good even in the scaled up raster version.

Vector tools in Photoshop

There are three sets of tools that create vector-based objects: Type, Pen, and Shapes. We'll look at the Type and Shape tools in more detail later in this chapter, for now we'll focus on key settings. The Pen tool and the Shape tools can create three different end results, depending on the choice you make in the Options Bar: Shape Layers, Path, or Fill Pixels.

- **Shape Layers**: A layer is automatically created and filled with the current Foreground color, and the vector shape you've drawn masks the layer.

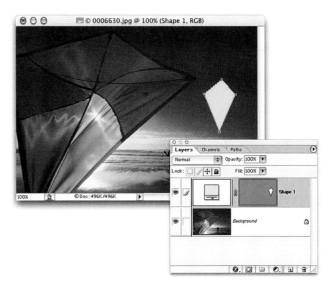

The vector shape can be edited with the Direct Selection tool and Pen tools (Add Anchor Point tool, Delete Anchor Point tool, Convert Point tool), as shown here:

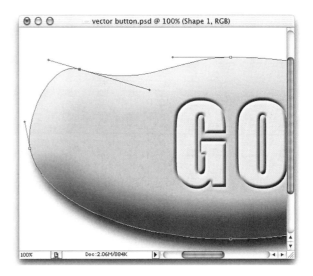

It is possible to select the shape with the Direct Selection tool, add an anchor point, and then alter the path of the shape. (Note how the Layer Effects are automatically updated.)

- **Path**: A Work Path is created in the Paths palette. Although the path is a form of vector, it does not output, unless you use it as a Clipping Path. Otherwise, the path is used to help make selections, or you can stroke or fill a path – but as raster art, not vector.

- **Fill Pixels**: Using this tool will create a raster object that is filled with the current Foreground color. A new layer is not automatically created (you have to create a new layer first if you want this paint on a new layer).

Although there are separate tools to Add Anchor Points, Delete Anchor Points, and Convert Points, you can also do all of these functions with one tool: the Pen tool. On a selected path, add an anchor point by positioning the Pen tool on the path until a plus sign appears beside the Pen tool, and then click to add an anchor point. To delete an existing anchor point, position the Pen tool over the anchor point until a minus sign appears, then click to delete the point. The Convert Point tool changes a curved anchor point to a straight point by clicking on the anchor point – to convert a straight point to a curved point, click and hold on the anchor point and drag out to create a curve. (Use the Pen tool with Opt/Alt held down to achieve the same result as the Convert Point tool).

Vectors and Illustrator

Illustrator is, by nature, a vector program – in fact there are only a few Illustrator functions that aren't vector-based. If you stick with only the vector functions you will end up with an extremely flexible, scaleable document. Rather than discuss all the vector tools, it may be of more benefit to take a look at the raster side of Illustrator. The following Illustrator techniques create raster objects:

- Effect > Stylize > Drop Shadow

- Effect > Stylize > Feather

- Effect > Stylize > Inner Glow

- Effect > Stylize > Outer Glow

- Effect > Blur > Gaussian Blur

- Effect > Blur > Radial Blur

- Effect > Pixelate effects

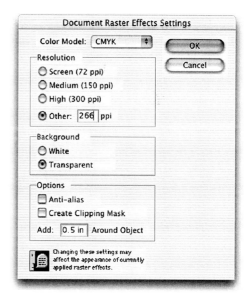

Use any of these effects and you will add a raster effect to the vector object – this means you are adding a restriction as to how much the artwork can be scaled, and potentially how it can be printed. Speaking of printing, when a raster effect is added, the quality of the raster effect is based on a setting under the Effect menu called Document Raster Effect Settings.

By default, this dialog box assumes all raster effects will be at screen quality – needless to say, this is not an appropriate setting for print. If you are preparing artwork for print, you should check and/or change the settings in this dialog box before adding any raster effects.

Channels

Every Photoshop document is made up of channels, which are used to store an image's color information – 1, 3, or 4 channels depending on the mode, as shown in the following images:

- Bitmap, Grayscale, Duotone, Indexed Color: 1 channel

- RGB Color, Lab Color: 3 channels

- CMYK Color: 4 channels

This channel information can be used for a number of purposes: editing the color information in a document, applying filters, or as a selection technique. The display of individual channels is based on a setting in Preferences > Display & Cursors: Color Channels in Color. If you check this box, the individual channels display in their color rather than in gray (the default setting). This of course is your choice, but I think most people ultimately choose to view channels as gray since Alpha Channels display in gray.

To be honest, most Photoshop users may not work with channels on a regular basis, rather, they'll make use of them when the need arises. For example, if you're working on a CMYK document and try to apply some filters (such as Lighting Effects), they simply don't work in that mode. Although you could change the mode to RGB, apply the filter, and change back to CMYK mode, this is unnecessary (and could cause color issues due to the differences between RGB and CMYK). Instead, use the individual channels to apply the filter. In the Channels palette, click on the Cyan channel to activate it alone, and then apply the filter. Then activate the Magenta channel and press CMD/CTRL+F to re-apply the last filter with the same settings. Repeat this for each channel. The net effect is the same as if you were able to apply the filter to the overall CMYK document.

> To speed things up, you could press CMD/CTRL and 1, 2, 3, 4 to activate the Cyan, Magenta, Yellow, and Black channels. It's also very important to note that this technique does not work as well with filters such as Render Clouds, since each time you run that filter you get a different, randomly generated result.

It is also possible to use individual color channels to adjust the overall color of the document. By looking at each color channel, sometimes it can help clarify the areas of a document that need to be addressed. For example, a very dark Magenta channel could suggest that there is too much Magenta in the image and this needs to be adjusted.

My goal in this section is not to discuss color correction techniques, but instead, the role of channels in color correction. The following method utilizes channels as a very visual method of adjusting a document by viewing both an individual channel and the composite image. Creating two views of the same document by going to the View menu and choosing Window > New Window sets up this technique. Keep one window in CMYK view, then activate the second window and in the Channels palette, click on one color channel. Use a command such as Curves to make an adjustment and with this dual window technique you'll be able to see both the adjustment on the individual channel and the composite image.

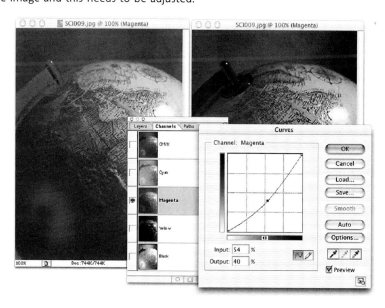

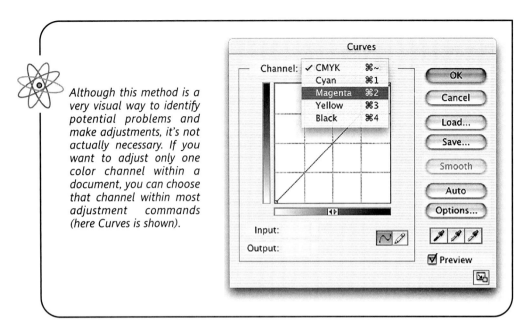

Although this method is a very visual way to identify potential problems and make adjustments, it's not actually necessary. If you want to adjust only one color channel within a document, you can choose that channel within most adjustment commands (here Curves is shown).

Selection storage with Alpha channels

Imagine your horror if you had spent an hour making a very complex selection, only to have your machine freeze, losing all that work. Rather than risk this happening, you could take advantage of a channel function known as an Alpha Channel. The name refers to the fact that these Alpha Channels are additional channels, above and beyond the built-in channels in every document, which can provide storage for selections so that they can be used again.

Here's how it works: make your selection:

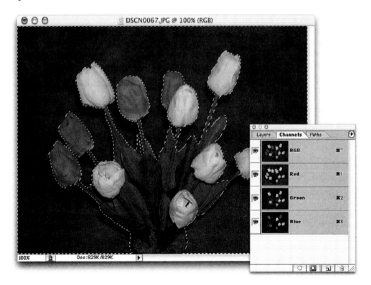

From the Select menu, choose Save Selection. A new channel is created – initially called Alpha 1 – that contains grayscale information that describes the selection: white represents the selection, black represents the unselected areas, and gray represents any feathered or partially selected areas.

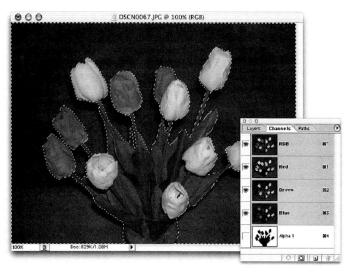

At this point, the Alpha Channel appears in the Channels palette, but is not yet a permanent part of the document, until the document is saved.

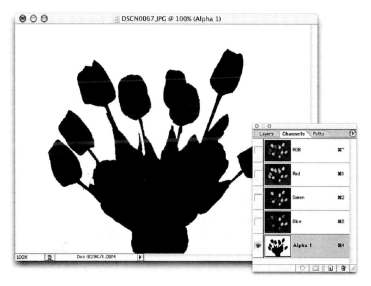

 To view the channel, hold down OPT/ALT and in the Channels palette, click on the Alpha Channel.

To view the Alpha Channel and the Composite image – to simulate Quick Mask – click on the Alpha Channel and click on the eyeball beside the RGB channel.

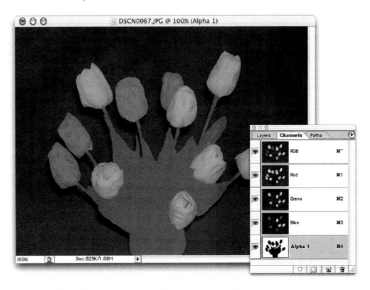

Once the Alpha Channel is saved in the document, it becomes, in effect, a storage place for your selection. To make a selection from the Alpha Channel, either choose Load Selection from the Select menu (and indicate which channel if you have multiple Alpha Channels), or CMD/CTRL-click on the Alpha Channel in the Channels palette.

There are a lot of possibilities to store selections, or even selections that are works in progress using Alpha Channels. Mind you, each Alpha Channel adds to your document file size, so the more channels, the bigger the file size. It is also important to note that not all file formats will allow Alpha Channels to be saved within the document. For example, if you try to save a document with an Alpha Channel as an EPS file, you won't be able to unless you save a copy and don't include the channel.

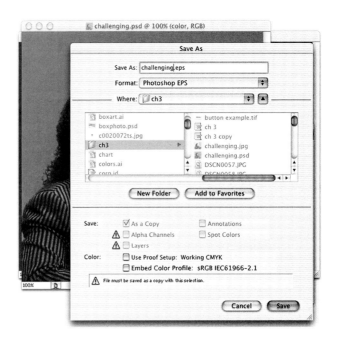

Channels can be duplicated, either within the same document or to other documents, and they can be deleted once they've served their purpose. To duplicate a channel (either a color or Alpha channel) activate the channel and from the Channels palette pop up menu choose Duplicate Channel. In the dialog box you can set the destination as the current document, another open document, or a new document.

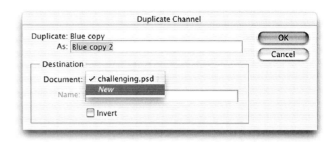

To delete an Alpha Channel (I can't think of too many reasons to delete a color channel) you can either drag it onto the Trash icon in the Channels palette, or hold down OPT/ALT and click on the Trash icon.

Using channels to make a selection

Here's a technique that can help with challenging selections such as fine details, blowing hair, leaves, etc. If you've tried the traditional selection methods and it's not working for you, here's how channels might help. In our discussion of Alpha Channels, we saw how a grayscale channel was created when we used Save Selection. We could then load that channel anytime we need that same area selected. Well, in this technique, we'll take the opposite approach: we'll use an existing channel to help us create an Alpha Channel, which we'll turn into a selection. Here's our challenge: select the woman in the image (keeping the hair detail) so that we can change the background behind her (this is image SFB13 from the Stock Photography 2 folder).

1. In the Channels palette, click on an individual color channel to view only that channel. What we're looking for is a channel that has good contrast between the woman's hair and the area outside her hair. Ideally, we want very dark hair and a very light area outside her hair. (More often than not it's either the Green or Blue channel)

2. This next step is vital – duplicate the channel you've chosen. (If you don't duplicate the channel and work on the original channel by mistake, you'll ruin your image).

3. Use the Levels command to increase the contrast in the channel – remember, ultimately we're aiming for a black silhouette of the woman with white everywhere else. To get us started, move the white triangle to the left to brighten the whites, and then move the black triangle to the right to darken the darks.

Throughout this step, your focus should be on the most challenging area – in this case her hair. Don't push the sliders too far or you could lose detail in the focus area. Remember don't worry about anything other than your focus area.

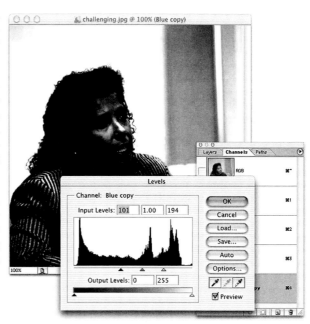

4. Now, paint with black and white to adjust this selection channel. Use whatever methods work best: Brush, select and fill...

5. To use this channel, activate the composite RGB channel, then CMD/CTRL-click on the channel you just created. If necessary (as in this example) inverse the selection (CMD/CTRL+SHIFT+I).

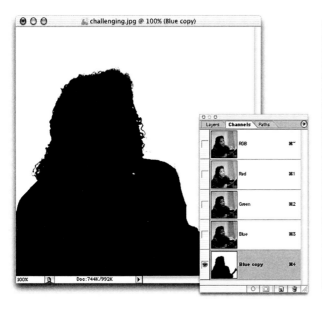

6. Duplicate the selected area onto its own layer (CMD/CTRL+J), then add a new layer (CMD/CTRL+SHIFT+N), and fill with a gradient.

Notice how the fine detail in her hair looks quite natural – I don't think you could get results like that from most typical selection techniques.

Another method to correct for the fringe is:

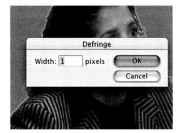

 As good as the selection from this technique might be, you might see a very slight fringe of the original background on the copied layer. To help remove the fringe, from the Layer menu choose Matting > Defringe. *In the dialog box enter a value of 1 or 2 and click OK. In many cases, this will fix the problem. If not, you may need to do some extra work to fix this problem.*

7. Make a rough selection around the edge of the layer. Make it slightly larger than you need.

8. From the Select menu choose Color Range. In the dialog box use the eyedropper to click on the fringe color. Since you have a selection, Color Range only looks inside this selection. Click OK.

9. Delete the selected area. Repeat if necessary.

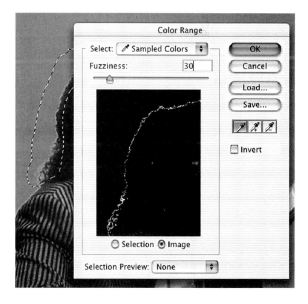

Color correction

There are a few areas where Photoshop is really the only choice, and one of those is color correction. Theoretically, you could make some minor adjustments to a raster image in Illustrator, but realistically, Photoshop is the place to do this kind of work. We're going to focus on two kinds of color correction here: making adjustments in RGB mode for digital output, and preparing for CMYK output on a printing press.

In general, we're going to try to use techniques where decisions are not left to our eyes, but are based on feedback we get from Photoshop. Why? If you make decisions based on what you see on your monitor, then you are not really correcting as much as you are adjusting – what looks better on your monitor may not look that way on another monitor, and it certainly won't print exactly the same as it looks. I suppose that you could argue that, when preparing images for an on-screen use such as PowerPoint or the Internet it's OK to use your eyes. You might be able to convince me of that argument, except, what if your monitor setting is a little off, or the sun is shining in your window, or you just came in from enjoying the sunshine outside? All of these factors can affect your on-screen perception of what you're seeing and how to improve it. Once you see how easy it can be to fix with Photoshop's help, I think you'll go with this approach.

 This section is not intended to make you an expert in color correction. That only comes with understanding some of the key concepts and lots (and lots) of practice. What we are trying to do here is introduce the concept of relying less on the on-screen look and more on using numbers and other feedback from Photoshop.

Correcting for digital output

What we're talking about here is preparing an image to be used on-screen or for output on a digital device such as a color ink jet or color laser printer. Rather than adjusting by eye, we'll use feedback from several Photoshop functions to help us correct the image in a few steps. We will still make some subjective judgments here and there, but overall we will rely on Photoshop to, in effect, tell us what to do. The steps will involve removing any color cast and adjusting the shadows, highlights, and midtones.

1. Crop the image to remove any unnecessary pixels. (Why correct pixels if you're not going to use them anyway?). I used image SFB08 from the Stock Photography 2 folder for this example.

2. Open the Curves dialog box (CMD/CTRL+M). We need to alter the settings for the eyedropper tools in this dialog box. Double-click on the black (shadow) eyedropper and in the Color Picker change the RBG values to: R=10, G=10, B=10. Click OK and double-click on the white (highlight) eyedropper and change its values to R=245, G=245, B=245. Finally, double-click on the gray (midtone) eyedropper and change its values to R=133, G=133, B=133.

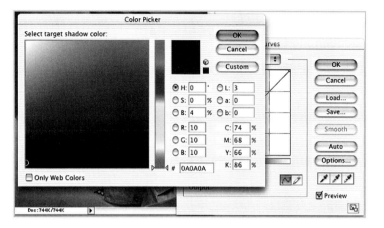

You only have to change these eyedropper settings once, they then become your on-going, default setting.

3. We need to use these eyedroppers to set the highlights and shadows. Rather than simply guess – which we could – here is when we'll get Photoshop's help. From the Layers palette, click on the Adjustment layer icon and add a Threshold Adjustment Layer. Drag the slider over to the far left, and then slowly drag over to the right until some pixels start to appear.

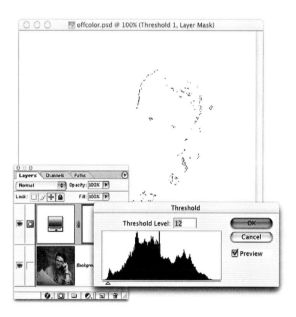

These are the darkest areas of your image. Click OK.

4. Choose the **Color Sampler** tool (under the Eyedropper tool). Click on the area you want to use as the darkest area.

5. Double-click on the Threshold layer in the Layers palette. Move the slider over to the far right, and then slowly drag to the left. The white areas that appear first are the brightest areas of the image. Click OK.

6. Use the Color Sampler tool to click on the area you want to use as the brightest area.

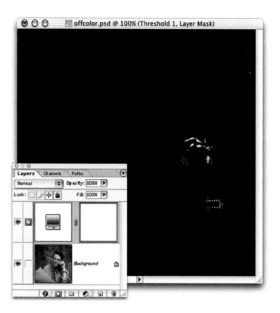

7. The Threshold layer has served its purpose, so you can delete it (or, if you think you might experiment further, you could hide it and click on the Background layer).

8. Press CMD/CTRL+M to open Curves. Click on the black eyedropper and position it over the first color sampler (it will have a 1 beside it). Click. Now click on the white eyedropper and click on top of the second color sampler. Finally, click on the gray eyedropper. Position the eyedropper over an area that appears to be neutral gray and click.

If you need help finding a neutral gray spot on your image, you can use the Info palette to help you. Before you use the Curves command, change the setting in the Info palette from RGB to K by clicking and holding on the eyedropper icon and choose Grayscale. Now, when you use the Curves command and the gray eyedropper, look for a spot where the K value is 50% (or as close as possible).

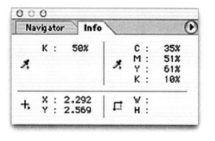

9. To remove the color samplers, click the Clear button on the Options Bar

To help line up the Curves eyedropppers with the Color Samplers, press CAPS LOCK – this will change the eyedropper to a precise cursor that you can line up exactly with the points you picked previously.

Particularly in images from digital cameras, you may find that flesh tones in the image still look a little reddish (yes, here we have to be a little subjective). Here's an easy way to deal with that:

10. Open the Hue/Saturation dialog box (CMD/CTRL+U).

11. From the pop up Edit menu, choose Reds (to affect only the red portions of the image).

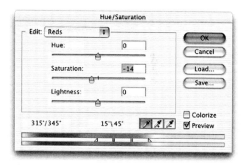

12. Lower the Saturation until the flesh tones lose some of the red.

13. Click OK.

If necessary, you could also make small, feathered selections around any really red problem areas and repeat the same technique.

This method of color correction offers one key advantage: it does not force you to make completely subjective choices, but gives you some help in finding the ideal shadow, highlight, and neutral points. If you want a bit more flexibility, you could run the Curves command as an Adjustment layer. The only really subjective choice is in dealing with flesh that's a little too red.

Correcting for print

In theory, you could use the procedure outlined above to prepare images for print. However, that method is really intended for digital output and more importantly perhaps, images that are in RGB mode. We need to take a look at a method to correct images intended for CMYK printing. Here it's important to note that on-going discussions with service bureaus and print shops are a vital part of this procedure. The method we're going to use is for CMYK documents, so needless to say, you'll have to convert your RGB images to CMYK before starting with these steps.

Stop! Before changing the mode from RGB to CMYK, we need to pause for a moment to discuss a form of Preference called Color Settings. The settings in this dialog box determine exactly how an RGB file is converted to CMYK. Although you could use the built-in setting (U.S. Prepress Defaults), I would recommend talking to your output friends and getting their advice as to what settings to use – they may even have a settings file they can send you that you can load into this dialog box. For now, we'll assume this has been done already and that we're working with appropriate Color Settings.

Note: When a document is changed from RGB to CMYK, several things happen:

1. The file size increases by one third due to the extra color channel.

2. Certain filters are no longer available (they only work in RGB mode).

3. Colors may shift (some colors that can display in RGB mode cannot be printed in CMYK).

This suggests that you should complete operations such as filters before moving on to this step.

Before we start we need to check a couple of settings. First the Eyedropper tool – with the Eyedropper tool activated, check the Options Bar. If necessary, change the setting from Point Sample to 3 by 3 Average. This will give us better readings from the Eyedropper (Point sample reads only one pixel, whereas 3 by 3 Average takes an average of a small area)

Then check the Info palette. Ideally we want the right hand measurement to be CMYK (it should be already) and the left hand measurement set to K. Do this by clicking and holding the eyedropper icon in the Info palette and choosing Grayscale. This will help us find appropriate spots to take measurements.

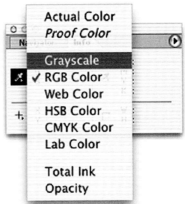

Here's an overview of this method of color correction: we'll take a series of Eyedropper readings to determine the average CMYK ink values in the document. Then we'll compare those settings with target CMYK values – values that we get (ideally) from our print shop, or failing that, using typical values. Finally, we'll use the Curves command to change the current settings to the target values.

Print Shops and Service Bureaus may refer to these target values by different names such as ink values, CMYK percentages, or black and white point values. If you ask for these values and they don't seem to know what you're looking for, you need to know the ideal CMYK percentages for shadow points and highlights – for the printing press your project will be printed on. If you still don't get a response, you can use these typical target values as a guide:

Coated stock: Highlights C5 M2 Y2 K0, Shadows C80 M70 Y70 K70.

Uncoated stock: Highlights C5 M2 Y2 K0, Shadows C70 M60 Y60 K75

Uncoated stock (newsprint): Highlights C5 M2 Y2 K0, Shadows C60 M52 Y52 K76

1. This first step takes a bit of time, but is key to making good decisions. Using the K% as a reference, find a series of shadow areas (90% K and above if possible) and make note of the CMYK values.

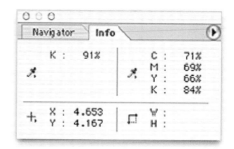

What you're really looking for is a trend – a recurring number or average. In a typical example you might measure five shadow areas and get Cyan values of 68, 67, 70, 68, 69. In a case like this, you'd use 68 as an average value that represents the current percentage of Cyan in the shadow areas. After some measuring, you'll end up with average shadow percentages for each of the four ink values. Then repeat the same procedure, measuring a number of highlight areas to get average numbers for all four inks. When you complete these steps, you'll have a summary of the current CMYK ink make up of your document.

For our example, we'll use these numbers as the current ink values:

Highlights: C3, M12, Y20, K0 and Shadows: C70, M69, Y72, K82.

2. Now we'll use the Curves command to make the current values match up to the target values. Open the Curves command (CMD/CTRL+M) and from the Channels menu, choose Cyan to work only with those ink values. For this example we need to shift the current Cyan shadow value from 70 (the current value) to 80 (the target value). Do this by positioning the cursor over the diagonal line (don't click, just drag) and drag up or down until the Input number at the bottom of the dialog box matches the current value (in this case 70). Click on the line to add a point, and then in the Output field, type in the target value (in this case 80).

This will shift the shadows from the current value to the target value.

3. Now we need to apply the same method to change the highlight values – with one minor difference. Unfortunately, once you've typed in the field to change the Output number, you'll no longer see the Input values change as you drag the mouse along the line. So, to change the highlight value, just click on the line, close to the bottom, to approximate the current value. When a new number appears in the Input field, change that number to the current value (in this case 3) and then in the Output field, type the target value (5 in our example).

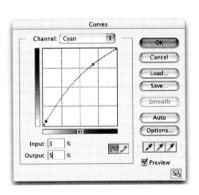

4. Once those steps are completed, move on to the Magenta channel by choosing it from the Channel menu in the Curves dialog box and repeat the same procedure (making the current shadow and highlight values match the target values)

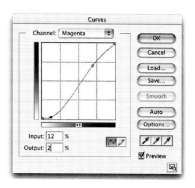

 It is not unusual for an image to look worse during this procedure. Don't worry! You're not finished yet, since you have only changed two of the four inks.

5. Repeat the same steps until you've adjusted the numbers for all four inks. If you like, you can check to see how you're doing while the Curves dialog box is open, by moving your mouse over to one of the places you measured and looking in the Info palette. You should see two sets of numbers separated by a slash – this represents the original number and the adjusted value.

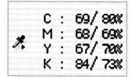

Hopefully, by the time you get to the Black channel, you should see after numbers that are very close to the target values. Don't worry if the numbers aren't exact matches, but we do want them to be pretty close to the target values.

 Print shops may also suggest using the Total Ink Coverage (or Density) as another form of target or reference. To check this value, change the values measured in the Info palette to Total Ink. Now the value will indicate the total ink percentage – in typical printing, you'll want values of between 240 and 295%, depending on the press, paper stock, etc.

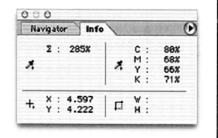

One final note: if you are having trouble getting the values to match in both shadows and highlights, concentrate on the highlights. In general, shadows can stand to be off by 5% without having a major impact on the image – the human eye is more sensitive to color variations in light areas than in darker areas

Components and re-purposing

Any time we can re-use design elements or automate our work, we should! Why recreate components if we can re-purpose objects and layers for other uses? In this section we'll take a look at some of the ways that we can take advantage of Illustrator and Photoshop's options for creating custom, re-useable elements.

Brushes

Illustrator brushes

Illustrator has a unique implementation of brushes – not only does the Paintbrush tool use the Brushes palette, rather, you can apply a brush to any path created with any tool.

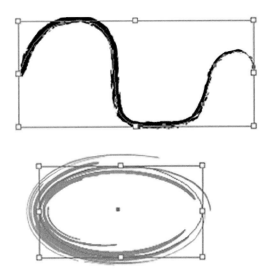

In addition, there are four types of brushes that offer a range of possibilities: Calligraphic, Art, Scatter, and Pattern. Basically, the reasons for using the different brushes are:

- Calligraphic brushes create variable width strokes that resemble working with a calligraphy pen.

- Art brushes stretch artwork along the length of a path.

- Scatter brushes disperse copies of artwork along a path.

- Pattern brushes paint a pattern (made up of individual tiles) that repeats along a path.

If you double-click on an existing brush to edit its options – depending on the type of brush, you'll get different options, as shown below for the Art brush and Calligraphic brush.

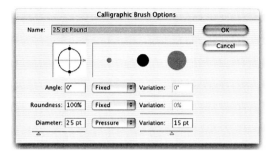

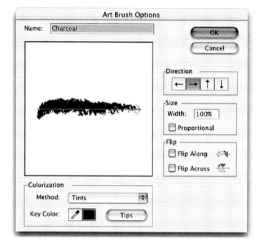

Any object can be turned into a brush, simply by selecting the object(s) and dragging the selection into the Brushes palette. A dialog box prompts you to choose which type of brush you want to create – depending on the objects, some choices may be grayed out.

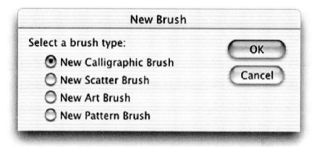

When you add a brush to the Brushes palette, it is added only to the current documents and will not be available in any other documents. It is possible to create a library of brushes that can be loaded into any document. Start with a new, blank document and create the brush(es) by dragging into the Brushes palette. Then save the document in the Brushes folder, found in the Presets folder in the Illustrator application folder. Quit and re-launch Illustrator, and look under Window > Brush Libraries *to load the brush library you saved.*

If you want a brush to be automatically available to every new document you create, the brush must be added to a special document called Adobe Illustrator Startup. Open this file from the Preset folder and then add a brush to the Brushes palette. After saving this document, your new brush will become a permanent addition to the Brushes palette. (There are two startup files, one for RGB files and one for CMYK documents)

Although you can apply a brush to any path, it is not possible to apply a brush to type, unless you convert the type to outlines. Of course, you would lose the ability to edit the text. Here's an interesting solution: with your text selected go to the Appearance palette and from the pop up menu choose Add a New Stroke. Then click on the brush to apply it to the new stroke, giving the illusion of text with a painted stroke.

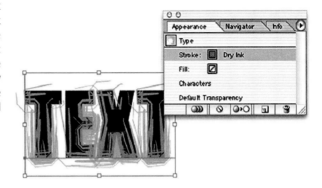

As shown here, edit the text and the brush stroke changes too.

Photoshop brushes

There are quite a number of tools in Photoshop that use brushes: Healing Brush, Brush, Pencil, Stamp tools, History brushes, Eraser tools, Blur, Sharpen, Smudge, Dodge, Burn, and Sponge. With the exception of the Pencil tool, all tools can use either a hard edged or soft edged brush (with the Pencil tool, all brushes change to hard edged). Although there are many options available to affect the performance of brushes, our main focus here is on creating custom brushes.

A brush can be created from anything that can be selected: an imported logo, painted shapes, or even type. Brushes are based on shades of gray: black will create solid colored areas, gray will create semi-transparent areas, and white will be transparent when painted.

1. To create a custom brush, start with a new layer and paint on that layer (you can also apply filters to the paint).

2. Hide any other layers and make a selection just larger than the brush.

3. From the Edit menu, choose Define Brush. Name your brush if you wish.

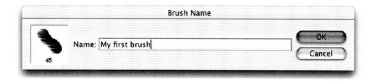

The new brush is added to the Brushes palette and, unlike Illustrator, is now available to each and every Photoshop document. Once a brush is created it becomes a permanent default brush, unless you reset the Brushes palette or make adjustments to the Preset Manager (more on that later).

Photoshop brushes are resolution-specific, meaning the brushes are created at the resolution of the document in which they were created. If you want the same brush at several resolutions, you would have to create the brush in a document that was created at the highest resolution, then resample down, create a second version of the brush, and so on.

To edit the performance of the brush, open the expanded view in the Brushes palette, which offers many editing options. Click on Brush Presets to view all the brushes, including a preview of how the brush will look (in this view you can edit the overall size of the brush).

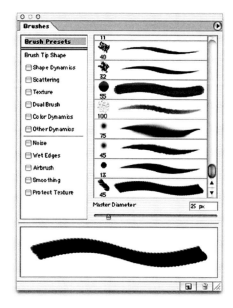

Clicking on the many other choices such as Shape Dynamics, Scattering, and Texture, allows you to adjust many other options to alter the performance of the brush.

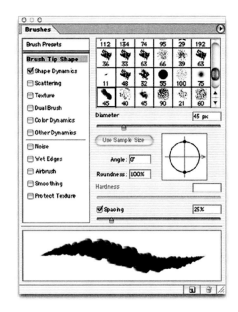

As an extra back-up plan, you may want to save your custom brushes so you can load them back in should you reset the palette. To do this, use the pop up menu in the Brushes palette, choose Save Brushes and name your brush set. This will save all the brushes in the palette, including the default brushes. To save only the custom brushes you've created, use the Preset Manager.

The Preset Manager controls the contents of a number of palettes, including Brushes, Swatches, Gradients, and Shapes. To create custom sets of brushes, go to Edit > Preset Manager and select Brushes as the Preset Type. Click on the first brush you want in your set, then SHIFT-click on each additional brush you want to add to the set.

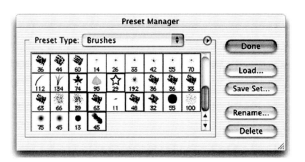

Click the Save Set button, name your set, and save (the path for where you have saved the brush set is Photoshop 7.0/Presets/Brushes, although it is not necessary. By saving the set in the Brushes folder, you'll never have to go looking to find the set(s) you've saved).

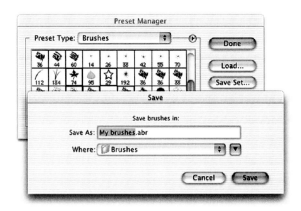

Should you want to change the order in which brushes appear in the Brushes palette, in the Preset Manager, CMD/CTRL-click on the brush and drag to change the order of brushes. (This also works with the other presets such as Swatches and Gradients).

Shapes

Photoshop comes with a series of custom shapes, both those built-in to the palette and additional shapes that can be loaded. As discussed earlier, these shapes are vectors, offering very flexible, scaleable objects. To pick from the custom shapes, choose the Custom Shape tool and then in the Options Bar, click on the custom tool icon to pop up the palette of shapes.

To load additional shapes, use the pop up menu from the palette of shapes, and choose from the list of shapes at the bottom of the menu. You can also very easily create your own custom shape, either by drawing it in Photoshop, or by copying and pasting from Illustrator.

1. To create your own custom shape, use the Pen tool (P) to draw a shape – you can do this either as a Path or a Shape Layer.

2. With the shape selected, choose Edit > Define Custom Shape. Name the Shape, click OK, and that's it!

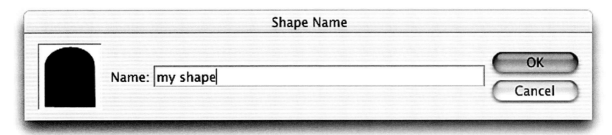

Now this shape is added to your Custom Shapes palette.

To take advantage of Illustrator's drawing capabilities, we can create artwork in Illustrator and copy and paste it to create a custom shape.

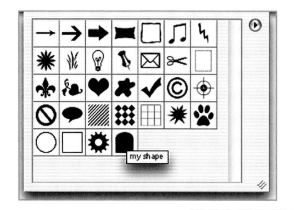

3. In Illustrator, select, and copy the artwork (CMD/CTRL+C).

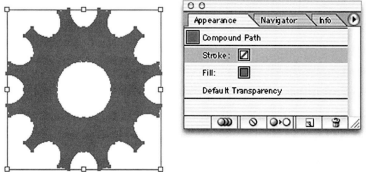

4. Switch to Photoshop, create a new document (CMD/CTRL+N), and Paste (CMD/CTRL+V). A dialog box appears offering several choices, to Paste As: Pixels, Path, or Shape Layer. Choose Shape Layer, which will create a new Shape Layer (no surprise there!). Then use the Define Custom Shape command from the Edit menu to add this Illustrator artwork to the Custom Shapes palette. Now choose this new custom shape and click and drag to create a new shape layer.

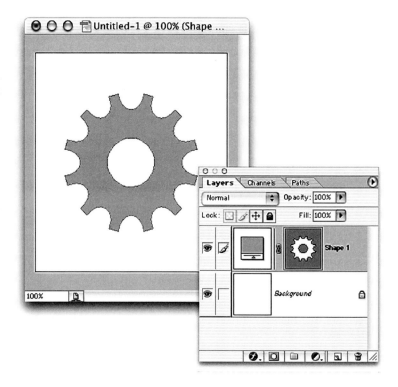

As with Brushes, you can use the Preset Manager to change the order of the Shapes, or to create your own set(s) of Shapes.

There's one other use of Shapes that offers an improvement over the typical way of working with text. If you create a Type layer and then attempt to use the Free Transform command, you'd find that two transformations – Distort and Perspective – are grayed out.

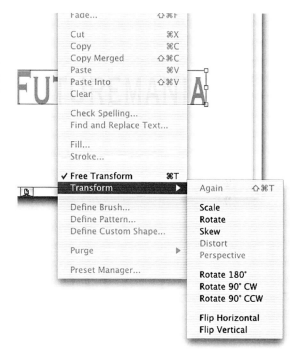

In order to be able to apply these transformations, the most commonly used solution is to rasterize the type. Although rasterizing does allow all transformations to be applied, when you apply transformations such as Perspective, the quality suffers.

Instead of rasterizing, you'll get better results if you convert the type to a shape. From the Layer menu, choose Type > Convert to Shape. Then apply Perspective, but since you are distorting vector shapes, the quality will be much higher.

At this point you could choose to rasterize the shape (Layer > Rasterize > Shape), and the quality will be much higher than you'd get by rasterizing and then transforming a type layer.

Styles

Both Illustrator and Photoshop have an incredibly powerful and practical function called Styles. The concept is very similar in both programs – save a look as a style and then apply it to another object or layer. Let's take a look at the similarities and differences between using Styles in these two programs.

Illustrator styles

Styles in Illustrator are very closely tied to the Appearance palette. Create a look for an object by using not only the basic fill and stroke, but by adding additional strokes and applying Effects. Here's a simple example:

1.   Create a basic shape such as an oval.

2.   Fill with red, Stroke with black with a Weight of 8pt.

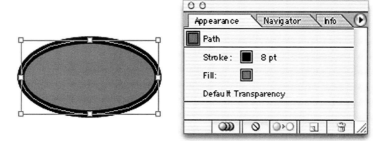

3.   From the Appearance palette pop up menu, choose Add New Stroke.

4.   Change the color of this second stroke to yellow and the Weight to 3pt.

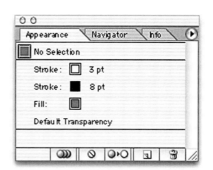

5.   Add another New Stroke, purple, Weight 1pt.

6. From the Effect menu, choose Distort & Transform > Roughen (use your own settings, here's what I used):

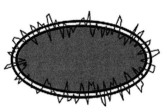

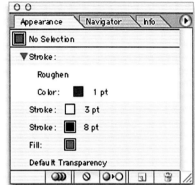

Once you're happy with the look of your oval we can turn this look into a Style.

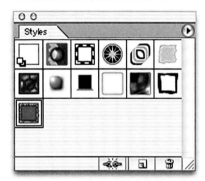

7. Click on the small swatch at the top the Appearance palette and drag it into the Styles palette.

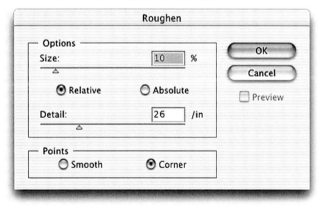

8. To apply this new style to another object, create a second object such as text. With the object selected, click on the style swatch to apply it to the object.

Take a look at the Appearance palette to view (or edit) the elements of this style.

A couple of important notes:

- In typical Illustrator fashion, any style you create is added only to the current document. To get access to your styles in other documents you can either save the document as a style library, or add your styles to the Illustrator Startup document. (See the section on Illustrator Brushes to see how to do this).

- If you load the extra Style libraries provided with Illustrator, and you apply a style to an object, use the Appearance palette to see how they did it and to edit any aspect of the style. (Double-click on any Effect to edit the settings).

Don't overlook an Effect called Transform (Effects > Distort & Transform). This powerful dialog box lets you add various effects such as multiple copies of the same object, complete with random scaling and rotation. Here's an example of the Transformation effect applied to a text object.

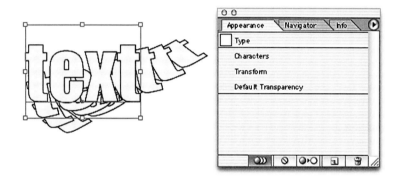

Take a look at the dialog box settings that were used to get this result.

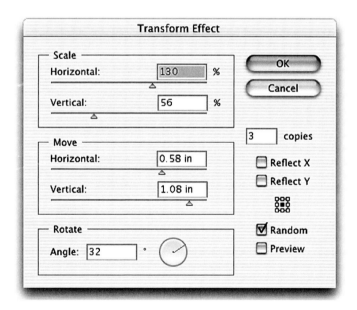

Of course, this could be made into a style – talk about great potential!

Photoshop styles

Photoshop styles are a great way of saving a set of Layer Styles so you can easily apply these effects to other layers. Now, let's try to clear up some of the confusing terminology in the world of Layer Styles, effects, and styles. When you add a Drop Shadow to a layer you are adding a Layer Style, as indicated by the dialog box.

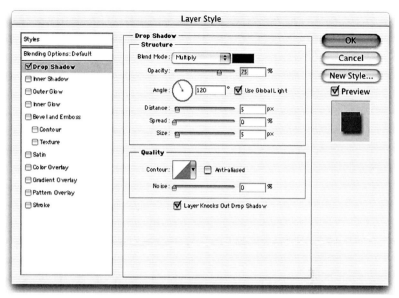

Once one or more Layer Styles have been applied to a layer, in the Layers palette they are known as Effects. Individual effects can be kept visible or hidden by clicking the Layer Styles icon beside the layer name or the entire look can be hidden by clicking off the eyeball beside Effects.

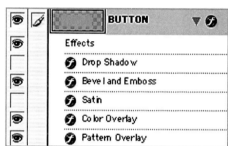

The Styles palette contains, well, styles, which is how collections of Layer Styles are saved.

1. To create a style, apply one or more Layer Styles to a layer. In this example, a number of effects were added to a type layer (as shown).

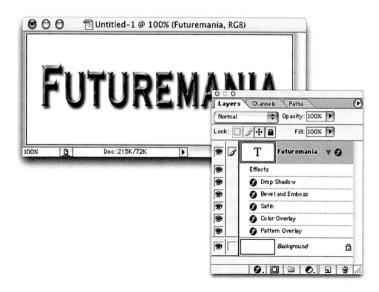

2.   From the Styles palette pop up menu, choose New Style. Name the style.

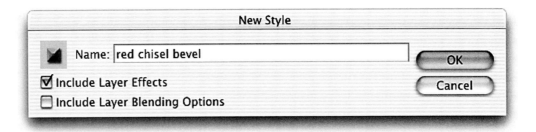

3.   Click OK and it is added to the Styles palette.

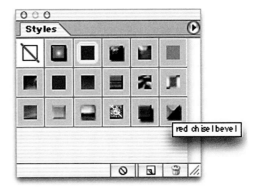

4.   Now that style can easily be applied to any layer. Create a new layer (CMD/CTRL+N) and add some paint, or use a Shape layer.

5.   Click on the swatch in the Styles palette to apply the style to the layer.

Once again, it's important to remember the difference between the way Illustrator and Photoshop deal with custom features such as brushes and styles. In Illustrator, you must take steps to ensure the custom settings are saved (as a library or as part of the Startup document). In Photoshop, these same custom features are automatically saved in the application, and you can save your creations as a custom set – if you choose to.

Gradients

The Gradient feature is so similar in both programs that we can explore them together. Perhaps the biggest difference is that Photoshop comes with a few more built-in gradients and more libraries that can be loaded. The real fun with gradients begins when we start to create our own.

Creating custom gradients

In Illustrator, expand the Gradient palette to show all options. Each time we want to change the color in our gradient, we add stops to the gradient bar.

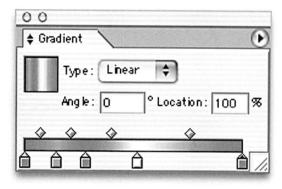

This can be done in one of two ways: dragging colors from the Swatches palette to the bottom of the gradient bar, or by clicking below the bar to add a stop, then double-clicking on the stop to edit the color. You can also duplicate color stops by holding down OPT/ALT and dragging the stop to copy it. Once the gradient is finished, click on the swatch on the Gradient palette and drag it into the Swatches palette.

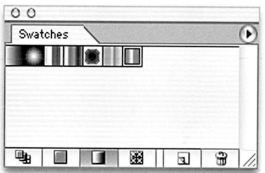

In Photoshop, activate the Gradient tool and in the Options Bar, click on the gradient editor to edit an existing, or create a new gradient.

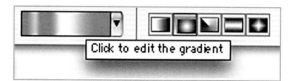

Use the same methods described above to add color stops.

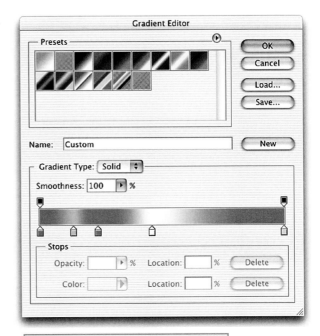

The main difference in Photoshop is that you can also choose to use the Foreground and Background colors when you're creating color stops, and that you can also set the transparency for each stop. Once the gradient is finished, click on the New button to add this gradient to the Presets.

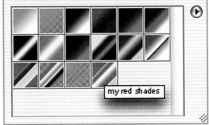

Once you have created a custom gradient, it becomes available within a Layer Style called Gradient Overlay.

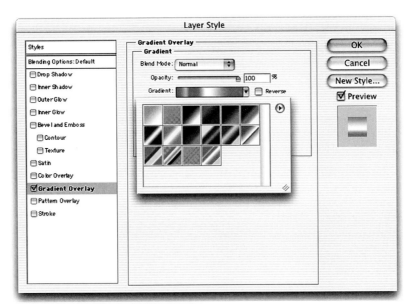

This is a very useful way to apply a gradient when there's a chance that you might want to edit the look of the gradient. For comparison purposes, here's an example where the Gradient tool was used to fill an object:

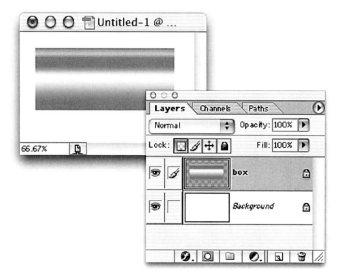

There's very little that can be done to this other than painting a new gradient. By applying a Gradient Overlay (from the Layer Styles pop up menu), the effect appears in the Layers palette, and can be edited. So, if you need more flexibility with gradients, use a Gradient Overlay.

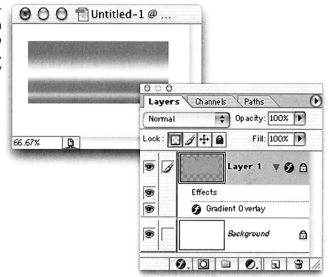

Patterns

Illustrator patterns

Before we get too far into a discussion of Illustrator patterns, it is important to note that unlike most Illustrator vector functions that print like a dream, patterns can cause potential printing problems. The bottom line is that patterns can be extremely useful, but that we need to pay careful attention to one key setting (we'll look at this later).

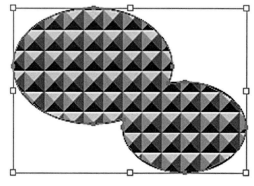

Any vector object can be made into a pattern – unless that object is already filled with a pattern. In general, patterns are made based on amounts of a square tile that will be repeated. To use one of the existing patterns, just select an object and click on a pattern in the Swatches palette.

To edit the pattern, drag it out of the Swatches palette onto the document. Use the Direct Selection tool (A) to select and edit the colors of the pattern tile.

Select all the parts of the pattern object and drag it into the Swatches palette to create a new pattern swatch.

Creating your own pattern from scratch can be as simple as creating an object and dragging that object into the Swatches palette. Here a circle was created and dragged into the Swatches palette, and a larger oval filled with the resulting pattern.

Notice how there is no space between the circles in the pattern since only the oval was used to create the pattern. To create space around the circles in the pattern we would add a square that's slightly larger than the circle (the more space you want between circles, the larger the square should be). Unless you want the square to appear as part of the pattern, the square should have no fill or stroke (here's an example shown in Outline view so you can see the circle and the square).

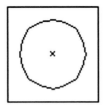

Here's the result of filling the oval with the new pattern:

It takes a little effort to create a more random effect in a pattern. One way to give yourself a good chance at success at getting that random effect is:

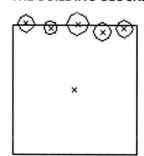

1. Create a square and change the fill and stroke to none.

2. Switch to Outline View (CMD/CTRL+Y) so that you can see what you're doing.

3. Start on one side of the square to create your pattern (I started with the top edge). Here I've created a series of circles of slightly different sizes. For now just concentrate on putting circles on the edge of the square. Don't forget to fill those circles with some color.

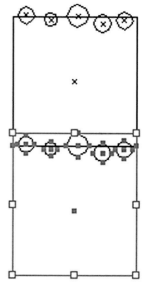

4. Select the square and the circles, hold down CMD/CTRL+OPT/ALT and start to drag the objects. Once you've started dragging, hold down SHIFT. (CMD/CTRL to get the Selection tool, OPT/ALT to make a copy and SHIFT to drag in a straight line). Keep dragging until the top of the square you're dragging lines up with the bottom of the original square.

5. Once the edges of the two squares line up, you can select and delete the square you copied, leaving the original squares with the circles on the top and bottom.

6. Repeat the same steps for the other sides: create (or copy) circles on to one side of the square, then drag a copy of the square and circles until the sides match up. Delete the square and the unnecessary circles.

    You'll end up with a square with random circles on all four sides.

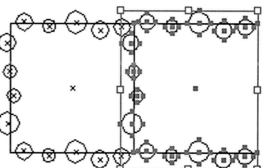

7. Fill in the middle of the square with more circles, being careful not to move the circles on the sides of the square (you should also avoid creating circles that touch the original circles).

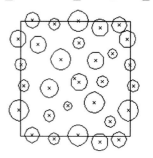

8. Finally, select the square and all circles and drag into the Swatches palette. Create a larger object and fill with your new pattern to see how well it worked.

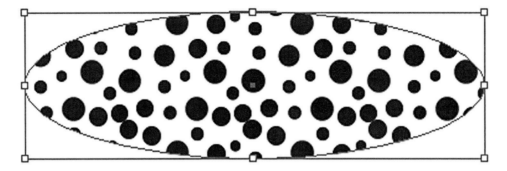

Yes, patterns can be a great way to create an effect, but, as mentioned before, there can be one possible problem. When you use transformation tools such as Scale and Rotate, be careful not to scale or rotate the pattern (this is an option in the transformation dialog boxes).

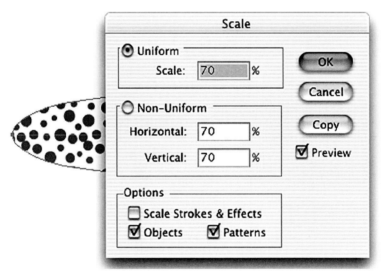

Although it would seem to make sense to transform the pattern along with the object, that has been known to cause printing problems. This could be a relatively minor problem such as taking longer to print, or worse, a PostScript error that will stop your job from printing. In general, it would be better to create a second, smaller pattern than to scale the pattern.

Along with filling an object with a pattern, you can also stroke with a pattern. Make the weight of the stroke thick enough to see the pattern. (The only potential problem is that some other applications don't handle patterned stroke very well – I would use patterned strokes only within Illustrator).

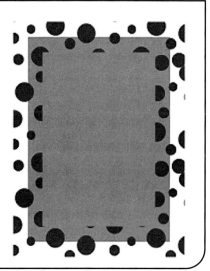

Photoshop patterns

If you can select it, you can make it into a Photoshop pattern – well, almost. As long as you use the Marquee tool with no feathering, you can select anything to create a repeating pattern. Once the pattern is created, you can paint with it, fill with it, and use it in Layer Styles.

The tools and commands that use Patterns are:

- Pattern Stamp tool (S)

- Paint Bucket tool (G)

- Edit > Fill

- Layer > Layer Style > Pattern Overlay

The process of creating a pattern is pretty straight-forward: use the Marquee tool to make a rectangular selection and from the Edit menu, choose Define Pattern. Name the pattern and it is added to the pattern presets, ready to use. It's important to note that the Layers palette has a big influence on the look of a pattern. If for example, you want to create a pattern that contains transparent areas, hide all layers other than the one containing what will be in your pattern. On the other hand, unlike most Photoshop functions that only work on one layer, when you choose the Define Pattern command, all visible layers will be part of the pattern. (You can also create a pattern that includes type without having to rasterize the type layer).

Here's a simple example of creating and using a pattern.

1. Create a new document that is .25 inches by .25 inches.

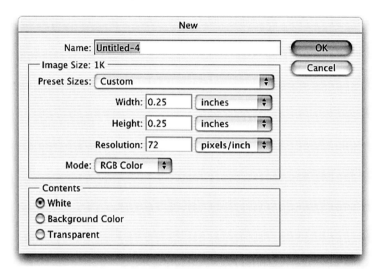

2. Add a new layer (CMD/CTRL+SHIFT+N) and hide the Background layer.

3. On the blank layer Select All (CMD/CTRL+A), pick white as the Foreground color, and from the Edit menu choose Stroke. Set the Width to 1 pixel and click OK.

4. Without deselecting, from the Edit menu, choose Define Pattern. Name the Pattern.

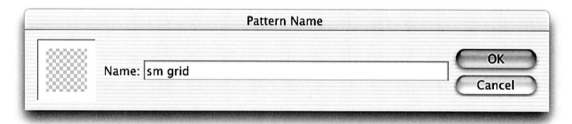

5. Make a new document (CMD/CTRL+N) that's larger than the original, for example 4 x 6 inches and fill it with black.

6. Add a new layer (CMD/CTRL+SHIFT+N) and from the Edit menu choose Fill (SHIFT+DELETE/BACKSPACE).

7. In the Fill dialog box change the Contents to Pattern and choose your pattern from the pattern presets.

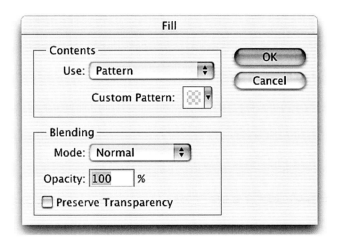

8. Add a Layer Mask and paint black with a large soft brush to hide the edges of the grid.

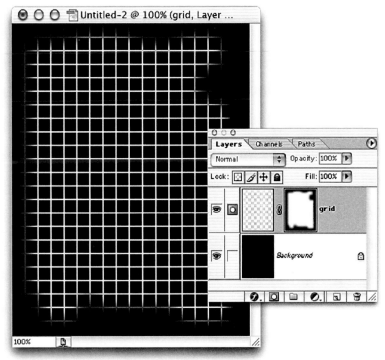

Here are two more examples that use the grid pattern we just created:

In this example a new layer was added to a painted background, and the Pattern Stamp tool was used to paint areas using the pattern. The settings for the Pattern Stamp (shown here) affected the way the grid was created.

In the following example, a rectangle was painted on a separate layer and two Layer Styles were added: Bevel and Emboss and Pattern Overlay. As you can see, the grid pattern was used, but with settings that scaled the pattern down, lowered the Opacity and changed the blending mode.

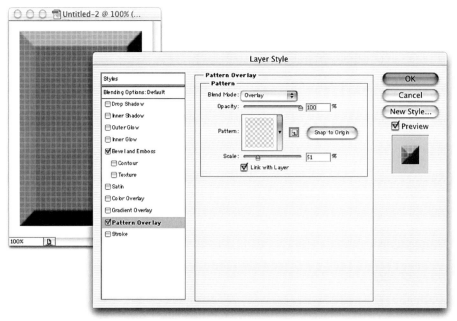

There's one other way to create a pattern, a filter called Pattern Maker. This filter takes some experimentation but luckily, it does much of the experimenting for you. To use this filter, open a document and then from the Filter menu choose Pattern Maker. Select an area in the preview that you want to use to generate a pattern.

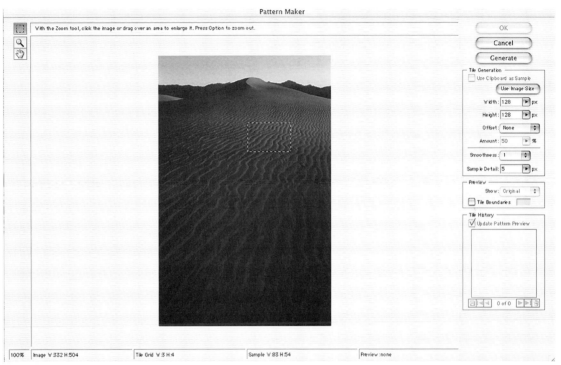

This is one of the areas where you'll have to experiment – on the same image, different sized selections will generate very different results. After you've selected are area, click the Generate button. The preview will change to show the repeating pattern that was generated.

To get another pattern from the same selection, press Generate Again. At the bottom of the dialog box all your patterns are stored until you close the window.

If you want to save any of the generated patterns, click on the disk symbol. At any time if you want to start over, hold down OPT/ALT and the Cancel button will change to Reset – click Reset to go back to square one (all generated patterns will be lost).

Actions

Although not really a component to use in a design, Actions can certainly streamline and automate the process of using components such as styles, layers, etc. An Action is like a macro – record a series of operations that you can playback to other images. You can create Actions to automate simple things, like creating a keyboard shortcut for a commonly used operation. Or, an Action can have many steps that can be customized. Both Illustrator and Photoshop have an Actions palette, and they look and act similarly. As shown here, you can view the Actions as a list where you can view each step, or in Button mode, where the palette turns into a clickable set of buttons.

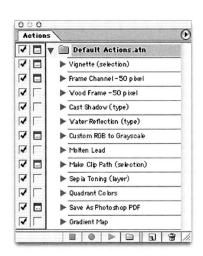

To work with Actions, it is recommended that you create a new set (folder) to hold your actions, just to keep them separate from the default actions. Then create a new Action by clicking on the **New Action** icon or using the pop up menu. Name your Action and allocate a Function key shortcut (if you want).

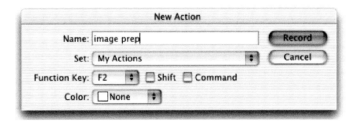

Click OK and the Action is automatically recording every operation you perform. Once you've completed all the steps, click the Stop button, or choose Stop recording from the pop up menu. Check the Actions palette to see your Action, with all the steps.

Once an Action has been recorded, you can skip a step by clicking off the checkmark beside that step.

For certain operations, such as filters, you can have the Action pause and open a dialog box to alter the settings for that command.

In Illustrator, Actions tend to be used mostly to add shortcuts to commands that don't have one, or to automate a series of operations such as cleaning up palettes. Although it is possible to record operations that involve creating objects, there are a number of operations that cannot be recorded. (It's pretty easy to tell if an operation can be included in an Action – try recording a step and check and see if it appears in the Actions palette).

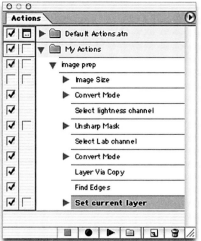

Photoshop Actions offer many more possibilities, particularly in the area of creating objects, layers, applying filters, etc. In addition, Photoshop has a command called Batch (File > Automate) that will apply an Action to a whole series of images in a folder.

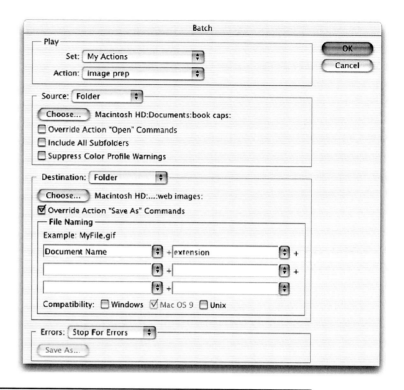

When using the Batch command, it is suggested that you create an after folder and save the results of the batch process into this folder. This eliminates the chance of over-writing the original documents as the batch is run.

Unfortunately, many Photoshop users seem to think of Actions strictly as a function designed for many images and/or for multi-step procedures. Actions can certainly be used for these purposes, but can also be very useful for smaller or short-term projects.

For example, I want to create a special effect that starts with type layers, but want to be able to experiment with different fonts. Rather than start over each time I want to try a different font, I'll use an Action to automate the process.

1.   Create a new document and add a type layer, typing the word ANTIQUE (use a fairly thick font and a large size).

2. Now we'll record the Action. In the Actions palette, click the **New Action** button. Call it Antique text and click OK to start recording.

3. Hold down CMD/CTRL and click on the type layer to load it as a selection.

4. From the Select menu choose Modify > Contract and enter 2 for the amount.

5. Press Q to switch to Quick Mask mode.

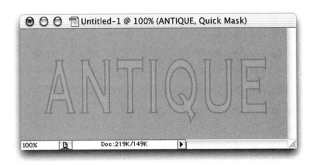

6. From the Filter menu, choose Brush Strokes > Spatter. Experiment with the settings to create a roughened edge.

7. Press Q to return to regular mode.

8. Click on the Add layer mask button at the bottom of the Layers palette and add a Drop Shadow.

9. In the Actions palette, press the Stop button.

Now we have an Action that allows us to experiment with different fonts and still end up with the antiqued look.

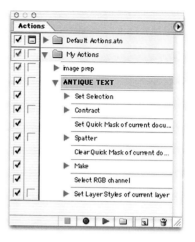

To try it, drag the Layer Mask icon to the trash and click Discard. Change the type to a different font, then click on the name of our Action and click the play button. The Action will automatically apply all the steps to turn this new font into the antiqued look.

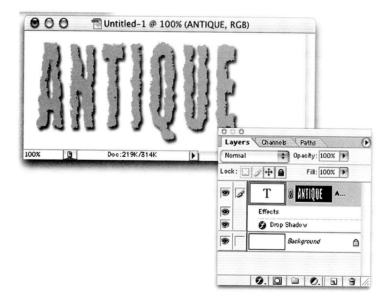

Each time you want to try a different font, throw away the Layer Mask and run the Action. You may not use this Action again after this project, but for the small amount of effort it takes to create the Action, it will still speed up the process of experimenting.

Achieving effects without presets

Although Illustrator and Photoshop each have preset, automated functions to create effects such as shadows and glows, sometimes the result may not be exactly what you have in mind. In these situations you may have to manually create the effect you want. In addition, as we discussed earlier, Illustrator creates effects such as drop shadows as raster effects – you may want to use only vector objects, so once again, you'd have to create this manually.

Vector shadows in Illustrator

Let's create a cast shadow with a simple object to demonstrate the process of making shadows using vectors in Illustrator. Create a copy of the object and fill with a gradient.

1. Create a simple object such as an oval and fill it with any color.

2. Select the Shear tool and click once on the bottom of the object to set this as the reference point. Move your mouse to the top of the object, hold down OPT/ALT to create a copy as you drag and click and drag to the right. Release the mouse, and then the key.

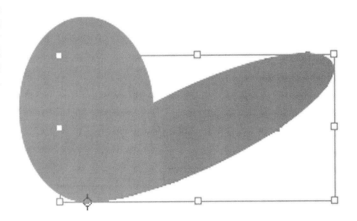

3. Press CMD/CTRL+SHIFT+[to send the shadow object to the back (or use the menu method: Object > Arrange > Send to Back). Fill with gray for now.

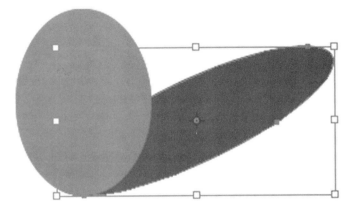

4.   Change the fill to the black and white gradient and use the Gradient tool (G) to drag from the top of the object to the base of it. Experiment with different gradient angles to create the faded effect you want.

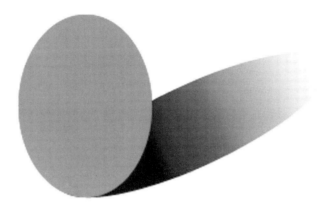

5.   If you are concerned about using raster effects, stop there. Otherwise, you could add a slight blur to the shadow object (Effect > Blur > Gaussian Blur).

Needless to say, you can apply this technique to a variety of objects (including text) and can adapt the steps to create different shadow effects.

Photoshop shadows

Yes, we can create drop shadows using Layer Styles, but what about cast shadows, or shadows that gradually fade out? There are still times when the manual method of creating shadows will give the best results. The simplest way is to duplicate a layer, fill it with a darker color, add a blur, transform, and fade it.

1.   Add a type layer to an image. This image also comes with Illustrator and can be found in the Stock Photography 1 folder (image number 0006618).

2.   Duplicate the type layer (CMD/CTRL+J). With the Eyedropper tool (I), pick up a dark area of the image to use as the shadow colour. Press OPT/ALT+SHIFT+DELETE/BACKSPACE to fill the pixels on the layer with this color.

3.   Move the copy behind the original type layer (CMD/CTRL+[).

4.   CTRL/right-click on the layer and choose rasterize layer from the Context Sensitive menu.

5.   Access Free Transform mode (CMD/CTRL+T) and CMD/CTRL-click on the handles to distort the layer to create the cast shadow look.

6. Now we'll create a displacement map to distort the shadow to follow the texture of the image. Hide the other layers so only the Background is visible. In the Channels palette, choose one of the channels with a good contrast in the key areas (in this case, the footprints on the beach).

7. From the Channels palette pop up menu, choose Duplicate Channel and choose New as the Destination.

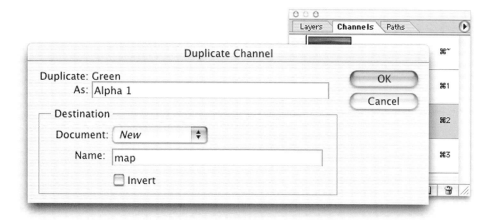

8. In that new document, run the Despeckle filter (Filter > Noise > Despeckle). Press CMD/CTRL+F twice to run the filter two more times. Save the document as a psd file called map.psd.

We use Despeckle rather than Blur to soften the image without losing detail.

9.   Make the shadow layer the active layer (and make sure it's visible). From the Filter menu choose Distort > Displace. You'll have to experiment with the settings, but generally, use low numbers with the Horizontal slightly less than the Vertical Scale.

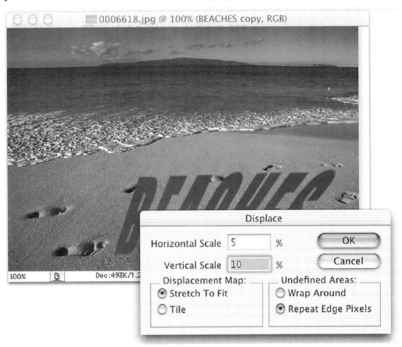

10.   Click OK and choose map.psd as the displacement map.

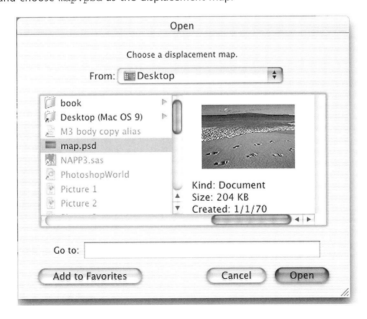

11. This will distort the shadow layer to follow the contours of the beach (Be prepared to undo and try different settings in the Displace filter).

12. Apply a Gaussian Blur (Filter > Blur > Gaussian Blur) to the shadow layer to soften the edges of the shadow.

13. Change the blending mode to Multiply and the layer Opacity to 70%.

14. Add a Layer Mask and use the Gradient tool (G) to paint a gradient on the layer mask to gradually fade out the shadow.

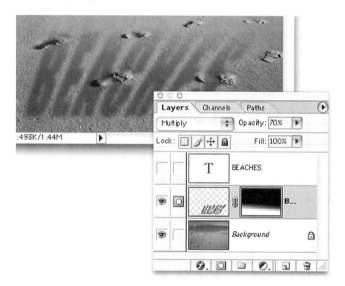

In this case, a Layer Mask was added to the type layer to make the type appear to sink into the sand.

*Another method of creating a cast shadow starts with the Drop Shadow Layer Style. C*TRL*/right-click on the Drop Shadow in the Layers palette and choose Create Layer. This will separate the Drop Shadow to put it on a separate layer. Then you can use Free Transform, etc., to alter the shadow.*

From the quick and dirty school of Photoshop, here's a method to add a shadow that's very quick, but not terribly flexible. With an object on a layer by itself, choose the Brush tool (B) and in the Options Bar, change the blending mode to Behind – this will, in effect, paint on the backside of the layer.

Reflections and shading

As wonderful as Layer Styles are, there are some effects that cannot be achieved with these styles, such as reflections and some forms of shading and highlights. Here are some ideas to get you started in creating realistic effects that cannot be created with Layer Styles alone.

Reflections

The basic idea here is to duplicate a layer, reflect it, and play with opacity, blurring, etc.

1.   Start with an object on a layer by itself and fill the Background layer with white. As shown here, make sure you have some Canvas space below the graphic to make room for the reflection. If you want to use the same image, this is 0006560 in the Stock Photography 1 folder.

2.   Press CMD/CTRL+T for Free Transform, then go to Edit > Transform > Flip Vertical. Press ENTER.

3.   Select the Move tool (V), hold down SHIFT, and drag the copy down until the bottoms line up.

4.   Lower the Opacity of the reflected layer and apply a Gaussian Blur of 3. Make a feathered Lasso selection around a portion of the layer (as shown) and apply a Gaussian blur of 6.

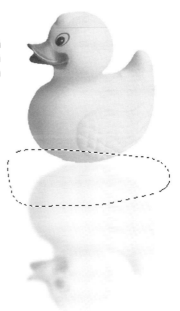

5. Move the selection down slightly (so it overlaps the position of the original selection) and re-apply the filter (CMD/CTRL+F). Continue moving the selection and re-applying the filter so that the further away from the original object you get, the blurrier it gets.

6. To tweak the effect, add a Layer Mask to the reflected layer and paint with black at a very low opacity to slightly hide some areas of the reflection.

7. Use the Marquee tool to select an area as shown (we'll use this to simulate the object sitting on a surface).

8. Add a new layer and fill the selection with a very pale color that's only slightly off white.

9. With the Elliptical Marquee tool, make a small oval selection that has a feather of around 10.

10. Make sure you're on the layer you just created, and then press CMD/CTRL+J to copy this selection onto its on layer.

11. Open the Levels command (CMD/CTRL+L) and drag the white output slider slightly to the left and the black input slider over to the right to create a somewhat darker version of the pale background.

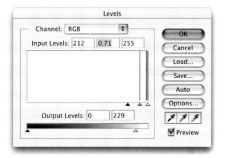

The finished image and Layers palette should look something like this:

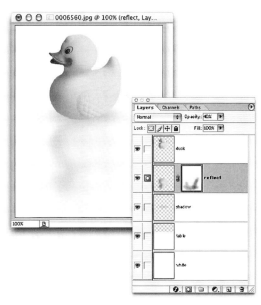

157

Shading

Here's a simple but effective technique to change the shading and lighting on an image. This example uses a photo of a wall with some Illustrator artwork pasted as a poster (I added some masking tape for good measure). I want to add some focus and drama, and thought of using the Lighting Effects filter, but frankly, it's overkill for this job and not as flexible either. Try this simple technique instead:

1. Open `wall.psd`, which is available to download from www.friendsofed.com, and on your image, make a circular selection with a feather of 20 – 25 pixels.

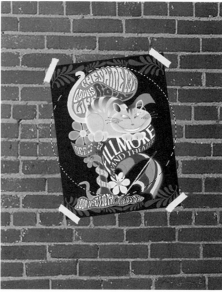

2. From the Adjustment layer menu at the bottom of the Layers palette, add a Levels adjustment. Use the white and gray input sliders to lighten the area (Note how a Layer Mask is automatically created from your selection).

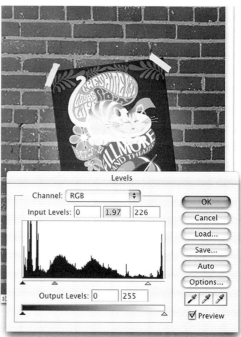

3. CMD/CTRL-click on the Layer Mask to load it as a selection. Inverse the selection (CMD/CTRL+SHIFT+I). Once again, add a Levels Adjustment layer. This time drag the black and gray sliders to the right to darken the image.

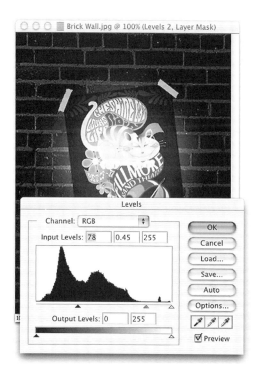

That's it! The advantage of this technique is the only option you have to edit is either (or both) Adjustment layers.

Your final image and Layers palette should look something like this:

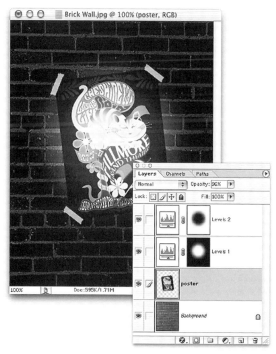

Working with type

Prior to Photoshop 6.0, there was one simple rule for using type: don't! It was pretty straightforward back then: Illustrator for type (since it was vector), Photoshop for special effects (raster is perfect for that). With the introduction of Photoshop 6.0, life with type changed quite dramatically, as Photoshop type became vector-based. This means you can create all kinds of interesting type effects in either Illustrator or Photoshop. The only catch is this: in order for Photoshop type to output in vector quality, it must be saved in either PSD or PDF format. If you save a Photoshop document in any other format such as TIFF, JPEG, etc, the text becomes rasterized. So, save a version as a PSD and save a copy in whatever other format you need.

Let's take a look at some of the more interesting type functions in Illustrator and Photoshop.

Illustrator type

No matter what you do to type in Illustrator, it will remain in vector format and will output at the highest quality – with two exceptions. If you rasterize the type you will, of course, lose the vector capability. Frankly there are very few – if any – situations where rasterizing type is necessary. In fact, you should basically avoid rasterizing type, since vector type gives so many more options. The other exception is really a partial exception: if you use a command called **Create Outlines**, type is converted to a graphic. It is still a vector object, but you lose the option to edit the font, size, or content of the type (there are some good reasons to use this command, but you'd be advised to copy the type and Create Outlines on the copy).

We're not going to explore the basics of using the Type tools as most of those functions are pretty intuitive but we will take a look at a couple of the more unusual type functions.

Text blocks

Most people probably wouldn't think of Illustrator as a page layout program, but it actually does a pretty good job (as long as you only want one page). You can't create columns of text per se, but you can use what Illustrator calls text blocks. Let's have a quick look at using text blocks.

1. Use the Type tool (T) and click and drag to create a rectangular text box.

2. From the File menu select Place to import a text file – Illustrator supports most standard text formats. (If you don't have any text to import, enter some text and then copy and paste until you fill the block).

3. With the Rectangle tool (M) drag a rectangle that will become the second column of text and select both the text block and the drawn rectangle.

Well folks, summer is just around the corner, and that means another very busy season for us all. I know I look forward with great anticipation to the summer concert series where we feature our brightest and best new performers. Another highlight of the summer will certainly be our biggest fund-raising effort ever – look for full details elsewhere in this newsletter.
As exciting a time as this is, we do need to be a little concerned over the recent drop in membership. As we all know, when the Taylor family moved away, that alone caused a drop of 9 members. Hopefully another large

4. From the Type menu choose Blocks > Link.

Well folks, summer is just around the corner, and that means another very busy season for us all. I know I look forward with great anticipation to the summer concert series where we feature our brightest and best new performers. Another highlight of the summer will certainly be our biggest fund-raising effort ever – look for full details elsewhere in this newsletter.
As exciting a time as this is, we do need to be a little concerned over the recent drop in membership. As we all know, when the Taylor family moved away, that alone caused a drop of 9 members. Hopefully another large

family will move into town and fill up some of that gap. A number of our younger members decided not to renew their memberships due to other commitments. Please be assured that your Executive is looking at ways to increase our member base, and we'd sure like your input in this area. Please talk to me with any ideas you might have.
I would like to congratulate the following junior members who recently won medals at the Hollingsworth-Middletown Regional Music Festival: Michael Renny, Gold Violin
Stephanie Smith, Gold Violin
Tyler Adams, Silver | Piano

5.   Edit the text in the first block and the text will re-flow in the second block.

6.   Use the Direct Selection tool (A) to edit the anchor points on the text blocks.

Well folks, summer is just around the corner, and that means another very busy season for us all. I know I look forward with great anticipation to the summer concert series where we feature our brightest and best new performers. Another highlight of the summer will certainly be our biggest fund-raising effort ever – look for full details elsewhere in this newsletter.
As exciting a time as this is, we do need to be a little concerned over the recent drop in membership. As we all know, when the Taylor family moved away, that

alone caused a drop of 9 members. Hopefully another large family will move into town and fill up some of that gap. A number of our younger members decided not to renew their memberships due to other commitments. Please be assured that your Executive is looking at ways to increase our member base, and we'd sure like your input in this area. Please talk to me with any ideas you might have, I would like to congratulate the following junior members who recently won medals at the

7.   If you like, add another shape and link it too – it doesn't have to be a rectangle.

Well folks, summer is just around the corner, and that means another very busy season for us all. I know I look forward with great anticipation to the summer concert series where we feature our brightest and best new performers. Another highlight of the summer will certainly be our biggest fund-raising effort ever – look for full details elsewhere in this newsletter.
As exciting a time as this is, we do need to be a little concerned over the recent drop in membership. As we all know, when the Taylor family moved away, that

alone caused a drop of 9 members. Hopefully another large family will move into town and fill up some of that gap. A number of our younger members decided not to renew their memberships due to other commitments. Please be assured that your Executive is looking at ways to increase our member base, and we'd sure like your input in this area. Please talk to me with any ideas you might have, I would like to congratulate the following junior members who recently won medals at the

Hollingsworth-Middletown Regional Music Festival: Michael Renny, Gold Violin Stephanie Smith, Gold Violin Tyler Adams, Silver Piano Julia Worth, Silver Vocal Soloist Tech Styles, Silver Vocal Group|

If you want to unlink the text blocks you can (Type > Blocks > Unlink), however, you'll end up with two blocks of text that look linked, but are not. Luckily, if you select the two blocks, you can use the Link command to re-establish the flow of text.

Text Wrap

I'd be the first one to admit that the **Text Wrap** function in Illustrator is not as elegant as in page layout software, but it works! The biggest challenge in working with this function is in editing the result, since the objects act as a group. In addition, it works best if you create the text wrap using an object that's slightly larger than the actual object around which you want the text to flow. Let's create a text wrap so we can see how it's done:

1. Draw the shape that you want to cause the text wrap (on top of the text blocks we created previously). In this example, I want the text to wrap around a spherical object so I've drawn a circle on top of my text blocks.

Well folks, summer is just around the corner, and that means another very busy season for us all. I know I look forward with great anticipation to the summer concert series where we feature our brightest best new perform Another highlig summer will c our biggest fe effort ever – l details elsewh newsletter.

As exciting a time a is, we do need to be a little concerned over the recent drop in membership. As we all know, when the Taylor family moved away, that

alone caused a drop of 9 members. Hopefully another large family will move into town and fill up some of that gap. A number of our younger members decided not to renew their emberships due to other mitments. Please be d that your Executive ing at ways to se our member base, e'd sure like your t in this area. Please k to me with any ideas you might have, I would like to congratulate the following junior members who recently won medals at the

2. Select the text blocks and the wrap object.

Well folks, summer is just around the corner, and that means another very busy season for us all. I know I look forward with great anticipation to the summer concert series where we feature our brightest and best new performers. Another highlight of the summer will certainly be our biggest fund-raising effort ever – look for full details elsewhere in this newsletter.

As exciting a time as this is, we do need to be a

little concerned over the recent drop in membership. As we all know, when the Taylor family moved away, that alone caused a drop of 9 members. Hopefully another large family will move into town and fill up some of that gap. A number of our younger members decided not to renew their memberships due to other commitments. Please be assured that your Executive is looking at ways to increase our member base, and we'd sure like your input in this area. Please talk to me with any ideas you

3.   From the Type menu, choose Wrap > Make.

4.   Change the fill and stroke of the wrap object to white so it can no longer be seen.

5.   Position the object on top of the wrap object and that's it!

Well folks, summer is just around the corner, and that means another very busy season for us all. I know I look forward with great anticipation to the summer concert series where we feature our brightest and best new performers. Another highlight of the summer will certainly be our biggest fund-raising effort ever – look for full details elsewhere in this newsletter. As exciting a time as this is, we do need to be a little concerned over the recent drop in membership. As we all know, when the Taylor family moved away, that alone caused a drop of 9 members. Hopefully another large family will move into town and fill up some of that gap. A number of our younger members decided not to renew their memberships due to other commitments. Please be assured that your Executive is looking at ways to increase our member base, and we'd sure like your input in this area. Please talk to me with any ideas you

To edit the text wrap, we'll need to move both the wrap object and the artwork. To do this, use the Group Selection tool and select both objects and re-position them – the text wrap will update.

Well folks, summer is just around the corner, and that means another very busy season for us all. I know I look forward with great anticipation to the summer concert series where we feature our brightest and bestinly be our biggest fund-raising effort ever – look for full details elsewhere in this newsletter. As exciting a time as this is, we do need to be a little concerned over the recent drop in membership. As we all know, when the Taylor family moved away, that alone caused a drop of 9 members. Hopefully another large family will move into town and fill up some of that gap. A number of our younger members decided not to renew their memberships due to other commitments. Please be assured that your Executive is looking at ways to increase our member base, and we'd sure like your input in this area. Please talk to me with any ideas you might have,

Tabs, rows, and columns

The controls over tabs in Illustrator are very intuitive – in fact, in some ways better than many text processors. Let's take a quick look at using tabs, and then turn the text block into rows and columns.

1. Create a text block and type in text with tabs in between numbers, creating several lines (ideally, use words of different lengths so that the tabs don't line up at first).

South Nepean United	11	3	4	37
Kanata Rangers 9	6	2	29	
Osgoode 6	6	5	23	
Gloucester Hornets White	7	8	0	14
Ottawa Internationals Red	5	12	0	10
Savin City 3	11	1	10	
Capital United 0	16	1		1

2. From the Window menu, choose Type > Tab Ruler.

3. Click on the tab ruler to add a series of right hand tabs until the text lines up (the tab stops, small arrows, show where your text is going to line up).

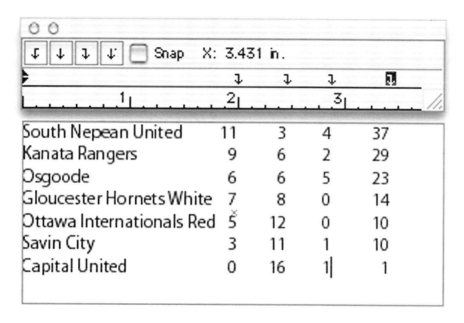

South Nepean United	11	3	4	37
Kanata Rangers	9	6	2	29
Osgoode	6	6	5	23
Gloucester Hornets White	7	8	0	14
Ottawa Internationals Red	5	12	0	10
Savin City	3	11	1	10
Capital United	0	16	1	1

4.   Now select Type > Rows & Columns.

5.   Make sure the Preview option is checked, and change the number of rows and/or columns until you get the result you want.

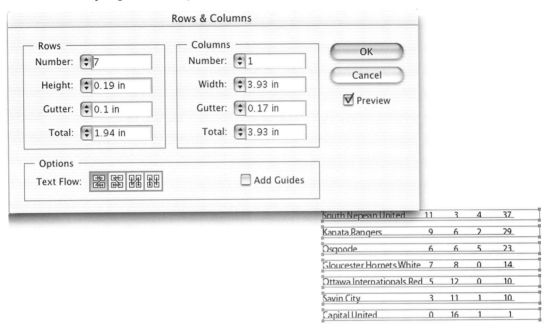

6.   Here, every second text block (a result of the Rows & Columns command) was selected and filled.

South Nepean United	11	3	4	37
Kanata Rangers	9	6	2	29
Osgoode	6	6	5	23
Gloucester Hornets White	7	8	0	14
Ottawa Internationals Red	5	12	0	10
Savin City	3	11	1	10
Capital United	0	16	1	1

Photoshop type

When working with type in Photoshop, your number one goal should be avoiding rasterizing the text if at all possible. Now, there will be times when you don't have any other choice but to rasterize the text. For example, as we discussed earlier, the Perspective and Distort transformations can only be applied to rasterized text. In these cases, you may want to make a copy of the Type layer and rasterize the copy, just as a back up plan.

It's important to note that, just because you get a dialog box saying you have to rasterize the type doesn't necessarily mean that is true.

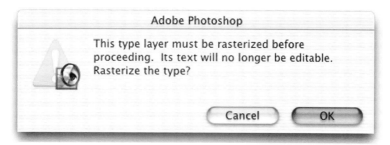

For example, try to apply a filter to a type layer and the dialog box will appear. Should you proceed and rasterize? Again, not unless you have to. In the section on Layer Clipping Groups, we looked at a technique that avoids having to rasterize but still gets the same end result as applying a filter to rasterized text. Painting on a type layer or applying a gradient also causes this warning box to open. Again, by using techniques such as Layer Clipping Groups, or even just a blank layer, this permanent step of rasterizing can be avoided.

On the other side of the coin, there are some pretty interesting type options that are available without rasterizing, such as Text Warp. This command applies a warp effect to a type layer, and both the type itself and the warping remain editable. With a type layer active – the text itself does not have to be selected – just click on the **Create warped text** button in the Options bar.

There are a number of different styles available in the Style drop-down box. Also, the settings for each of these styles can be adjusted using the sliders and boxes found in the Warp Text dialog box. Take advantage of the live preview to try different settings.

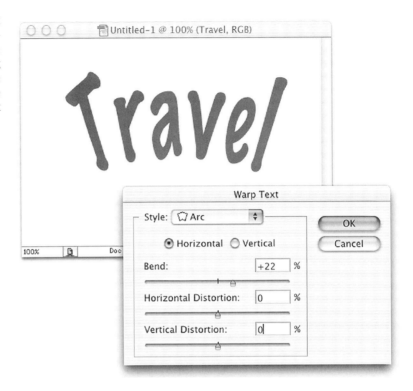

Unfortunately, it is only possible to apply one warp effect to a type layer. As long as you see the warp symbol in the Layers palette, you can click on the warp button to edit the warp.

Paragraph text

Don't feel restricted to using one or two words of text on a layer – you can also create paragraph text. Instead of clicking once with the Type tool, click and drag with it as if you are drawing a rectangle. This becomes a text block that will cause the text to automatically flow from line to line without carriage returns.

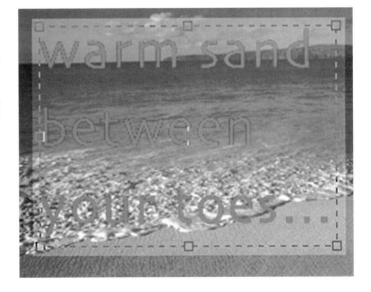

You can edit the text or the size of the box (by dragging the handles) and the text re-flows. If you need to create a paragraph text box of a specific size, hold down OPT/ALT and click with the Type tool. A dialog box will prompt you to enter a size (don't worry if it's in pixels, just type in if you want inches).

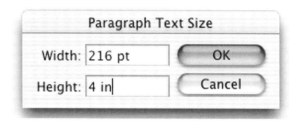

Once the text is created as a paragraph, we can take full advantage of the Character and Paragraph palettes.

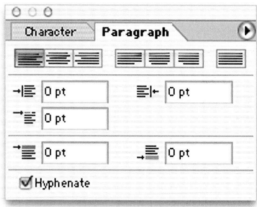

To convert a regular type layer (called Point text) to paragraph text, just make sure the type layer is active and choose Layer > Type > Convert to Paragraph Text. To convert the other direction (paragraph into point type) use the same approach, except the menu command will say Convert to Point Text.

Type tips

Here are a few quick tips that should help speed things up – or solve problems you may run into.

Changing the color of highlighted text

There's a simple answer to the puzzling question – how can I see the color of text when it's highlighted? This is an odd situation that can come up quite often: in some situations, you need to highlight text to change its color. However, when the text is highlighted, it's next to impossible to see the actual color when you're seeing a weird, color negative effect.

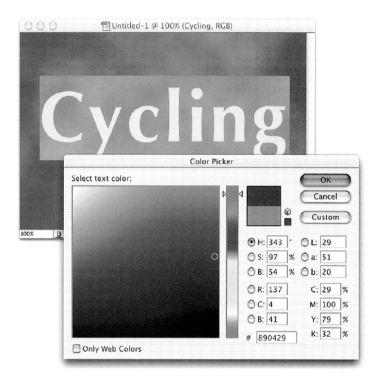

The way around this? With the text highlighted, press CMD/CTRL+H to Hide Extras – in this case the extra is the highlight. Now you can see the color you're choosing.

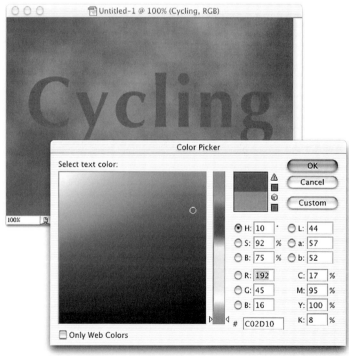

In many instances, you don't need to highlight the text to change its color. With the type layer active, just choose your color and press OPT/ALT+DELETE/BACKSPACE.

Editing multiple type layers

This shortcut can save a lot of time in situations when you have many type layers and you want to edit them all at one, to change the font for example.

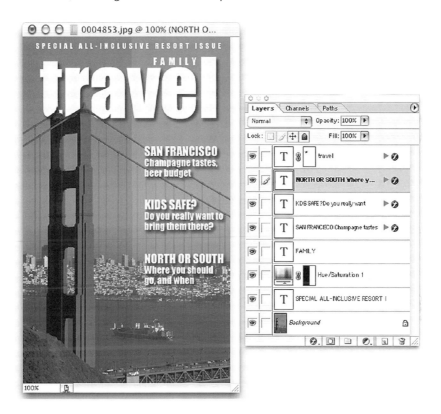

In the above example, there are six type layers, all of which share the same font, but are different sizes. I'd like to experiment with different fonts – very quickly. Rather than selecting and changing each type layer, use this trick: Make sure no text is highlighted, but that one of the type layers is active. Link all the type layers that you want to edit. Then hold down SHIFT and from the Options bar, choose a different font, and watch as all fonts change automatically. (You can also change other options such as size, tracking, etc., with this technique).

Browsing through fonts

Want to see what your type layer would look like in a variety of fonts – quickly? Try this. Activate the type layer and make sure the Type tool (T) is active (you don't have to highlight the text). In the Options bar, click once in the font field, and then press the up or down arrow keys to scroll through the fonts and watch the type layer change on the fly.

Or, if you know what font you want to pick (from your very long list of choices), once again, activate the type layer and make sure the Type tool is active. Click once in the font field, then press the first letter (or two) of the font you want. The text will not change automatically, so you must press ENTER to confirm your choice.

Conclusion

Photoshop and Illustrator share many similar features and functions. Throughout this chapter we have examined these carefully to better understand the distinctions between the two, to see where one application might be better suited to one task than another. With the essential building blocks clearly understood then we can best exploit the two applications to achieve optimum results.

After all this theory I'm sure you are waiting to get stuck in to some practical work. Over the next few chapters we'll look at Photoshop and Illustrator working in perfect harmony in some real-world practical examples.

4 Creating a Corporate Identity

A business's corporate identity becomes its own shop window and portrays an image of that business to the potential customer. In many cases that corporate identity, be it the logo, letterhead, or website, can make the difference between turning the potential customer into a buying customer or losing them to a competitor. It is easy to understand therefore why corporations allocate vast budgets, seemingly disproportionately, on creating the corporate image.

History shows that most of the successful business logos through the ages are comprised of simple, bold shapes that catch the eye. The design itself may be quite abstract and initially appear to have little to do with the business service or product, but it is this abstract quality that can have the most time enduring impact once the association has been forged. A contemporary example of this could be Nike's logo. Its origins are indeed abstract, but the logo is now omnipresent. Nike was the Greek goddess of victory, and after a success in battle the victors would proudly call out the word "Nike". The "swoosh" design represents one of the goddess' wings. The Mercedes car company logo shares a similar distinction in that the original concept behind the logo has been lost, but the abstract image is powerful enough to make the association in the viewer's mind.

This is what the game is all about. Make the image simple enough and strong enough to catch the viewer's attention and ensure that image appears everywhere, that the business has a presence. The creation of shapes for logos is where Illustrator excels. In fact, you do not even need to be able to draw in order to create professional looking logos. All the tools are at your disposal, it's just a matter of knowing how to combine them to achieve the effect and that's exactly what you are going to learn in this chapter.

But why use Illustrator and not Photoshop? Illustrator as you know is a vector application and vector artwork can be scaled up or down to suit your final needs without loss of quality. As previously mentioned, the business logo needs to appear wherever the business has a presence. The logo on a business card or letterhead may be less than an inch in size, but the same logo could be several feet in size on an exhibition display or the side of a delivery van. As long as the logo has been created in a vector application this will not pose a problem as the logo can be resized without any loss of its original integrity.

A logo created in a bitmap application, such as Photoshop, would not only take longer to create, (given that the creation and transforming tools are not as efficient as Illustrator's), but resizing that logo would incur a loss of quality, and also result in a larger file size.

In terms of using the logo for the business web site, you will of course need to use a bitmap version, unless you are using the Flash SWF or Adobe SVG format, but it is still easier to create the original artwork in Illustrator and rasterize it (convert it to a bitmap) for use on the web page. This means you could use the same artwork and rasterize it as many times as necessary at different sizes.

The scenario

Our task is to create the corporate identity of *The Music Factory*, a business selling musical instruments in their own store and on the Web. The elements required by the business will include a logo, a business card, and a quarter page display advert suitable for magazine publishing.

As with any business, budgets must be tightly controlled and to minimize costs it has been decided to produce the logo using a single spot color. So our first task is to set up the page with just the required spot color in the swatches palette. This is good practice as it prevents accidental use of an incorrect color. It also reduces the all-important file size by excluding irrelevant color information in the swatches palette.

Setting up the document for spot colors

We're designing for print, so the color mode will be CMYK, the optimum format for print work.

1.   Create a new CMYK document (the default page size is fine to work with).

We first need to delete all the default swatches apart from the registration color swatch and the white swatch, which will be used for unpainted areas of the artwork.

2.   Select the black swatch in the Swatches palette, then press and hold the SHIFT key and select the last swatch in the palette. (Make sure your Swatches palette is set to view all swatches, including gradients and patterns, otherwise you will only be deleting the solid colors). With all the swatches selected, click the trash icon at the bottom of the palette. You will be asked to confirm deletion of swatches. Click Yes.

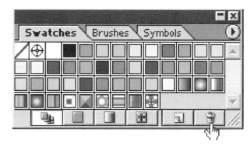

Next we are going to load the required spot color.

3.   Go to Window > Swatch Libraries > Pantone Solid Coated. The Swatch Libraries contain a number of pantone palettes, including Process, Pastel, Metallic, and many others. The palette you choose depends on the finished effect you are trying to achieve.

The Pantone Solid palette opens as a separate palette. The color we are going to use is **Pantone Process Black C**.

4.   Click in the Find Field at the top of the palette and type B. The first letter of the word black is all that is required to find our color. The color name appears in the field and the color appears highlighted in the palette. Here, I'm viewing the palette in List mode, but naturally you can choose to view thumbnails instead by selecting this in the palette menu.

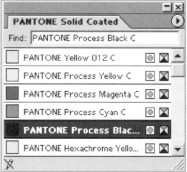

5.   To add the Pantone Process Black C to the document Swatches palette, click on its name in the Pantone palette and it will then appear in the main document Swatches palette. You can now close the Pantone palette.

Creating the company logo

This picture is the finished logo that you will be creating from scratch.

There are many ways of approaching this project. The aim is to use the most efficient techniques, ensuring that you complete the work in minutes rather than hours. To use processes that ensure precision and accuracy in your finished artwork, which will not only be pleasing on the eye but also avoid potential postscript printing errors.

Creating the body of the guitar with the Pen tool

It would require impressive eye to hand co-ordination and an enviable flair for drawing to achieve the perfect symmetry of a guitar, so we are not even going to attempt it. Any time symmetry is required the technique of choice is to create half the shape and use the Reflect tool to create the perfect other half. That is how we will approach it, but first we need to create the soft curves of one half of the guitar with the Pen tool.

Open the file called guitarbody.ai from the download folder.

The file is zoomed in to 400%. A template has been created on a locked layer displaying the optimum positions to click and drag with the Pen tool to create the left half of the guitar. Think of this as a sophisticated join the dots puzzle. As with any artwork involving the Pen tool, fewer anchor points result in smoother curves, smaller file size, and, because the file is simpler, less chance of errors when printing. This shape will use just four anchor points to complete one half of the guitar.

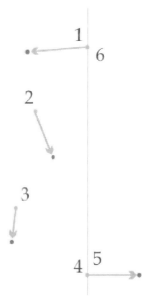

In the file, but obviously not shown here, you'll see a mixture of colors. Green dots show you where to click. Red dots show you where to drag to before releasing the mouse button. The blue guideline running down the middle of the page defines the exact center of the guitar and will be used as a reference point later when we have to reflect the other half of the guitar. The blue guideline will also help you define exactly where to click when you start and finish the shape. This will be important to avoid any gaps showing between the two halves of the guitar.

Let's get started.

1. Select the Pen tool (P). Make sure you have the layer named artwork selected. Starting at position number 1, click and drag from the green dot to the red dot. Continue this process until you complete dot number 4.

    Right, we'll just pause here to consider our next click. We need a straight segment between dot 5 and 6, so that we have an even reflection, therefore we need to create a corner anchor point. When you dragged from dot number 4 you automatically created a smooth anchor point, but we're now going to countermand this, and convert it into a corner anchor point.

2. Press and hold the Opt/Alt key to automatically create a corner anchor point and with the Pen tool click dot 5. (The same dot is used for clicks 4 and 5). This will result in a straight segment when you click dot number 6. Alternatively you could hover over dot 4/5, until the small corner anchor sign appears beneath the Pen, click now to create a corner anchor point.

3. Click dot number 6 (same as dot number 1) making sure you are over the original anchor point to complete the shape. Look to see when the cursor has changed to a circle, which indicates that the path is about to be closed.

4. Zoom in to check that the two anchor points directly on top of the vertical blue guide are correctly positioned. If you clicked slightly to the left or right of the guide, use the **Direct Selection** tool (A) to drag the point into position. This will ensure when you reflect the other side of the guitar there will be no gaps in the middle.

This is how your finished artwork should look. I have hidden the template layer in this picture so just the artwork and vertical blue guideline remain visible.

Creating the neck of the guitar

We are going to stick with the policy of drawing half of the symmetrical shape for the guitar neck.

1. Using the **Rectangle** tool (M), create a rectangle with a black stroke and no fill with a Width of 0.138 in and a Height of 1.35 in (as you know you click on the workspace to bring up the Rectangle options box to set these dimensions).

2. Make sure **Snap to Point** is enabled from the View menu and snap the edge of the rectangle to the blue vertical guide as in the picture. The bottom of the neck should just overlap the body of the guitar. It is vital that the right edge of the rectangle is snapped directly to the guide, so the anchor points actually sit on the guideline. If not, the two halves of the neck won't align correctly when the other half is reflected.

The neck needs to taper gently towards the top. This is an ideal task for the **Reshape** tool. The Reshape tool allows you to create anchor points and move them with greater fluidity than conventional anchor points. Although they offer a little less precision, they can be easier to use when creating free flowing shapes.

3. Before using the Reshape tool, the object being edited needs to be selected with the Direct Selection tool. This is so that you can edit part of the object without all the anchor points being affected. Select the guitar neck with the Direct Selection tool (A). Make sure all four anchor points are white, confirming they are not selected. From the toolbox, select the Reshape tool. It lives behind the Scale tool.

4. Click on the stroke of the guitar neck as indicated in the picture below to make the anchor point.

With the same tool, drag the anchor point a short distance to the right to create the tapered effect. Use the picture as a reference on how much to drag.

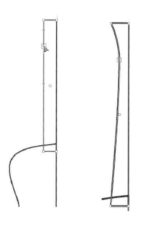

Creating the other half of the guitar

Now that the left side is complete, we are going to use the **Reflect** tool to flip and duplicate the shape. As with all of the transformation tools, the Reflect tool performs its function based on a point of origin. By default, this point of origin is the center of the object's bounding box. In order to create a symmetrical object it will be necessary to change the point of origin in order for the two halves to join up correctly. Let's work through that process.

1. Select both the guitar body and neck using the Selection tool (A), and then select the Reflect tool (O) from the toolbox. It lives behind the Rotate tool.

After selecting the Reflect tool you will see the point of origin appear as a target symbol, based on the center point of both of the selected objects.

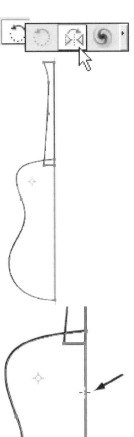

2. Now, we need to change the point of origin. This is where the blue guideline will help us. The guide defines the line over which we need to flip the left side of the guitar. (If the blue guideline were not in place, then it would of course be possible to use smart guides to help us define the point of reflection). Press and hold the OPT/ALT key and click anywhere on the guideline to reposition the point of origin, holding down the OPT/ALT key will open up the Reflect tool dialog box, an alternative to double-clicking on the tool in the toolbox.

3. We need to reflect a duplicate over the vertical axis at an angle of 90 degrees. Make sure the Preview button is checked, so that you verify that your point of origin is correct, and click the Copy button to create the duplicate.

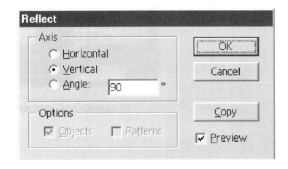

The end result is a perfectly symmetrical guitar.

*There are a number of options open to you to "clean up" artwork rather than start-ing from scratch. Using the **Average** command (Object > Path > Average) allows you to align selected anchor points along a vertical, horizontal, or any other axis. In instances where anchor points have not joined resulting in open paths when a closed path was desired, use the Join command to automatically join two endpoints (Object > Path > Join) or use the keyboard shortcut CMD/CTRL+J. If too many anchor points is the problem, the quickest way to rectify it is to use the **Delete Anchor Point** tool. This is the pen with the minus sign, found within the Pen tool location in the toolbox.*

Combining all the shapes with Pathfinders

Although the guitar artwork could be used as it is, it doesn't yet qualify as professionally finished artwork. The problem is that it is a collection of four shapes. This means there are a number of line segments and anchor points that are superfluous and only serve to add to the file size and potentially cause problems for printers. The file size issue may not seem a major issue with such a simple file, but as your project grows and becomes more complex, maintaining sleek file sizes is crucial.

This is where the Pathfinder commands can come to the rescue. One simple pathfinder can clean up all four shapes and convert them into one single piece of neat artwork.

If the Pathfinder palette is not open, go to Window > Pathfinder (SHIFT+F9).

1.   Select all four shapes of the guitar.

2.   In the Pathfinder palette, click the first icon in the first row as shown below. This is the **Add to Shape Area** pathfinder that will unite all the shapes and remove any overlapping segments and anchor points.

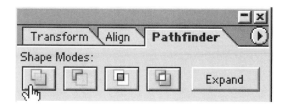

The **Expand** button now becomes active as seen in the above picture. The pathfinder process will only be completed once the Expand button has been clicked. Until you click the Expand button, you are left with a compound shape. The compound shape, although appearing to be one entity is actually the original shape with all the overlapping lines and anchor points no longer visible, but the shapes can still be edited individually using the Direct Selection tool or the Group Selection tool. The image below demonstrates this principle.

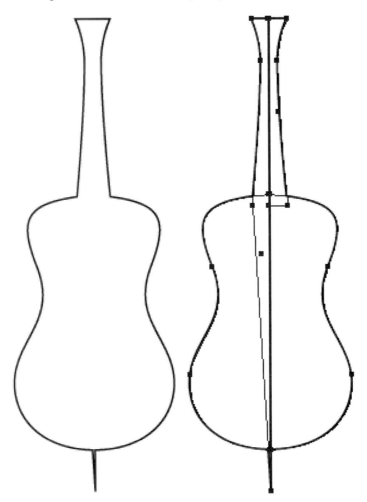

Both pieces of artwork have had the pathfinder as above applied, but neither has been expanded yet. The shape on the left has been deselected, so all we can see is an apparently single shape resembling a cello with a spike protruding from the bottom, rather than a guitar. The shape on the right has been selected with the Direct Selection tool and reveals how moving one of the original anchor points has created the spike. All the anchor points and lines can be edited in the same way even though they may not be visible once the shape has been deselected.

3.   Click the Expand button now to complete the Pathfinder command.

Creating the ellipse

In the final design, the guitar appears to be seated within an elliptical disc that hides the bottom of the guitar. This 3D illusion can be achieved quickly and accurately, once again with the aid of the pathfinders.

First we need to create the elliptical disc.

1. In a blank part of the page create an ellipse with a black stroke and no fill with a Width of 2.127 in, and a Height of 1.377 in.

> *In case you are wondering where the measurements originate from, the entire logo was created freely by creating shapes directly on the page and scaling them to form an aesthetically pleasing shape. The only reason they are being quoted in this case is so that you can follow along and reproduce identical artwork. When creating your own projects you will most likely create elements without worrying about their measurements in the early stages.*

2. Rotate the ellipse to an angle of –37.613 degrees. The easiest way to do this is to use the Transform palette. Your ellipse should look like the image here:

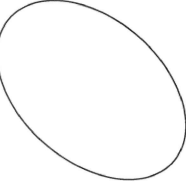

The ellipse has a smaller ellipse within in it that is off center creating the flat disc effect. We are going to use a command that will create a duplicate at a precise offset from the original in one step.

3. Ensure that the ellipse is selected and then go to Object > Path > Offset Path. In the Offset Path dialog box that opens, entering a negative number in the Offset field will create a duplicate object that is smaller than the original object. In this case, I have entered a value of –0.12 in, so the duplicate ellipse will be 0.12 in smaller than the original.

The Joins drop-down box has no effect with this elliptical shape, but let's take a brief look at the available options:

- **Miter**: Creates a stroke with pointed corners.

- **Bevel**: Creates squared off corners.

- **Round**: Creates rounded corners.

Miter limit is the method by which Illustrator defines whether a mitered join or a beveled join should be created. The range is 1 to 500 with 4 being the default. If the default is used, once the length of the point becomes four times the weight of the stroke, a bevel join will replace a miter join.

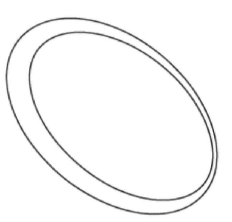

4.   Click OK to confirm the command.

5.   Keeping the smaller ellipse selected, press the right arrow key on the keyboard six times to nudge the shape to the right. You should be left with your artwork looking like the image here.

Combining the guitar and ellipse

The two major pieces of the logo are now ready to be brought together. We are now going to place the ellipse over the guitar. You could place the objects by eye, but it will be much more precise if you enter co-ordinates for positioning to match my artwork, so we'll do it this way.

1.   We'll start by synchronizing our canvases, by making sure that you have the same zero point that I'm using. If you haven't changed the zero point of the page it will still be using the default, which is the bottom left corner of the page. If you have changed the zero point, simply double-click in the top left corner of the page where the two rulers meet to reset the page to the default.

2.   Select the guitar, and then enter 4 in the X field and 6 in the Y field in the Transform palette, as in the picture below. The diagram to the left of the X and Y field in the Transform palette is the objects reference point. This controls which point of the object is used in order to take measurements. Make sure the center dot is selected as in the example otherwise your positioning will not match mine.

3. Now select the ellipse and enter the following values in the X and Y fields: X= 3.889 in, and Y= 5.253 in.

Your artwork should now be perfectly placed as in the example shown here:

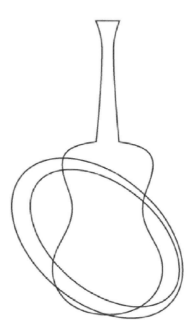

A similar situation now exists as when we brought the various pieces of the guitar together. We need to lose all the superfluous lines and anchor points, but this time we also need to create the illusion that the ellipse is a hoop and the guitar is positioned inside the hoop, so part of it is in front of the guitar and part of it behind. Once again a pathfinder will help us create this illusion.

We composed the artwork using strokes with no fills. This made it easier to draw and manipulate the shapes. However, the final logo uses filled shapes with no strokes, so we are going to use a nifty series of shortcuts to convert the shapes from black stroked objects to black filled objects.

Here goes.

1. Select both the guitar and ellipse shapes. As you know, if your stroke color is behind your fill color box, as in the picture below, then your stroke color is not active. Press X on the keyboard to bring the stroke box to the front and therefore activate it.

2. Press the / key on the keyboard to apply no color to the stroke.

3. Press X again to bring the fill color box to the front and activate it.

4.   Press the , key to fill the selected objects with our black fill color.

You should now have shapes with black fills and no strokes.

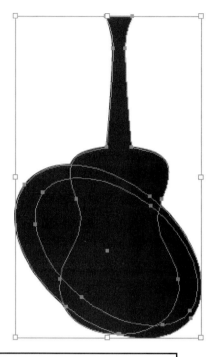

 This keyboard sequence provides the fastest method for adding and removing color from fills and strokes. There are actually three keys in total that provide color functions and they all sit together consecutively. You've seen how the , and / work. The . key that sits in between these two applies a gradient fill to selected objects.

Now that the color is set, we need to dissect the shapes to create the illusion that the ellipse is wrapped around the guitar. Pathfinders will make this easy.

We are going to use the pathfinder called **Divide** as indicated:

You don't need to remember all the symbol icons on the Pathfinder palette, just hover the mouse cursor over the icon and a tool tip will appear, as long as this is enabled. If not, Press CMD/CTRL+K to open the General Preferences dialog box and put a check mark in the Show Tool Tips check box.

The Divide pathfinder works by dividing all overlapping shapes into separate filled shapes that are grouped and not overlapping. This is perfect for the task in hand.

1. Select both of the shapes and click the Divide pathfinder button. The difference you see on screen will be very subtle. A few extra anchor points will appear where required to construct any new independent shapes.

    Because both of the shapes are black, if you deselect the object you will only see one black mass. So we are going to create a rectangle with a mid gray color that sits behind the object and makes it easier to edit from here onwards. This rectangle will also become part of the finished logo.

2. Create a black filled rectangle with no stroke and the following dimensions and positioning:

    Width   3.1 in
    Height   4.0 in
    X position   3.825 in
    Y position   5.7 in

    This places the rectangle directly on top of the logo, so we need to send it to the back. Press CMD/CTRL+SHIFT+[to send the rectangle to the back .You won't notice a difference, of course as the rectangle is also black, so we need to adjust the color.

3. Make sure the rectangle is still selected and use the Color palette to reduce the tint to 50%, resulting in a gray color.

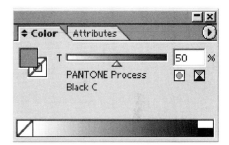

    Your artwork should now look like this picture:

The pathfinder action has now made it very easy for us to apply a white fill color to selected areas and create the final illusion. Each independent shape within the group as a whole can be selected by using the Group Selection tool. We are going to use that tool now to select individual elements and color them with a white fill. There is also one element that we are going to delete altogether.

4. Select the Group Selection tool and click the neck of the guitar. This will select only the individual component as it was divided by the Pathfinder command. Apply a white fill to the shape so your artwork resembles the example below.

5. Continue this process, selecting and filling with white using the following sequence of pictures as a guide to which objects to select and color.

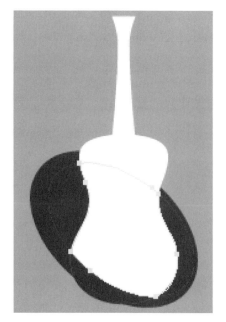

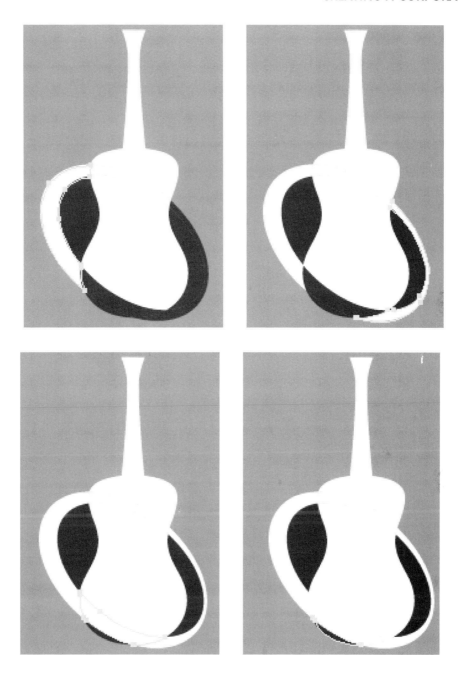

6. The last picture shows the bottom left corner of the guitar selected. This element is not needed as we want the guitar to appear as if it is hidden inside the ellipse, so rather than filling this shape with white, simply delete it and you will be left with the logo resembling the picture below.

It's really coming together now, but if you look closely you will see a hairline where the ellipse cuts through at the top and the bottom of the guitar. This is easily fixed by reversing the process we carried out earlier. We dissected the overlapping shapes with the Divide pathfinder, now we are going to combine certain elements again so we are left with clean, efficient shapes.

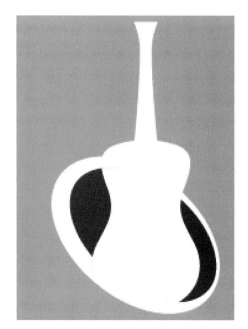

7. The guitar is now comprised of four shapes. Select all four shapes with the Group Selection tool. The shapes are highlighted in the following example.

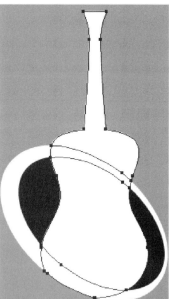

8. In the Pathfinder palette, click the **Add to shape area** icon. Then click the Expand button to confirm the action. This will combine all four shapes into one.

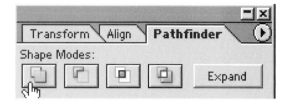

9. Select the rectangle and return its color to 100% black.

Finally we need to add a couple of points of detail to the guitar: an oval, to represent the acoustic hole, and a rectangle for the board to which the strings are attached. To create these shapes we'll use the Ellipse tool, and the Rectangle tool respectively

10. The problem with these elements is that they need to be in the precise center of the guitar, so you need to position the cursor over the center vertical guideline and hold down the OPT/ALT key as you drag the mouse out. This forces the shape to be drawn from the center so there is no alignment to worry about.

11. That's the guitar and ellipse elements of the logo complete, so now make sure you save the file before proceeding. (You don't need reminding about that though – you've been doing frequent saves all along haven't you?)

Creating the musical notes

1. Create a new layer in the file and name it "music notes". This is the layer we will work on. To prevent any accidental editing of our existing artwork, lock the main artwork layer by clicking the empty gray box to the left of the layer name. This reveals the lock icon as in the picture here.

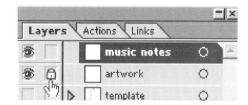

We could draw the complete musical note using the pen, but why create extra work when we can use the Ellipse tool to get us started.

2. On a blank part of the page create an ellipse with a black stroke and no fill with the following measurements: Width = 0.135 in, Height = 0.108 in

3. Rotate the ellipse to an angle of 15.6 degrees.

We are going to use the Pen tool to create the tail of the music note, but we need to do it in such a way so the whole music note can be combined into one shape easily without any fragments jutting out. The most precise way to do this is to have the first anchor point for the tail being one of the existing anchor points in the ellipse.

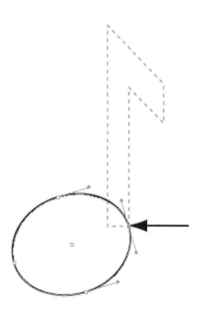

4. Using the Pen tool (P), place the cursor over the anchor point as illustrated in the picture below. If you have not changed the default preferences for the Pen tool, you will notice a minus sign appear next to the cursor. This means that if you click you will delete the existing anchor point and so destroy the ellipse shape, which is not what we want to achieve. To override this, keep the SHIFT key pressed as you click to make your first anchor point with the Pen tool.

This is a really handy trick - it allows you to start an independent shape with perfect accuracy based on the ellipse's anchor point, but without deleting its anchor point. This also means you do not have to change the preferences, but keep the useful functionality of being able to delete and add anchor points when necessary by just clicking on a point or line segment.

5. After making your first anchor point, continue clicking using the dotted line in the above example as a guide. Keep the SHIFT key pressed as you click which will constrain the angles to increments of 45 degrees. Click on the first anchor point in your new shape to create a closed path.

Your finished artwork should look similar to the image here. Your dimensions may differ slightly, but the important thing is that the first anchor point you made is directly over the ellipse's anchor point.

6.   To combine the shapes use the Pathfinder Add to Shape area icon as before, then click the Expand button to confirm the action.

7.   Apply a black fill and no stroke. Eventually the music notes will be white on a black background, but we are filling them with black for the moment so they show up on our white page.

As a result of applying the pathfinder, a number of additional points may have been added that serve no purpose, so we need to clean these up.

8.   Select the music note and go to Object > Path > Simplify. In the dialog box drag the Curve Precision slider to 100%. This maintains the integrity of the original curves. Lower settings will reduce the amount of points but also change the original shape. Drag the Angle Threshold slider to 180 degrees. This controls the smoothness of corners. In my example, these settings have reduced the amount of anchor points from 32 to 11 without affecting the shape.

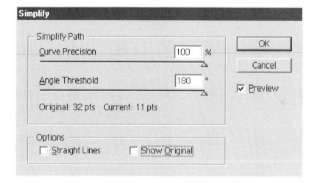

9.   To complete the musical note element, select the note with the Selection tool (V), then click on its side, and drag away from it, keeping the OPT/ALT key pressed as you do so. Position the two notes in a similar configuration to the following picture, select both of them and go to Object > Group to group them.

Rotating the musical notes around the guitar

The notes will form a semi-circle on the left side of the logo. Despite the precision with which they are distributed the process is unbelievably simple, fast, and accurate.

We'll create a white stroked circle to define the path that we would like the notes to take. This circle is not part of the logo but merely serves as a guide to follow.

1. Position the two music notes on the black background. This will be the first pair. Apply a white fill so they are visible. Use the example above as a guide.

2. Create the circle using the original vertical guide as a starting point. Holding down the OPT/ALT key, drag to create the circle from the center. The size of the circle must be gauged by eye assessing how you would like the semi-circular shape of the music notes to flow. Again use the above example to guide you.

3. Once the circle is complete, keep it selected so that its center point is visible, and then drag a horizontal guide onto the page so it intersects with the circle's center point. You should be left with a circle with both guides criss-crossing through its center. That is all you need to set up the rotating music notes.

4. Now that we have the guides and a center point in position, these can be used as a reference in determining how the music notes will be controlled as they are rotated. We therefore no longer need the white circle so that can be deleted.

5. Select the music notes, and then using the **Rotate** tool (R), hold down the OPT/ALT key and click the point where the guidelines cross. This point becomes the new point of origin for the grouped music notes. This means we are able to rotate the notes around this point and achieve a perfect semi-circular flow. Holding down the OPT/ALT key causes the Rotate dialog box to open where a precise value can be entered. Enter 20.19 degrees. I have used a precise value in this case purely for the object of enabling you to recreate the artwork exactly. Click the Copy button and a duplicate will appear rotated at an angle of 20.19 degrees.

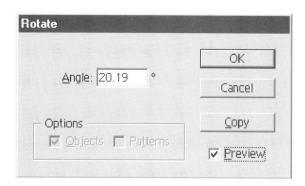

From a designer's point of view you may find it preferable to use this method, judging the rotated duplicates by eye. If you would like to use precise numbers to create the circle of objects a simple bit of math will help you out. As an example, let's say you want nine objects to form a semi-circle, equally spaced on the left. Divide 180 (the degrees of half of a circle) by 8 (the number of duplicates required, the ninth one will be the original shape you start with), this gives you 22.5. Position the original object at the top of where you would like your semi-circle to begin. With the Rotate tool, OPT/ALT-click somewhere below the object in a perfect vertical line (Use smart guides or create a vertical guide) then type 22.5 in the rotation in the degrees field of the Rotate dialog box and click the Copy button. Finally press CMD/CTRL+D seven times to repeat the process, leaving you with nine objects.

6. Before doing anything else, press CMD/CTRL+D. This is the keyboard shortcut for Object > Transform > Transform Again and repeats the last transformation you applied. In this instance it produces another duplicate at 20.19 degrees. Repeat the same shortcut until you have created a semi circle of music notes as below.

Adding the text

1. Using the **Type** tool (T), click on a blank part of the screen. Type the company name *The Music Factory*. At this stage your text should be black.

2. Open the Character palette by going to Window > Type > Character, (CTRL/CMD+T). Select the text, and from the Character palette choose the font Book Antiqua. If you don't have that font, select one of your choice. The font size I used was 22 point. To space the letters out a little I set the Tracking to 75.

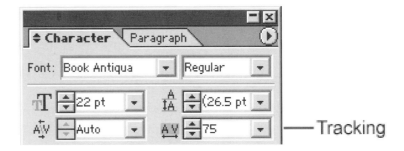

3. We want the text to be centered horizontally on top of the logo's black rectangle. To do this accurately, click on the black rectangle and take a reading of the X co-ordinate from the Transform palette. In my example it is 3.825 in. Select the text and type the same value into the X field of the Transform palette. The vertical position can be done by eye, but to match my artwork, enter 3.956 in into the Y field of the Transform palette. Finally, change the color of the text to white.

4. Now you need to create a white filled rectangle with the following dimensions and co-ordinates. Your co-ordinates may alter slightly; the important point is that the rectangle should sit over the word Factory.

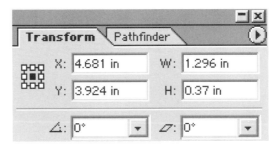

5. Send the white rectangle behind the text, select the word Factory, and change its color to black.

That's it we're finished. As the logo is a vector we are free to scale it up or down as necessary without losing any quality.

Embellishing vector artwork in Photoshop

There are times when, budget permitting, you may want to add a bit of sparkle to your logo. This may be for a special color feature in a printed publication, a web site feature, or a video or screen presentation. Illustrator's arsenal of tools and filters offer a broad range of options, but it still won't give you the almost limitless choice of possibilities that Photoshop can offer.

In the next exercise we are going to use part of the logo you created in the previous section and jazz it up in Photoshop for an on screen presentation.

Open the file called `logo_embellish.ai`, this is the logo without the text.

This is the finished effect we are going to create. The true impact of the effect will be appreciated when you complete the exercise and the metallic effect gradient colors show through on your screen.

In order to apply the effect we need to keep the guitar separate from the background. The guitar has been placed on its own layer and the black background sits on the bottom layer. By creating artwork on layers we can export the file as a Photoshop PSD file and keep the layers intact, thereby avoiding the need to make a separate selection in Photoshop. The process of exporting the Illustrator file rasterizes (converts to bitmap) the Illustrator artwork, but keeps the original Illustrator file in its original vector format so you can use it again for other purposes.

1. Go to File > Export. Select PhotoShop (PSD) from the Save as Type drop-down box and choose a location on your computer in which to save the file. You will be opening it in Photoshop in a moment.

2. In the Options dialog box that opens apply the following settings and click OK.

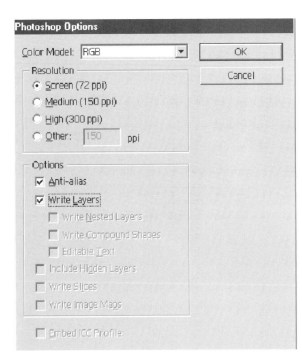

RGB is the chosen color model and 72 ppi the chosen resolution because this version will be used for on screen media only. Anti-alias creates the illusion of smooth edges when the artwork is rasterized and Write Layers is selected to keep the layers intact.

3. In Photoshop, open the file you have just saved.

The file is now a PSD file and the layers have been preserved exactly as they were in Illustrator. This allows us to benefit from the transparency within layers and apply some layer effects without having to make any selections.

4. Select the layer called artwork. Click the **Add a layer style** button at the bottom of the Layers palette and choose Bevel and Emboss from the pop up menu.

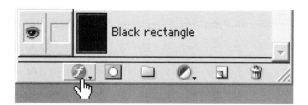

5. In the dialog box that opens select Inner Bevel as the Style and Chisel Hard as the Technique. All the actual settings can be applied from the picture below. Most settings are as the default with the exception of the Gloss Contour. I wanted a shiny chrome effect so I selected the option as pictured below by clicking the Gloss Contour drop-down box.

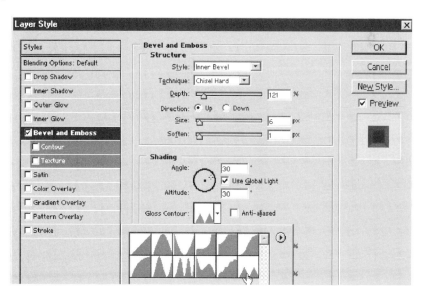

6.   Next click the Gradient Overlay check box from the left of the dialog box, and then click the words Gradient Overlay and the dialog box will update to display the gradient settings as pictured below. Select the rainbow gradient from the Gradient drop-down box. Click OK to apply the settings.

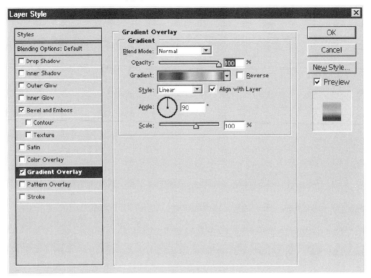

And there's the jazzy, embellished version of the logo complete, demonstrating a perfect marriage between vector and bitmap graphics. If we were going to use this logo in an on screen presentation or for the web, we would need to save it in a suitable compressed format, but that's all coming up when we look at working for the Web in part 6.

In the next section we will use the original black and white logo as part of the company business card.

Creating a business card

Open the file called `bizcard.ai` from the download folder. This file contains the complete logo that you have just created. It has been scaled to fit on a standard 3.5 by 2 inch business card. The ultra-pale gray area to the right of the logo has been created just so you can identify the true size of the card. The final card will be just black and white. At the foot of the page are the text blocks that will be positioned once the card is set up.

Select the card and you will see in the Info palette that the size is bigger than the finished size we want to create. The reason for this is due to a factor called **bleed**. The bleed allows for a margin of error when cutting the artwork from the master sheet. In this case we will have a white sheet of paper with a black left edge to the artwork. If we created the artwork exactly the same size as the required dimensions, there would be a risk that the machine cutting up the cards could be slightly out of alignment. This would result in a strip of the original white paper showing on one or more edges of the card. The bleed margin avoids this, ensuring the color of your card runs right to the edge in every case.

1. Make the new zero point the top left corner of the business card. When setting the point to an object as you are doing now, you will find the cross hairs at the tip of the cursor snap to the corner of the object. To make sure it has worked, look for zero on both rulers to make sure they are lined up with the top edge and left edge of the business card.

    We are now going to place guides on the page to mark the bleed and the true finished size of the card.

2. Drag a guide onto the page from the vertical ruler. As you drag, keep the SHIFT key pressed. This forces the guide to snap to the increments of the ruler. Place the guide on the zero point of the top, horizontal ruler. This lines up with the left edge of the artwork.

    We need another three guides, one each for the top, bottom, and right edge of the artwork.

3. Drag another guide from the left ruler and position it on the 4 in mark of the top ruler. This is the right edge of the artwork. Hold down the SHIFT key as you drag so the guide will snap into place on the 4 in ruler increment.

4. Drag a guide from the top ruler and position it on the zero mark on the left vertical ruler.

5. Drag the last guide from the top ruler and position it on the 2.5 in mark on the left vertical ruler.

    Your artwork should look like the picture below.

The next set of guides will be used to define the actual card that will be cut out. For accurate positioning of the guides use the Transform palette

6.   Drag one guide from the left hand ruler and place it anywhere on the page. In the Transform palette, type 0.125 in the X box. This defines a one eighth inch bleed from the left of the card.

7.   Drag another guide from the left hand ruler, positioning anywhere as before. In the Transform palette, type 3.875 in the X box. This creates a one eighth inch bleed from the right.

Now we need to do the same thing to create a one eighth inch bleed at the top and the bottom of the card.

8.   Drag a guide from the top ruler this time, positioning it anywhere on the page. In the Transform palette, type -0.125 in the Y box. In case you are wondering why you typed a negative number this time, bear in mind the page zero point is the top left of the business card. Any location above the zero point will be a positive number and locations below the zero point are negative numbers. You could of course have set the page zero point to the bottom left of the card, but for many people it is more logical to measure from the top left corner. It's a personal thing and you can make your own decision on this in your own projects.

9.   Finally drag another guide from the top ruler and type -2.375 (don't forget the minus) in the Y box of the Transform palette to position it.

This completes a full set of bleed and trim guides identifying the area in which we can work. All we need to do now is add some crop marks to notify the printer where he has to trim.

To avoid doing this frequently, make a template with the size and guides already set for different client's business cards, and save the template in an easy to find folder. This will enable speedier creation of business cards.

To create the crop marks, we need a rectangle that will define the boundaries of the finished business card.

10. Create a rectangle that sits on the innermost guides. The fill and stroke color do not matter as these will disappear when the crop marks are created. To make sure the rectangle is correctly positioned use the Transform palette. Make sure the Transform palette reference point is set to the top left corner, as in the picture below. Enter 0.125 in in the X field and -0.125 in in the Y field. This ensures the rectangle is perfectly positioned on the innermost guides.

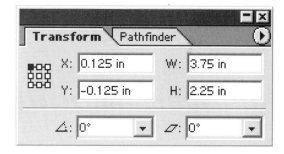

11. With the rectangle selected, go to Object > Crop Marks > Make. The crop marks will replace the selected rectangle.

If you need to edit the Crop marks, go to Object > Crop Marks > Release.

All that remains is to set the text. The text blocks have already been created and can be found at the bottom of the page.

12. With the Type tool (T), select the text stating Dan Sharpe, then go to the Paragraph palette. Click the **Align Right** button. We are going to align all text by its right edge.

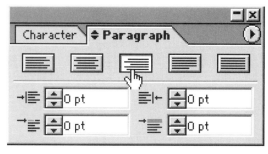

13. Do the same for the address text block.

     The telephone number is too close to the last line of the address, so we are going to increase the leading to create a larger gap. Leading or line spacing defines the size of the space between the baselines of consecutive lines of text.

14. With the Type tool, select the telephone number line of text and increase the Leading to 16 pt from the Character palette.

     To position the text blocks we will use a single guide and position the right edge against it.

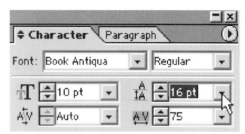

15. Drag a guide onto the page from the vertical ruler and use the Transform palette to position by entering 3.8 in in the X field. Drag the two text blocks onto the card snapping the right edges of each text block against the guide. Use the picture below to gauge the vertical positioning on the card.

16. Finally delete the guide you just created, so they are not confused with the trim and bleed guides, then use the Group Selection tool to select the right half of the business card and apply a white fill.

That's the business card complete.

Working with Photoshop images in Illustrator

It is undoubtedly the ultimate partnership in any publishing environment. Preparing bitmap images in Photoshop, then importing them into Illustrator utilizes the best of what both applications have to offer. In this section we are going to look at the process of importing bitmap images into Illustrator and then defining which parts of the bitmap are visible through the use of clipping masks and compound paths.

An ideal scenario in which this process will be used is in the production a magazine display advert.

Open the file called `display_advert.ai` from the download folder.

The picture above is the first advert we are going to produce, but first we have to bring the bitmap image into Illustrator.

The first question to address is what file format can or should be used.

There are many file formats that Illustrator is capable of importing. On a professional level the following four are the most commonly used:

- **EPS (Encapsulated PostScript)**: Typically, this format is used to transfer PostScript language artwork between applications. EPS files can contain a single image or a combination of photographic images, text, and vector artwork. The ability of this format to contain both vector and bitmap graphics is due to it being based on the PostScript language, a language created by Adobe.

- **PDF (Portable Document Format)**: Similar to the EPS format in that it can represent both vector and bitmap graphics, but additionally it can also contain electronic document search and navigation features just like a web page. To use these features the user requires the free Adobe Acrobat reader plug-in. Any images or text contained within a PDF document can be opened and used within Illustrator.

- **PSD (Photoshop Document)**: This is the native file format of Photoshop. Saving a Photoshop document in its native format preserves all the functionality offered by the program.

- **Tiff (Tagged Image Format)**: Tiff is a widely supported cross platform bitmap image format, capable of using the RGB, CMYK, and Grayscale color models. It is one of the most commonly used formats for transferring bitmap images between bitmap and page layout programs. The format also supports a lossless compression utility called LZW. This serves the function of reducing the size of the file without degrading the quality of the image. Also a popular format for scanning as virtually all desktop scanners are capable of producing TIFF images, which can then be shared with other applications.

As already mentioned, this list is not exhaustive, but covers the main formats you will come across in any commercial operation. As a general reference, Illustrator also supports the following formats: SVG/SVGZ, Pict, BMP, GIF 89a, JPEG, PCX, PNG, and many others.

There is an important distinction between file formats for print and formats for the Web. The two most common formats for print are EPS and TIFF. EPS files are generally much larger than TIFF but will often be more suitable if the file contains postscript data. JPEG and GIF are the two most popular formats for the Web. It is possible to print with these formats but not recommended. JPEG uses a lossy form of compression, which can result in blurriness, pixelation, and digital artifacts on the image. GIF can only use a maximum of 256 colors giving the appearance of speckled color or jagged edges. Despite this, both formats excel on the Web due to their very high rates of compression resulting in tiny file sizes.

Once you have an image in a suitable format, which is most likely to be one of the top four professional options, the next thing is to get it into Illustrator in some way and that's what we are going to do now.

Placing files

There are two ways of bringing images into Illustrator. The first of these methods is known as **Placing**. The Place command, as the name suggests places files from other applications into an existing Illustrator file.

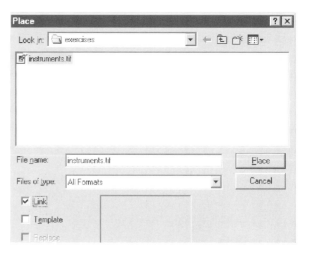

1. Go to File > Place. This opens the Place dialog box. Navigate to the download folder and select the file called `instruments.tif`. Beneath the Files of type drop-down box you will see a **Link** check box.

The Link check box is checked and enabled by default, meaning the file will be linked. Linked files remain independent of the Illustrator file, which results in a smaller Illustrator file. This is one of the primary benefits of linking files. Imagine your Illustrator file is 1mb and the image you place is 50mb, by linking the image to the Illustrator file you have avoided creating a file that weighs in at 51mb. Instead the 1mb Illustrator file shows a relatively small increase in file size to account for the linked file.

So what happens if you don't have the Link check box enabled? In this instance, the image you place will be **Embedded**. Embedding an image physically imports the image into the Illustrator file, making it a part of the file in the same way as if you had created an object in Illustrator. To use the above example of the 1mb Illustrator file and the 50mb image, in the case of the Embedded image, you would end up with a 51mb file. The down side of this being you have a large file to manipulate and use up more system resources.

2. With the Link box checked, click the Place button and the bitmap will be placed within the Illustrator file.

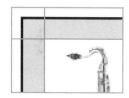

3. Position the bitmap so its left corner snaps to the guides, which have been positioned ready for the image.

Managing linked and embedded images

The process of linking and embedding images is not a complex one in itself. But like so many computerized processes, the simpler they are, the greater scope they offer for problems further down the publishing line.

Here is a typical scenario: You create an advert that includes a number of linked images. Remember, by linking an image you do not physically embed it into the Illustrator document. Strictly speaking it is not there and all you are seeing on screen is a preview of an image that resides somewhere outside of the Illustrator document. You finish working on the file and in the frenzy that often accompanies the delivery of the file to the printer, you only send the Illustrator file and not the images, as they are still independent images. A checklist of images used and their location would reduce the chance of such last minute panics. During the creation of the file, it would also be beneficial if there was some way of choosing, monitoring, updating, and replacing images that are linked to or embedded in the Illustrator file.

Fortunately, all these options are available to you through the **Links palette**. As well as these useful functions, the Links palette allows you to assess if the link to an image is broken or missing as well as enabling you to get information about linked or embedded image characteristics, and finally open the linked image and its application.

Updating links through the Links palette preferences

So what's so great about being able to update links automatically? Well, if you have a Photoshop image that has been linked to an Illustrator file and you subsequently decide to edit the Photoshop image in some way, that image can be updated without having to this is an enormous time saver not to mention removing the tedium from a labor-intensive task. Let's set this up now.

1. Create a new CMYK page using the default size.

2. Go to Edit > Preferences > Files & Clipboard. Look at the Update Links drop-down box in the dialog box that opens

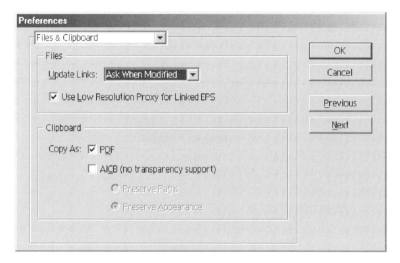

The Update Links drop-down box offers the following choices:

-   **Automatically**: Updates linked images automatically when the original files are edited.

-   **Manually**: This option leaves linked images unmodified when the original files are changed.

-   **Ask When Modified**: This option displays a dialog box when the original files are changed in some way prompting you to answer Yes to update an image that was modified and No to leave it unchanged.

The option you choose will largely depend on the way you work. If you are likely to modify images a lot in Photoshop, then automatically updating would make sense.

3. In this instance, choose Ask When Modified, which is the default and click OK.

Creating clipping masks

All bitmap images are square or rectangular because they are based on pixels and pixels are square. So what if we want our bitmap image to be some shape other than a square or rectangle. This problem is easily solved by the use of a **clipping mask**. As the name suggests, a clipping mask clips away all the parts of the image you don't want and leaves you with the parts that you do want to see. A clipping mask can be any shape, so all the shape creation tools and commands are at your disposal. In addition to this, clipping masks are vector based they won't have pixelated edges if you adjust the size of the mask.

We are going to create a mask so our magazine advert displays the photo as an ellipse rather than a rectangle.

1. In the `display_advert.ai` file, create an ellipse a little smaller than the instruments photo. The color is not important as both stroke and fill will be removed when the mask command is applied.

2. Position the ellipse on top of the photo, and then select both the photo and the ellipse.

3. Go to Object > Clipping Mask > Make (CTRL/CMD+7). That's all there is to it. You have created the finished image as shown below.

Even if you have not positioned the elements correctly, nothing has been deleted. You can still move the image around to fine tune which parts of it show by using the Direct Selection tool.

It is just as easy to remove the photo from the mask.

4. Using the Selection tool (V), select the photo. The Selection tool selects both the photo and the original mask object. Go to Object > Clipping Mask > Release. The original ellipse is still there, it has just had the stroke and fill removed.

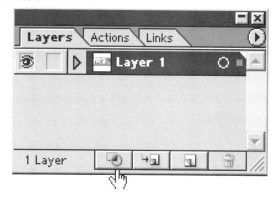

Additionally, clipping masks can be created by using the icon at the foot of the Layers palette rather than going through the menu commands. The set up of the artwork remains the same. The photograph should be below the object that will become the mask and both objects should be on the same layer. There is no need to select any objects, but make sure the relevant layer is active. Clicking the icon as in the picture below will create the clipping mask.

Creating complex clipping masks

Open the file called `display_advert2.ai` from the download folder.

This file contains a number of star objects. Each star needs to be an individual mask that shows different parts of the single bitmap image. This is where the problem lies. It isn't possible to use multiple objects as one mask using the conventional methods. To achieve this we need to combine all of the stars as a compound path. We were looking at various compound paths during the construction of the logo. This time we will use the Compound Path command from the Object menu. The essential principle remains the same. Overlapping lines and points will be removed, but even if there are no overlaps the fact that the objects have been combined means we can use these objects as if they were one and so create a clipping mask with them.

The file has been created with all the elements in place. All you have to do is create the Compound path and then the clipping mask. If you wish, to prove the point, try creating a clipping mask with all of the stars using the same procedure as previous and you will see it is impossible.

1.   Select all the stars, and then go to Object > Compound Path > Make. Nothing appears to have changed. As the stars are not overlapping there is nothing to see, but the stars have now been united as a Compound path.

2. Select the stars, any one will do and the photo, then go to Object > Clipping Mask > Make.

3. Releasing the mask is exactly the same process as when you released an ordinary mask.

Using these techniques means you are no longer limited to one format of bitmap image and the true power of bitmaps and vectors combined can be truly realized.

Conclusion

In this chapter, you have learned to bring together the strengths of Photoshop and Illustrator to create some of the vital components of an organization's corporate identity. These techniques form the foundation of any project involving brand creation and advertising literature. The ability to be spontaneous and creative while ensuring precision and accuracy are maintained is one of the many benefits you will enjoy from mastering these techniques.

5 Building a company web site

The array of applications and tools available for the production of web graphics and web pages can seem overwhelming. Within the Adobe stable alone, the decision on whether to use Illustrator, Photoshop, ImageReady, or all three can become a stumbling block. Over recent upgrades the three applications have come closer together resulting in a number of processes overlapping, particularly in regard to the web.

So which application do you use to create a web page? The honest answer is any one or all three! A more productive answer requires a little analysis of what your web page is going to look like and where the artwork is coming from.

There's no escaping the fact that Illustrator is still a vector program and Photoshop and ImageReady are bitmap programs. This gives you your first clue as to where to start working. For instance, will the style of your pages dictate that the bulk of the artwork must be created as vectors? If the use of pathfinders, blends, and simple line artwork will feature heavily, then Illustrator is the program to use. All the slicing and compression tools and commands found in Photoshop and ImageReady are also in Illustrator, so there is no need to switch programs to output your finished files.

Another reason to use Illustrator would be if you wanted to take advantage of the SVG or SWF vector formats either for static or animated graphics, both of which will be covered in this chapter.

Web pages designed around a lot of photographic material or with interfaces requiring heavy use of filters for bevels, shadows, textures, etc., would be more suited to Photoshop. Finally, ImageReady's strength is in the creation of rollovers and animation.

Admittedly this summary pigeon-holes each application a little too neatly, but it does serve to make some kind of distinction between the three to give us a good starting point. In reality, the desired web page design may require the use of all three applications depending on what you need to achieve. Knowing the strength of each is the secret to a streamlined and efficient workflow resulting in the ultimate web design toolbox.

The exercise we are about to work through will demonstrate these strengths and equip you with the knowledge you need to make these decisions in your own projects. We are going to build the interface for the "Music Factory" home page. This follows on from the Music Factory logo you built in part 4, but don't worry if you are not working through the chapters in order, the files you need to start can be downloaded from www.friendsofed.com.

The web page we build is going to exploit all the greatest assets of each of the three applications so you can gain hands on experience of using the programs in tandem.

The picture below is the finished web page as viewed in a browser. The printed page can't show the dynamic elements on the actual web page. If you have downloaded the folder called mf_home_complete, open the page called index.HTML in a browser and you will see the rollovers on the text buttons and the animated buttons that make up the photographic images on the left of the page.

As with any design project, you will probably work out your rough sketches on paper and have a clear plan to work from prior to starting work on the computer. Fortunately for you, I've already done that – so without further ado, let's get started.

Preparing the logo using Illustrator

The Music Factory guitar logo is currently a vector graphic. I want to use the music notes that rotate to the left of the guitar as a navigational element on the web page but they need to be simplified first so as not to create the feel of too much clutter when combined with other elements on the web page.

The fact that the logo is already in vector format and the need to rotate objects by a set number of degrees means that Illustrator, and its precision transform tools, is the clear choice for this first stage of the web page.

Open the file called `mf_home.ai.`

The art board of this page has been set to 760 x 420 pixels. I have used this size as I intend to target a screen resolution of 800 x 600. The reason behind the smaller size of the art board is the fact that the browser icons and menus effectively reduce the workable size of the target screen.

Three elements appear on the page, the guitar logo, a single music note, and the company name. The company name is on its own layer as we will be repositioning it within the context of the finished page later.

The zero point has been set to the top left corner of the page. This is good policy for web pages as all web page elements are measured from this point.

The first thing to do is define the center of the page with a guide. This will be used to position the guitar and, shortly, to rotate the music notes.

1.   Drag a vertical guide to position 380 on the X-axis. The most precise way is to use the Transform palette.

     I want the bottom of the guitar to lie a little over three quarters of the way down the page, so we'll use a guide to mark the position.

2.   Drag a horizontal guide down to -330 on the Y-axis. You wouldn't necessarily need to use this guide if you were positioning the guitar by eye, I have used it here so your finished design will replicate mine.

3.   Position the guitar so that its bottom edge rests on the horizontal guide and the center of the guitars acoustic hole is resting on the vertical guide, as shown in this picture:

Just so there is no mistake with the positioning you can type the following co-ordinates into the Transform palette so you have a carbon copy of my artwork. (Make sure the Transform palette reference point is in the center.)

X = 372.5 px
Y = -215.868 px (Don't forget the minus in front of this value)

To create the semi-circle of music notes on the left of the guitar, a point of origin needs to be decided upon that will act as the center point from where the notes can radiate. Think of a bicycle wheel, the hub is the center point, the spokes radiate out from the center and the tire itself provides the guide where the music notes will sit, except we are only going to use one half of the wheel.

The only point we need to mark is the true center of our imaginary wheel. This depends on how you would like the music notes to rotate. I would like the center to be just below the acoustic hole of the guitar.

4. Drag a horizontal guide to location -241 px on the Y scale, as shown on the diagram here:

Now we have a center point where the horizontal and vertical guides meet. This will be our point of origin for the semi-circle rotation of music notes.

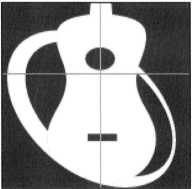

5. Position the music note on the horizontal guide, as shown. This is the easiest one to position manually because there will be five notes equally spaced, with the middle one of the five notes sitting right on the horizontal guide.

Once again for the sake of replicating my artwork the precise co-ordinates for the music note are as follows:

X scale = 286.425 px
Y scale = -232.907 px

This is the only note that will be positioned manually as all the others will be rotated and duplicated at the same time, with the measurements taken from the co-ordinates of the first note. All the duplicates will be rotated from the point of origin where the guides

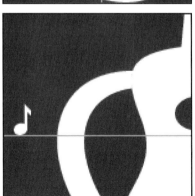

6. To rotate a duplicate, select the music note, hold down the Opt/Alt key and click the point where the blue vertical and horizontal guides meet. Enabling Smart guides (Cmd/Ctrl+U) will help you click directly on the *intersection* of the guides. In the Rotate dialog box type 30 in the Angle field and click the Copy button.

   When deciding by how many degrees to rotate, my calculations started with the number of music notes, which is 5. The area of a circle I wanted to cover was about one third or 120 degrees. I divided the 120 by 4, 4 being the number of spaces between the 5 notes, which gave me 30 degrees.

7. Press Cmd/Ctrl+D four times to generate the four additional notes, each rotated at 30 degrees.

8. Select all five notes, with the Rotate tool (R), Opt/Alt-click where the guides intersect again and type -60 in the Rotate dialog box Angle field and click OK. This rotates the all five notes backward so that they are sitting in the correct position.

   The first and last two notes are at the wrong angle. I want them all to be upright the same as the middle note. We'll use the Transform tool to correct this.

9. Select the top music note and type 60 in the Transform palette rotate field. For the second note type 30, the middle note needs no adjustment. The fourth note is −30 and the fifth is −60. Now all the notes are correctly oriented with the page.

   All that remains is to distribute them so that they are equally spaced.

10. Select all the notes and use the Align palette to vertically distribute the notes from the center.

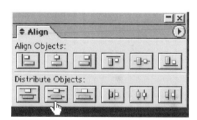

   This is how your artwork should be looking:

   The web page is going to have rollovers and other animated image links, and that's where ImageReady comes in. While we are there we will also add the text, other images, and slice up the page so the HTML document can be created. That's a lot of steps, but before we do any of that, we are going to export our Illustrator file as a PSD. That way we can keep the layers intact and we will have the basic outline of the page ready to build on.

11. Clear the guides, then go to File > Export and save as a Photoshop PSD document at 72 ppi, RGB, Anti alias and Write layers checked. (These are the same settings as when you exported the logo in Part 4 prior to embellishing it).

Adding further elements in ImageReady

Launch ImageReady and open the PSD file that you just exported from Illustrator. We now have the basis of the web page. The artwork layer contains the black background, guitar logo, and music notes. These are correctly positioned so they don't need to be on a separate layer. The Music Factory text logo does have its own layer, as it needs to be positioned within the context of other elements as they are added later.

First we need some guides on the page prior to adding text and images. The preparatory work for this was done on paper to define the space and layout.

1. Drag out three vertical guides and position them at 15, 130, and 630 on the X-axis. Use the Info palette to check the position as you drag. Measurements are always in pixels in ImageReady and the point of origin is the top left corner of the page by default.

2. Drag out two vertical guides and position them at 10 and 70 on the Y-axis. Then drag five more that align with the bottom of each music note. Your page should now resemble the picture below.

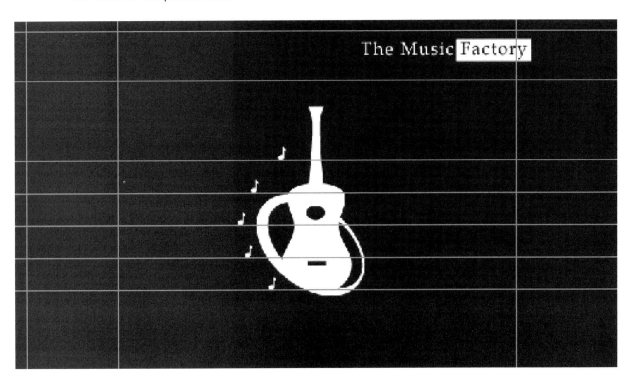

Adding and positioning the text

As with Photoshop, text is automatically generated on a new layer in ImageReady. This is vital if we want to create rollover text buttons, which is what we are ultimately going to do. For the moment we are going to create the top line of text buttons that will sit on the second horizontal guide.

1. Type the following words, each as a separate layer. I used Franklin Gothic medium, size 14 px, Tracking set to 100, and color white, but use a font of your choice if you do not have that one. A quick way to create multiple text items on separate layers without going back to the toolbox each time is to type one item then CMD/CTRL-click on the page to deselect the Type tool. Click on the page again and you can start typing a new item, which will appear on a new layer.

   About us
   Stores
   News
   Lessons
   Contact.

2. Place the baseline of each text item on the second horizontal guide. Position "About us" against the second vertical and "Contact" against the third vertical guide, as shown in the image below:

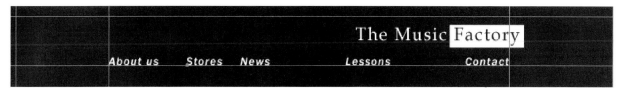

   You will notice that I haven't bothered to space the words evenly. We'll use an automatic function for that. Only the first and last text items need to be positioned. These positions define the outer parameters and all other linked items are evenly distributed between the first and last.

3. Link all five Type layers from within the Layers palette. When layers are linked, the Align and Distribute commands become available on the Tool Options bar at the top of the screen. Click the Distribute Horizontal center button.

   Next we need the text links that will line up with the music notes forming a gentle curve. Take a look at the finished web page picture at the start of this chapter if you want to refresh your memory as to how the text needs to look.

4. Type the following words, each on a separate layer as before. The same text attributes were used.

   Strings
   Keyboards
   Percussion
   Woodwind
   Guitars.

You are typing the words in reverse order as they appear on the page, Guitars is at the top of the page and Strings at the bottom. By typing from the bottom up, the Layers palette stacking order will be in the same order as the text appears on the page. Apart from being more logical when editing, it will be easier to follow when creating rollovers.

5. Position the baseline of each word on the each of the horizontal guides so they are touching the music note in each case.

6. Select each Type layer in turn and press the SHIFT and left arrow key on your keyboard. This moves the text 10 pixels to the left of the music note in each case so there is a consistent amount of space between the word and note for all the instrument categories.

Here's how the page should be looking so far with the guides hidden. Save the page to update the changes.

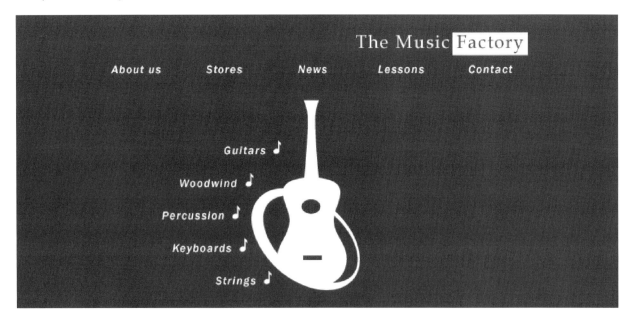

Adding additional image elements

We are going to add one static image and two images that will animate when the user places the cursor over them. We will be creating these shortly, but first we need to prepare them in an easy to use format and lay them out on the page.

1. Keep the web page open, as we need to come back to it in a moment. Now open the file called `sax_small.psd`.

    In case you are wondering if Photoshop has a role to play in all this, I used Photoshop for the preparation of this and the other images you are about to open. Although many of Photoshop's filters and effects are in ImageReady, some are unique to Photoshop, such as the Color Balance command, which was used on this image for color correction. This further reinforces the fact that although there is much crossover between the three applications, there are times when only one will do a specific job.

2. With the sax file active go the File menu and choose Place. Choose the file called `drums small.psd`. When the Open button is clicked you will be presented with the following dialog box. Accept the default. This will place the new file on top of the current file based on the top left corner of the image window. Both images are identical in size so one layer will be right on top of another.

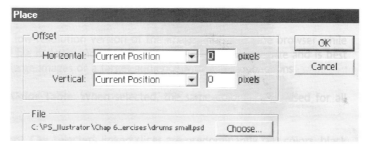

3. Repeat the process placing the file called `guitar small.psd`.

    You now have three images each on separate layers in one file. These three layers are going to be used to make an animating rollover. In order to transfer all three layers as one entity into our master web page we are going to make a layer set.

4. Select the top layer, and then click the **Create a new set** icon at the bottom of the Layers palette.

5. Double-click the words `Set 1` to rename it "instruments". Drag each image thumbnail in the Layers palette onto the layer set icon to add it to the set. Close the layer set by clicking the drop-down arrow next to the word instruments.

    We now need to transfer the entire layer set from its current file to the web page file. This is a quick and simple process. Make sure you can see the web page file on the screen.

6. Working from the three instruments file, drag the layer set folder from the Layers palette onto the web page file and position it anywhere on the left of the page. You have now transferred all three layers from one file to another and kept them as one entity so that they can be positioned on the page as if they were one. More importantly when we come to build the animation it will be very easy to navigate around as we have the components neatly packaged in one layer set.

7. We need one more sequence of animated images. Open the file called `IanJames_a.psd`.

   Using the same process as you used for the instruments, place within this file the files named `IanJames_b.psd`, and `IanJames_c.psd`. Create a layer set for the three layers, name the set "Ian James", drag the set into the web page file and position it on the left of the page.

   Now the image components can be positioned and captioned.

8. Place the left edge of the Ian James image against the first vertical guide and the bottom of the image sitting on the horizontal guide that was used for Guitars. Make sure Snap to > Guides is enabled from the View menu to help you with positioning.

   Continuing the layout, the instruments image set has been positioned again against the first vertical guide and resting on the horizontal guide used for Strings.

9. New Type layers have also been created, "Gig Guide" and "Classic Range". Both were aligned against the same vertical guide and touching the bottom of their respective images. The text was lowered down the page by pressing SHIFT and the down arrow key to move the text 10 pixels down.

10. The use of guides for lining up more than one element not only contributes to a more aesthetically pleasing and uniform design but, in the case of web page design, also assists in creating a less complex HTML table. The true benefit of this last point will vary depending on your perspective. Seasoned coders will have a bias towards tight, economical script whereas designers will often opt for getting the design right irrespective of the state of the code. Excessive code will add to the file size, but code is still smaller in size than images. A more serious consideration is that complex HTML tables are more difficult to edit than simple

ones, but as ImageReady is going to do the HTML creation for you anyway, this does not seem a relevant point in this context.

We have just one more image to add. This is a single, static image and so it can be placed directly into the web page file.

11. Place the file called Sax player.psd. When the Place dialog box opens, type the following settings this time. This will place the file centered vertically and the left edge of the image will be 525 pixels from the left of the screen, which is just over two thirds along.

Finally we need to position the Music Factory text logo in the top right of the page.

12. Position the logo so that its top edge is against the top horizontal guide and its horizontal placing is above the sax player image.

This completes the design and layout of the page. Your page should look like the picture below – now don't forget to save it!

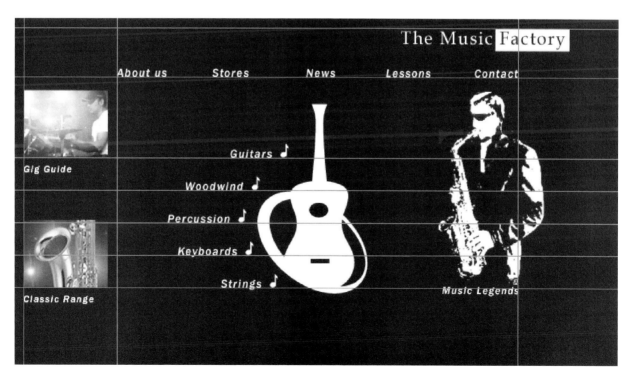

Slicing the image

Slicing an image is the process of cutting up areas of the image into a configuration that will be converted into independent images and integrated together in tables to form a HTML file.

But why slice up the image in the first place? It would be quite possible to simply save the entire page in a browser compatible format and use that on the web. However this would pose a number of problems: first, we plan to use image rollovers on the page. Any element designated as an image rollover needs to be isolated as an independent graphic. Even if no rollovers were planned, there are large areas of solid black on the page. If we were to convert these areas into graphics, we would add to the file size of the page unnecessarily. It is far better to designate these areas as "blank" areas and provide the black color through the HTML code. Even if the entire page consisted of one large photographic image, it would still be preferable to slice the image, as the download of the sliced graphics would be quicker than one large single graphic. Finally, image links of any kind should also be independent graphics, otherwise you will be forced to use image maps to create graphic hyperlinks. So the reasons for slicing are either desirable or absolutely necessary depending on your design and functions.

1. Select the **Slice** tool (K) from the toolbox. There are two tools in this tool location. The Slice tool makes the initial slice, the **Slice Select** tool edits and repositions slices.

    Our objective is to create slices of all the text and image elements, leaving blank areas as they are. Let's start logically with the first element at the top of the page, the Music Factory text logo.

2. Using the Slice tool, place the cursor at the top left corner of the Music Factory text and drag diagonally towards the bottom right corner of the text logo – try to go as close as possible to the image area. The picture here shows the logo after being sliced. If you have not sliced close enough to the edge, using the same tool you can drag the yellow square handles to redefine the slice.

    The entire page has now been sliced up into five slices. At present, only the slice you created is editable, the other four slices have been created automatically and have been designed around the one you created.

3. The next elements we'll slice are the text buttons starting with About us. Slice each word, using the horizontal guide on the baseline of the text as a guide whilst you slice. Continue slicing each word up to and including the Contact image. After you have created the first slice for About us, you will see blue guides above and below each word to help you create slices in a straight line. The picture below shows the five text images sliced, each slice bearing an automated number.

4. Create slices for the two images on the left of the screen, the drummer and saxophone images, and the two captions under each image. Below they have been sliced and appear as numbers 23, 26, 29, and 31.

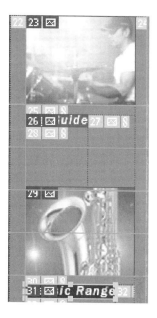

5. We're almost done. Slice the instrument category words next, Guitars, Woodwind, etc., but also include in the slice the music note also. This will become part of the active link when the user clicks it. Remember to slice as close to the word and music note as possible. Here's the complete guitar and music note slice:

6. The slicing of the guitar logo is a little trickier and needs a bit of analysis. It will help if we recap on what the ultimate goal is. We are trying to isolate all the image areas from the plain black areas. The guitar logo is an irregular shape and the slices defining the instrument category words have made the shape even more irregular. The way around this is to define a number of slices around the guitar logo, trying to be as economical as possible with the amount of slices.

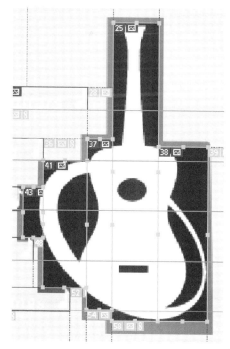

This picture shows the completed slices. I have faded back the background area to emphasize the guitar slices only. Five slices have been used around the guitar, numbered 25, 37, 38, 41, and 43. Too many slices and the page would become unnecessarily complicated as well as taking longer to slice. Your slices may differ slightly depending on how you have created the other slices around the guitar, but as long as you follow the general principle, your artwork will be fine.

7. Finally slice the sax player graphic. This is straightforward and one rectangular slice can be used around the graphic.

8. Now all the slices are complete, clear the guides (we are finished with them) and save the PSD to update the changes.

This is how the sliced page should be looking:

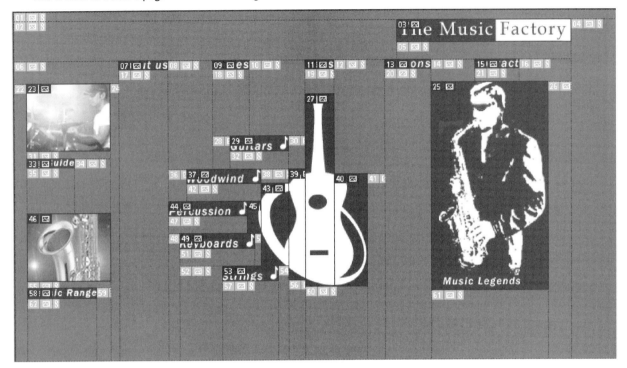

Once again don't worry if yours looks a little different, as long as you have a similar pattern of slices, you are on the right track.

Creating rollovers in ImageReady

Now that the slices are complete we are ready to start creating rollovers prior to the final optimizing and saving of images.

If you are new to the concept of rollovers, these are the images, such as text and buttons, that change color on a web page when you place the cursor over or click them. In the early days of rollovers, they were criticized for being gimmicky, but they have become a valuable aid to navigation and user feedback. JavaScript is the language that provides the functionality for rollovers of this kind to work. Not a language to be trifled with if you have no desires to get involved with scripting, but don't worry - ImageReady will write all the necessary JavaScript for you.

We're going to start by turning the top line of text into rollovers, starting with the words; About us.

1.   Select the About us layer in the Layers palette.

If the Rollovers palette is not on your screen go to Window > Rollovers. The Rollovers palette displays all the slices you created as a separate layer. This layer is simply called a slice.

2.   Using the **Slice Select** tool (SHIFT+K), select the About us slice on the page. Once you select the slice on the page, the Rollovers palette will jump to the relevant layer slice.

The name that appears in the Rollovers palette slice is the name of the file and the slice number. We can make this easier to work with by renaming the layer slice to reflect its content.

3.   Double-click the layer slice in the Rollovers palette and you will be able to rename it. Type "About us" as the name.

4.   Click the **Create rollover state** button at the bottom of the Rollovers palette.

This has created a rollover state. A state is the word used for the new sub-layer that appears in the Rollovers palette. By default the first state to be created is an Over state, which defines the version of the image when the user places the mouse "over" the image. At present the current state and the Over state of the image are identical so there is no effect to see. We are going to change the Over state to a different color.

5.   Make sure the Over state is selected in the Rollovers palette then click the Add a layer style icon at the bottom of the Layers palette and select Color Overlay from the pop-up menu.

6.   In the Color Overlay palette that appears select red as the rollover color. Look back in the Rollovers palette and you will see the Over state now displays in red but the original maintains its color.

If you only want an Over state, that is all you have to do. In this case, however, we'll create another state, one that changes color when the user clicks the mouse button. A word of warning though – for every state, another graphic must be created and preloaded from the server. If your navigation panel contains 10 unique text buttons and each button has two additional states, 30 graphics will have to be downloaded. Even if the graphics are small in file size they all go towards increasing the overall page size and thus, file size. As long as you aware of this and correctly assess your target audiences ability to download the web page you have created, you have done your job professionally.

7. Click the Create rollover state button again. The next state to be created is a **Down** State. This refers to when the user presses the mouse button "down". As before, in the Layers palette **click the Add a Layer Style icon and choose Color Overlay.** In the Color Overlay palette select a dark red as the Down State color.

8. Repeat steps 1 to 7 for each of the text images including the instrument categories, guitars, woodwind, etc.

To see your rollovers working without having to view them in a browser click the **Preview Document** icon in the main toolbox or use the keyboard shortcut Y.

You can now try out the rollover effects.

Once you are in preview mode you will be prevented from carrying out other functions so when you have finished previewing either press Y, the Esc key, or click the **Cancel Preview** icon towards the top right of the screen to return to normal editing mode.

Editing rollover states

When you create new states, ImageReady automatically allocates the type of state in a logical sequence based on the order in which the user would use a button. The mouse action known as an Event in JavaScript coding describes how the mouse interacts with the graphic. For example, Over (when the mouse cursor is over the graphic) is followed by Down (when the mouse button is pressed down and the cursor is over the graphic) which is followed by Selected (when the mouse button has been pressed and released). All these states can be changed depending on the effect you wish to achieve.

There are a number of ways to change the mouse action within each state by doing any of the following. For example if you wanted to change the Down state to a Click state:

1. CMD/right-click Down state in the Rollovers palette (click the words Down state) and select Click from the pop-up menu.

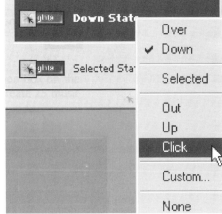

2. CMD/right-click the State layer (not the word), select Set State from the pop-up menu and then choose Click.

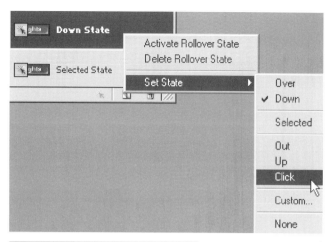

3. Click the pop-up menu in the top right corner of the Rollovers palette and select Rollover State Options. This will reveal the options dialog box.

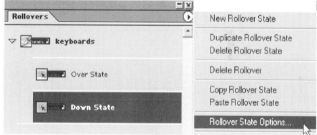

4. Double-click the Down State sub-layer to bring up the Rollover State Options dialog box.

In the last two cases you will be offered a selection of different states from which to choose. Although most options are self explanatory, some provide a very subtle difference in the way they function.

- **Over:** Image becomes active when the mouse cursor is over the image and the mouse button is not pressed.

- **Down:** Image becomes active when the mouse cursor is over the image and the mouse button is pressed down. The image remains active while the mouse button is pressed.

- **Click:** Image becomes active when the mouse cursor is over the image and the mouse button is clicked, which means that the mouse button must be pressed down and released before the state is activated.

- **Custom:** If you know how to write JavaScript code and have embedded the code onto the HTML document, you can use this option to activate a named image when the user performs the action as designated in the JavaScript code.

- **None:** Maintains the state in its current image form, which can be used at a later time. This option will not create an image when the final optimized file is saved.

- **Selected**: Image becomes active after the mouse button is clicked. This state will remain until the user activates another Selected rollover state. However other rollover states can still be operational while the Selected state is active. For example, you would still want other rollover buttons to become active in the Up state on the web page.

If you wanted the selected state to be active as soon as the page loads in the browser, or when previewing in ImageReady, double-click the state sub-layer and check the box labeled **Use as Default Selected State**.

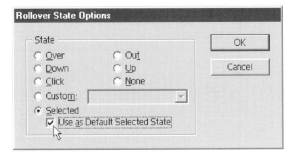

When you add a Selected state to a rollover, if you choose Click or Up for any of the other states, you will see a warning triangle appear in that sub-layer. This means the Selected state will override the Click and/or Up state.

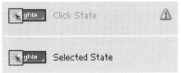

- **Out:** Literally, this means when the mouse curser is "out" or outside of the image and not touching it. It could describe the image before the user has actually even touched the mouse, so the normal initial state would normally be used instead of using this state.

- **Up:** As with the previous option, this refers to when the user has released the mouse button, so the mouse button is in the up position, which also describes the mouse button in its dormant mode, so again, the normal initial state is normally used instead of this state.

It is important to be aware that different types and versions of browsers interpret JavaScript slightly differently. The events such as Down, Click, and Up may respond differently to clicks and double-clicks. The only way to assess what the user will see is to test the page in a variety of browsers, concentrating on the browsers that you believe your target audience will be using.

Let's have a quick review of where we have got to in ImageReady so far. We have laid out the page with all the necessary elements. We have sliced the page into components ready for export and we have generated rollovers for the text buttons. The two photographic images on the left of the page are going to be a slightly more complex type of rollover image. We are going to make these into animated rollovers.

Animation in ImageReady

We have already completed some animations. The text rollovers are animated, but for many people animation implies a little more action than just a simple two color switch. The kind of animation ImageReady excels at is GIF animation. This is a common animation format that requires no plug-ins, is cross platform, and works well even on older browsers. Using ImageReady to combine a GIF animation with a JavaScript rollover can give you some pretty sophisticated effects with a little planning.

The idea is for the user to place the cursor over one of the thumbnail images, (the drummer or the saxophone) causing the image to animate, playing a sequence of different images. When the mouse cursor is moved away from the image the animation will stop playing. This is the reason you created the two independent layer sets called Ian James and instruments and dragged them over to the main web page file. The images within each layer set will be the images that play.

1. To start with, in the Layers palette expand the layer set called Ian James. This reveals the three independent layers that make up the set. Rename the layers "green", "red", and "purple" to reflect the color of each image. This is just to make things easier as we create the animation.

2. Ensure the Ian James layer set is still selected, and then use the Slice Select tool (K) to select the drummer image slice on the page. In the Rollovers palette the layer slice will now be selected. Rename the layer slice "Ian James" as you did earlier with the text images.

3. Click the Create rollover state button at the bottom of the Rollovers palette. As before this creates an Over state. Leave this Over state selected.

4. In the Animation palette (Window > Animation), click the **Duplicates current frame** button at the bottom of the palette.

    We now have two frames, both showing the same top layer which is green (Assuming yours are in the same order as mine).

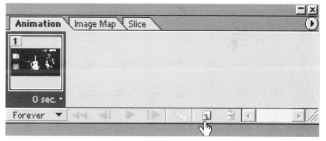

5. Hide the green layer in the Layers palette. Frame 2 will now use the red layer, which is the next in the layer stack. You will see the image update on the page.

6. Click the Duplicate current frame button in the Animation palette again to create a third frame, then hide the red layer in the Layers palette. Frame 3 will now use the purple layer as that is the next one in the stack.

    That's it – we're done. Press Y to go into preview mode, place the cursor over the drummer and you'll see the animation play, revealing a colored strobe light effect, perfect for our musical audience.

(Remember to press Y again to leave preview mode).

7.   Repeat steps 1 to 6 for the instruments layer set.

Changing the animation speed

The Ian James animation works well at its default speed because of the strobe light effect. The instruments are little different as these are all different images and they play a bit too fast to be recognizable, so we are going to change the timing.

1.   In the Rollovers palette select the Over State of the instruments slice.

2.   This reveals the three frames in the Animation palette. While holding down the SHIFT key, select all three frames then click the frame delay timer at the bottom of any of the frames. Select 0.2 seconds from the pop-up. This creates a 0.2 second time delay on all of the selected frames.

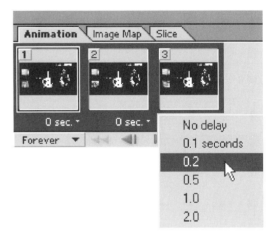

We are going to come back to animation shortly and look at tweening, but first we need to finish off the page so it's ready for publishing.

Assigning URLs to slices

At present, our web page is purely graphic. Although we have seen the text and images animate, they don't actually link to any other pages or web sites, so that's our next task.

1.   Using the Slice Select tool (K), select the About us slice on the page.

2.   In the Slice palette (Window > Slice) type the name of the page into the URL field. Normal convention applies here with regard to paths. The picture below shows a page called aboutus.htm in the URL field. This assumes that, when saved, this web page will be placed in the same folder as the aboutus.htm page. If different folders are being used, then the appropriate path must be typed in full. For example if the aboutus.htm page were in a folder called Text, I would need to type: Text/aboutus.htm.

If an image were to link to an external web site, the full absolute URL would need to be typed. For example to link to the friends of ED web site, I would type: http://www.friendsofed.com.

The **Target** drop-down box is for use with Frameset web sites. If the linked page were to be displayed in a frame called main, the word main could be typed in the Target field.

This process would need to be repeated for each slice that links to a URL.

Once the page has been saved as HTML, it can be opened in popular web design applications, such as Dreamweaver and GoLive, where further editing can take place such as linking images to other pages within the site or external web sites. Of course the HTML page can even be opened in a standard text editor like Wordpad or SimpleText on the Mac for editing. We will save the HTML file at the end of the next section.

Optimizing images for the web

The battle to find a balance between acceptable image quality and acceptable file size is common in web design circles. The inescapable fact is that bitmap images are large. Vector images are far smaller but only two vector formats are supported in the popular browsers, Flash SWF and SVG and both of these require plug-ins (which are increasingly widespread in their distribution). Even if by law every browser had to be capable of displaying SWF and SVG formats, vector graphics are not really geared up for photographic images.

So the answer is compression algorithms. These are responsible for converting your unwieldy bitmap image and converting it into something of a fraction of its original size.

The question is - which compression algorithm to use? Use the wrong one and you will end up with a file that is still large and also looks poor in quality. So let's have a look at the two main file formats that use compression and are supported by the popular browsers.

Compressed file formats

JPG (Joint Photographic experts Group) This is currently the format of choice for photographic images or any image with a continuous tone. JPGs are capable of displaying millions of colors, which makes them ideal for photographs. It uses a powerful compression algorithm that drastically reduces the size of the file. However all this comes at a price. The JPG format is known as a Lossy format. The greater compression you apply, the greater the degradation of the photo. This degradation normally manifests as blurriness, pixelation, or small artifacts appearing on the image. A balance is required between the amount of compression and the visual quality.

GIF (Graphic Interchange Format) For non-photographic images such as company logos, graphs, text, in fact any artwork that contains areas of flat color as in traditional vector artwork, this is the format to use. The GIF format is a lossless form of compression unlike the JPG. The negative aspect of GIFs is the fact that it is only capable of displaying 256 colors. For this reason it is not really suitable for photographic images. The compression algorithm used by GIF is capable of shrinking flat color artwork to almost impossible file sizes. The fewer colors in your artwork, the smaller the file will be.

Armed with this knowledge, take a quick glance at your web page and the question of which compression format to use is fairly cut and dried. The bulk of the page uses solid, flat color, ideal for the GIF format. The drummer and saxophone images on the left are photographic so fit neatly into the JPG format, but not so fast... we have a little conflict here. Remember these images are animated. GIF animations to be precise and as the name suggests, we can only use GIFs. So we have to start by breaking the rules and converting a photographic image into a GIF.

Using the Optimize palette

At the top left corner of the screen you will see four tabs. Click the Optimized tab. This shows us a preview of the images as we carry out optimization. 2-up and 4-up display two and four windows respectively so you can assess different degrees of compression in one screen view when you want to really fine tune and squeeze out the last byte. This is the same as the Save for Web window in Photoshop and Illustrator.

If the Optimize palette is not visible, open it from the Window menu now.

Let's set out the parameters for what we need to do, based on what we know so far.

- We are only using the GIF format.

- This format can use up to 256 colors only.

- The fewer colors we use, the smaller the file will be, but the visual quality will suffer.

Based on this summary, it's fair to say that the text images, the logos, and the sax player probably share a similar number of colors. The photo images are clearly different so we will deal with those separately.

To save time and work we can define an optimization setting for all the similar slices in one go.

1. Using the Slice Select tool (K) select all the slices containing black and white artwork. This includes all the words, the guitar logo, the Music Factory text, and the sax player. Hold the SHIFT key to select multiple slices.

2. Go to Slices > Link slices. Now the slices are linked we can apply a compression setting to any one slice and the same setting will be applied to all other linked slices. The linked slices now share a common color as an indicator that they are linked.

3. Select any of the linked slices and press CMD/CTRL+H to hide the slices and allow you to see the artwork without being obscured by the slices. You can reveal the slices again just by clicking any slice with the Slice Select tool.

4. Take a look in the Optimize palette. This is where you control how many colors to use. Also open the Color Table palette from the Window menu if it is not open. These two palettes can be used in tandem to define numbers of colors.

If your Optimize palette looks different from the one here click the pop-up menu button in the top right corner of the palette and choose Show Options

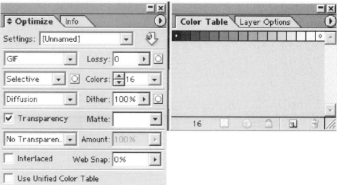

Select the GIF option and the palette displays the options as shown in the picture. 16 colors have been specified in this instance, so the color table palette displays 16 colors.

The drop-down box displaying Selective is known as the **Color Reduction Algorithm**. This applies different preset methods to make its selection of color based on a maximum number that you set. In the case of simple flat color artwork, there is little visible difference between the different methods These methods come into their own if you have complex vector artwork with gradients and blends or were attempting to save a photograph as a GIF format.

The following summarizes how each of the methods works:

- **Perceptual**: Gives priority to colors that are more sensitive to the human eye.

- **Selective**: Similar to Perceptual, but has a bias to broad areas of color and also preserves Web safe colors. Using this method normally produces images with the greatest color integrity. Selective is the option of choice in Illustrator.

- **Adaptive**: This option only samples colors from the visible spectrum that are concentrated in the image, so if an image contains predominantly reds and yellows, only reds and yellows will be sampled.

- **Web**: Only uses the standard 216 web safe color palette. The web safe palette consists of colors that will not dither on monitors capable of displaying only 256 colors.

In addition there are further options to refine image quality and file size:

- The **Lossy** drop-down box allows you to define a degree of further compression. As you discovered earlier, the GIF format is a lossless compression format by nature. If you need to shrink the file further, this option will introduce a lossy function. The higher the setting, the smaller the file size, but quality will suffer. Use with caution, if at all.

- The **Diffusion** drop-down box creates dithering, which is something we are always trying to avoid on 256 display monitors, and the reason for the creation of the web safe color palette. So why would we want to intentionally create it? For flat color artwork such as our logo, we wouldn't. Simple flat artwork works best without dithering. In the case of the photographic images on the page or if we had a gradient that could not be reproduced because there are not enough colors within the range of 256, then dithering would help to create the illusion. The options available in this drop-down box are summarized below:

  - **Diffusion**: Works by applying a random pattern of pixels of different shades across adjacent pixels.

  - **Pattern**: Similar to Diffusion but this setting applies a halftone-like square pattern in an attempt to interpret colors that cannot be created.

◼ **Noise**: Works in a very similar way to Diffusion but this option does not apply its effect across adjacent pixels. This can result in a less blocky effect compared to the Diffusion method.

Whichever option you choose, depending on your image, the effect may be so subtle that it looks like splitting hairs.

◼ Working in tandem with Diffusion is the **Dither** box. If you have applied any of the settings other than No Dither, this box will become enabled and allow you to set the amount up to 100%. Higher settings result in a more pronounced effect.

◼ **Web Snap** relates to web safe colors. Set the box to 100 to use only colors from the web safe palette. The lower the setting, the lower the tolerance will be in shifting colors to the nearest web safe equivalent. If you do not intend to use the web safe palette, make sure this box is set to 0.

◼ **Transparency**: Checking this box preserves any transparent areas in the image.

◼ **Matte** enables you to substitute the transparent areas in the image with a color of your choice. In practical terms, this usually means matching the color of the web page background. If the web page background was red and we wanted our logo to sit seamlessly on the red background, we can select a red from this box and the anti-aliased pixels around the edges of the artwork would have the correct shades of red to match the background perfectly.

◼ **Interlaced**: A low-resolution version of the image appears in the browser while the full image file is downloading. This option does increase file size and is best kept for very large images or a target audience with slow connections.

◼ **Use Unified Color Table**: When selected, the same color table is used for all rollover states.

1. Let's experiment. Our selected, linked slices are predominantly two colors, black and white. Try selecting two colors from the colors drop-down box. You will notice the text and edges of the other artwork become very jagged and grainy. With only two colors it is not possible to produce the required anti-aliasing to create the illusion of smooth edges. However the file size is tiny. The bottom left of the window shows you the original and optimized file sizes. In this case we have reduced the selected slices from 590k to 5.542k

~590K / 5.542K GIF ▼

2. Now try increasing the colors to 256 colors. We get smooth edges but the file size leaps to over 30k for the selected slices.

3. The surest technique is to destroy the quality to an unacceptable standard then gradually increase colors until you can no longer see an improvement by adding more colors. For these selected slices try 16 colors.

4. Select the photo images on the left of the page and link them by going to the Slices menu again. A different link color is displayed. 16 colors produces a grainy result for these images. Try 64 and you will get an acceptable image without too much of an overhead in file size.

    We have now applied gif settings to all the image areas on the page. Finally we need to deal with the non-image areas. This accounts for any plain black areas.

5. Shift-select all the plain black slices. Go to the Slice palette and select No Image from the Type drop-down box. Also select black as the color from the BG drop-down box. This will fill each table cell with a black background color.

This action creates a file with the absolute minimum file size and no unnecessary graphics.

Saving the optimized images and HTML page

This is the final task. The preparation is complete, all that remains is for ImageReady to create the required images files, HTML, and JavaScript code to operate the rollovers. Before we give that command we just need to check a few settings to ensure the files are created the way we would like them.

1. Go to File > Output Settings > Slices.

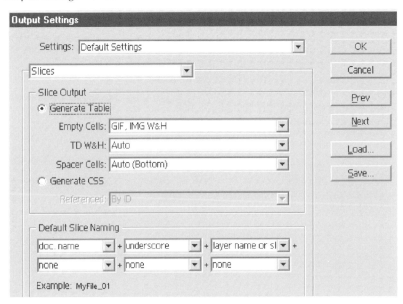

2. Make sure the Generate Table option is selected. This is the default option and creates the most compatible HTML for different browsers. Keep the defaults selected for maximum compatibility.

3. Click the drop-down box that displays the word Slices and choose Background. In the BG Color drop-down box choose black as the color. This will create the page with a black background that will blend seamlessly with our HTML table for computers with a higher resolution than our target resolution size.

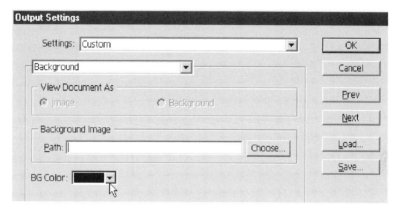

4. Click OK to close the dialog box.

5. Create a folder somewhere on your computer named Music Factory web. The purpose of this is to keep the HTML and images folder that will be created neatly in one location.

6. Go to File > Save As. Save the file as a PSD calling it index into the folder you just created. You now have the master PSD file for future editing.

7. Now to create the optimized files: go to File > Save Optimized As. Navigate to the same folder. Automatically the file will be called index.HTML. The file name *index* is used by most servers to define the first or home page of a web site. Make sure the settings are as shown in the picture here. Click Save and the HTML file, image files, and an image folder will be generated.

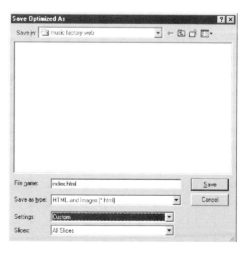

8. Take a look in the folder you created and you will see the `index.HTML` file and the images folder containing all the images optimized at the compression settings that you specified. Assuming you have a browser installed on your computer, double-click the HTML file and your web page will open in the browser where you can see the rollovers and animation working.

    We need one small HTML tweak to make this page look better on computers with higher screen resolutions. The market analysis for the target audience for this site told me a screen resolution of 800 by 600 pixels is required. If you have this screen resolution or smaller, the page should look just as it was intended. If you have a larger resolution, 1024 by 768 or even greater, the page sits up in the top left corner of the screen. The higher the resolution, the more blank space there will be on the right and bottom of the web page.

    One simple way to resolve this problem is to center the HTML table within the page. Then the page will always be centered horizontally irrespective of the resolution of the users computer, providing some balance to the page. I say simple, but it does entail some manual HTML editing, there's no real need for this to bother you, however, you'll be surprised how simple some basic HTML editing is - you may even want to learn it yourself after this. Of course if you use Dreamweaver, GoLive, or similar programs, they can be used just as easily.

9. Open the HTML page in Wordpad or Notepad on a PC or SimpleText on a Mac. Scroll down the page or use the search or find function to find the following line of code.

    ```
    <TABLE WIDTH=760 BORDER=0 CELLPADDING=0 CELLSPACING=0>
    ```

    Add the words `ALIGN="CENTER"` so your complete line looks exactly the same as the following line. If you are outside the US, note the spelling of "center" uses the American variant.

    ```
    <TABLE WIDTH=760 BORDER=0 CELLPADDING=0 CELLSPACING=0
    ALIGN="CENTER">
    ```

10. Save the page to update it, then open the page in the browser again or refresh it if it is already open in the browser.

Now the page is centered horizontally. Even if you expand and contract the width of the browser window the web page will gracefully move with it remaining in the center.

That is the web page complete. If you want to edit the web page in the future, open the original PSD file in ImageReady, carry out any editing and redefine slices if necessary, then go to File > Save Optimized to recreate the images and HTML file.

Other animation techniques

Tweening animation in ImageReady

The GIF animations we have created so far have relied upon existing layers, which were converted into self-contained animations. ImageReady also provides a fast, highly functional method of creating gif animations called **tweening**, which doesn't rely on existing layers. All you need to create is the first and last frame of the animation and ImageReady creates all the in-between frames, hence the name. Anyone familiar with applications such as Macromedia Flash will have already come into contact with the concept of tweening, but if you haven't, now is your chance to find out what it's all about.

We are going to use the Music Factory logo as a banner advert that will be displayed on selected web sites as a simple fading image. In these more informed and sophisticated days of the Web it might be fair to say that flashing logos are kitsch, but fading logos suggest a reserved subtlety. You can decide, but either way, tweening is going to make our life a lot easier in the creation of this animation.

1.   Open the file called `Logo_fade.psd` in ImageReady.

Take a look in the Layers palette. You will notice that this file has only one layer above the black background layer and that's all we need to get started, so already our workload has been reduced.

2.   In the Animation palette, click the new frame button at the bottom of the palette. This creates frame 2, which is a duplicate of frame 1.

3.   Make sure frame 2 is selected. In the Layers palette reduce the layer Opacity to 0%. This effectively makes frame 2 invisible, but does not affect frame 1 in any way.

4.   Select frame 1 in the Animation palette, click the pop-up menu button in the top right corner of the palette, and select Tween.

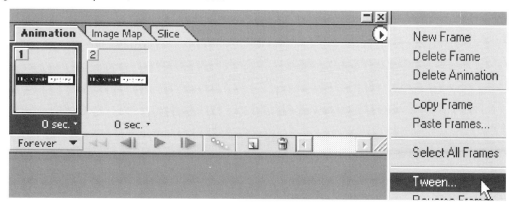

5.   In the Tween dialog box apply the settings as shown:

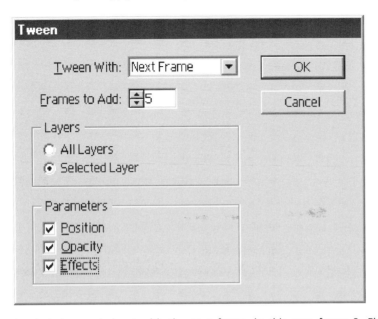

Tweening is being carried out with the next frame, in this case frame 2. Five frames are being added, making seven in total. Use caution when deciding how many frames to add. The more frames you use, the smoother and more fluent the animation will be, but this also means you are using more frames which will add to the file size and take longer to download. Just as with any image, the target audience must be kept in mind and a suitable balance should be found between quality and file size.

Only the selected layer is being tweened as the bottom, black layer remains visible all the time. The Parameters section enables you to define which parameters can be changeable.

6.   Click the play button on the Animation palette to see the animation play. The image fades out and then repeats in a permanent loop.

As an alternative to the logo suddenly appearing again and then fading out, how about if we make it also fade in - creating a more relaxed pulsating effect? We can do this without creating any more artwork or tweening. All we have to do is modify the existing animation.

7.   Select frame 1, then SHIFT-select frame 7 so all the frames are selected. Click the pop-up menu button in the top right corner of the palette and select Copy Frames.

8. Click the same button again and select Paste Frames. In the Paste Frames dialog box, select the Paste After Selection option. This pastes the copied frames immediately after the current selected seven frames.

We now have 14 frames of animation that play twice in succession each time fading in, disappearing and fading in again. It's not quite what we want. The idea is for the animation to fade out and fade in again.

9. Select frames 8 to 14, just select frame 8 then SHIFT-select frame 14. These are the pasted frames. Click the pop-up menu button and select Reverse Frames.

Now the animation fades out and in fluently. The animation default is to play forever. If you wish it to play once only or any number of times, click the pop-up menu in the bottom left corner of the palette and select Once or Other to enter the required number of times.

Saving the animation follows the same process as when you created the web page. Save the PSD in case you want to edit the master animation in the future, then choose the desired amount of colors in the Optimize palette and Save Optimized to output the finished GIF file to be embedded in the web page.

Using Illustrator to create vector animation in Flash SWF format

Macromedia Flash is a stand-alone application that is used to create animation for web sites and on screen presentations, among other things. Unlike their humble GIF counterparts, Flash animations can be highly complex and sophisticated, they use vector technology, so potentially the file size can be far smaller whilst retaining all the high quality, scalable benefits of vector artwork.

Of course nothing is perfect, and the downside of this is that Flash files require a plug-in on the user's computer before the content can be viewed. However, because of the acceptance of Flash as an Internet standard, the latest browsers and computer operating systems now include the Flash plug-in as standard. Therefore the problem of compatibility is not the major issue it used to be, but you need to be aware of the computer set up of your target web audience - there are still are lot of older browsers out there.

Illustrator is capable of exporting layered files in SWF format, the compressed format of Macromedia Flash. We are going to create a simple vector animation in Illustrator for a web site and take advantage of the popularity of Flash by saving our file in the Flash format, thereby giving us animation that will be readily accessible to a broad web audience.

Open the file called `Logo_fade.ai`.

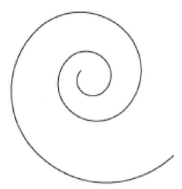

We are going to create an animation of a music note fading away into the distance in a decreasing spiral pattern. This could be used as a banner animation, the kind you see you see typically on web pages.

I have created the starting artwork. The music note came from the logo you created in part 4. The spiral stroke was created using the Spiral tool - unsurprisingly.

The creative use of the **Blend** tool is the secret behind creating fast animations that can be saved in the Flash Format.

Let's create a blend between the two music notes and then apply the blend to the spiral.

1.   First we need to set up the Blend tool so it works the way we want it to. Double-click the Blend tool in the toolbox.

2.   Apply the settings as in the image below. Make sure the Orientation box on the left is clicked as shown. Click OK. This sets up the Blend tool to create 25 music notes between the first and last note.

3.   Click the music note on the left, and then click the note on the right. Click anywhere on the main body of the note, not on the edge or an anchor point.

You should see a blend gradually increasing in size from left to right as in the picture below:

We now need to apply the blend to follow the spiral.

4.   Select the whole blend and the spiral. As there is nothing else on the page you can press CMD/CTRL+A. This command will select all the artwork on the page.

5.   Go to Object > Blend > Replace Spine.

This is how the blend should now look:

The idea is for the music notes to appear as if they disappearing into the distance so we need to change the color of the last note to match the background color.

6.   Using the Direct Selection tool (A), select the last, smallest note in the blend and change its fill color to white.

The whole blend will update, each note gradually changing from a black note at the beginning to a white note at the end of the blend. The smallest note was at the left of the screen when we created the blend. When the animation plays it will play from left to right by default. This means the notes will appear to come towards us rather than going away from us. All we need to do is reverse the blend.

7.   Go to Object > Blend > Reverse front to back.

The blend is now complete.

Next, we need to use the Layers palette to create separate sub-layers of each music note in the blend. This process is similar to the concept of a strip of film in a projector. Each independent sub-layer becomes a picture in a sequence that will create the illusion of movement.

8. Look in the Layers palette. Expand the Artwork layer to reveal the Blend layer.

9. Click the Blend layer to select it, then click the pop up menu button in the top right corner of the Layers palette and select Release to Layers (Sequence) from the pop up menu

    Your Layers palette will now display a number of additional sub-layers, each one containing one of the music notes in sequence. If you were to select the other Release to Layers option (Build), each sub-layer would appear in a cumulative manner with the artwork building up until every object appears in the last sub-layer.

    That's the production side finished. All we have to do now is save in the Flash format, apply the settings, and then we can view the finished animation.

10. Go to File >Export. Select Macromedia Flash (SWF) from the Save as Type drop-down box. Type "Myspiral" into the File Name box and select a location in which to save the file. Click the Save button.

11. The final dialog box shows the Flash Options. This is where we define the quality and performance settings.

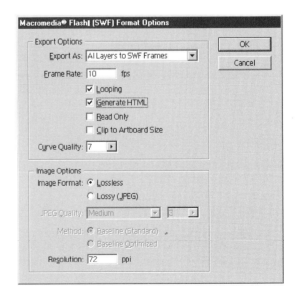

This is the breakdown of what these settings will do:

- **Export As** drop-down box:

    - **AI File to SWF File**: Exports the artwork to a single frame. All the artwork will be visible as one image so it is not suitable for animation.

    - **AI Layers to SWF Frames**: Exports each layer to a separate frame, as in projector film. This is what we need to create animation.

    - **AI Layers to SWF Files:** Exports each layer to a separate SWF file. If you had 10 layers, this option will create 10 independent SWF files, each with one frame and the artwork from one of the layers.

- **Frame Rate**: This defines the rate at which the animation will play. Technically, the faster the frame rate, the more fluent the animation will be. For example, in Flash the default frame rate is 12 frames per second. This means 12 frames or pictures will be played or seen by the user in one second. The more pictures you can see in one second, the more life-like the animation will be. It's really the difference between a Charlie Chaplin movie where the movement is very jerky because fewer frames were used and today's film that depicts real live movement. So if we set our animation to 24 frames per second, do we see more fluent movement? Technically, yes - as I mentioned above. In reality, not everyone viewing your animation over the web will have a computer geared up for animation. The faster the computer's processor, the more capable it will be of playing your animation at the desired frame rate. If the computer can't play at the pace you have set, it will still play but much slower. Your 24 frames per second animation could end up playing at 6 frames per second. For this reason, Flash set the default to 12 frames per second and it would be wise not to exceed this unless you are certain of your target audience. Again, a corporate Intranet would be the only place where you could be certain of the capabilities of everyone's computer. Very simple animations consisting of a few objects and limited movement can quite happily play at less than 12 frames per second. The one we are creating now will be set to just 10 frames per second.

- **Looping**: Automatically plays your animation in a loop so that it keeps playing as if you were winding it back to the start and playing it each time.

- **Generate HTML**: In most cases the animation will be viewed in a browser. An HTML file will be needed for this to happen. Selecting this option forces Illustrator to create the HTML file for you.

- **Read Only**: Prevents users from editing the exported SWF file.

- **Clip to Artboard Size**: Exports all the artwork on the artboard to the SWF file. Any artwork outside the artboard will be clipped.

- **Curve Quality**: Defines how accurately curves are followed. A low number will create the curves in the SWF file with slightly less precision, but the file will be smaller. A higher number increases the precision in following the original curve, but results in a larger file size.

- **Image Format**: Defines how bitmap artwork is compressed to reduce file size.

- **Lossless**: Maintains the highest image quality but creates a large SWF file.

- **Lossy (JPEG)**: Creates a smaller SWF file but can result in imperfections appearing in the image.

- **Resolution**: Sets the resolution for bitmap images. 72 ppi is the maximum required if there is no intention to print the image.

Apply the settings as shown above and Click OK.

The folder in which you saved the artwork now has two additional files. Both are called "Myspiral" one is an SWF format, the other is an HTML file. Have a look at these files in your folder now.

Before you can view either of the files you must have the Flash plug-in installed on your computer. If you have one of the latest browsers or a fairly new computer you probably have it installed already. If you don't have the plug-in, you can download the latest version from http://www.macromedia.com/downloads/.

12. Double-click the Myspiral HTML file.

     Your browser should have launched and you will be seeing the animation play. If you don't see the animation but the browser opens it means you do not have the plug-in and you will need to download it.

13. Close the browser, then go back to your folder where the two "Myspiral" files are located. Double-click the SWF file this time. As long as you have the Flash plug-in installed, the file will open in the Flash Player. The Flash Player is an application designed to play Flash content. For this reason, the SWF format is great for sending animations by email. As long as the recipient has the plug-in, they can play your animation in the Flash Player without having to launch a browser and as this file weighs in at 2.35k it's not going to keep anyone waiting as they download it.

Creating SVG web graphics

The **SVG – Scalable Vector Graphics** is a vector file format based on **XML – Extensible Mark-up Language** and was designed primarily for viewing vector graphics through a browser on the web. SVG enables Web developers and designers to create dynamically generated high-quality graphics from real-time data with precise structural and visual control.

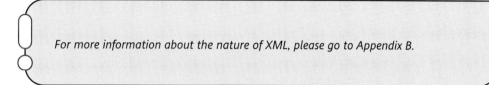

For more information about the nature of XML, please go to Appendix B.

All the popular and widely supported file formats on the web are bitmap file formats (with the exception of Flash's SWF format that we just looked at). You will be aware now of the deficiencies of bitmaps. File sizes are generally larger and they lack the scalability of vector formats. This is one of the reasons for the existence of the SVG format. The ability to preserve the crisp smooth edges of a vector graphic as well as scale it without loss of quality seems a natural development for graphics on the web. Think of the benefits, for example, a vector graphic of a map being viewed in a browser on a web site. If you want to zoom in closer to see the name of a road, you simply zoom in as you would as if you were in Illustrator and you see a close up view without any loss of quality.

From a designer's point of view, SVG allows you to have a greater degree of control over your web page layout and use any fonts you choose by embedding them in the file. As SVG is written in XML, it is possible to link content to e-commerce systems and databases for efficient dynamically updateable web sites. Interactivity plays a strong role in SVG and by using languages such as JavaScript, Java, and Microsoft's Visual Basic, entire web applications and interfaces can be built.

This all sounds like a great innovation for the web and a step in the right direction, but it comes at a price. As with the Flash SWF format SVG content requires a plug-in to enable a user to view it. No one actually owns the web, which is a good thing. But the downside of this fact is that there are many technologies and protocols being developed by different companies and organizations whom are all competing in order to become a "Web standard". This situation means there is a huge breadth of choice for the user, but the benefits of choice also means we are able to use different bits of software. Unless a user has the bit of software necessary to view the graphics that I have created in a certain format, they won't be able to see my work. The lack of single web ownership means there is no law or policy that says you must use this particular software and hardware set up or you can't play.

This situation presents a problem to the web developer and designer. Before deciding on which kind of formats to use within their web site, some research will need to be conducted into their target audience to assess what percentage of their audience is likely to have the required software setup.

Assuming SVG is right for your kind of audience, let's create and save some SVG artwork.

Essentially, SVG is just plain text. So SVG code can be edited with a text editor. As a designer, you will most likely prefer to use a graphics application to create your shapes and colors and that's where Illustrator excels.

Open the file called `Electra.ai`.

Maps, technical drawings, illustrations, graphs, the list goes on, are all prime examples of where it would be preferable to maintain the vector characteristics of the artwork. When viewed in a browser that supports the SVG format the user will be able to zoom in closer to see fine detail. This guitar is simplified but irrespective of the complexity of the drawing, the vector detail will be maintained. It should be noted however that the more complex the vector artwork, the greater its file size. As we are discussing artwork that will be downloaded over a potentially slow connection, depending on your target audience, it will be good practice to be conscious of the finished file size.

Saving artwork as SVG

We are now going to save this file in SVG format.

Go to File > Save As.

In the Save As dialog box, the Save as Type drop-down box displays the available formats. There are two versions of SVG. The first SVG in the list is the standard SVG format. The second option, SVG compressed (SVGZ) can reduce file sizes by 50% to 80%, so that is the option we are going to choose. Choose a location on your computer to save the file. Leave the file name as Electra and click the Save button.

The SVG Options box opens so let's look at the settings in this dialog box:

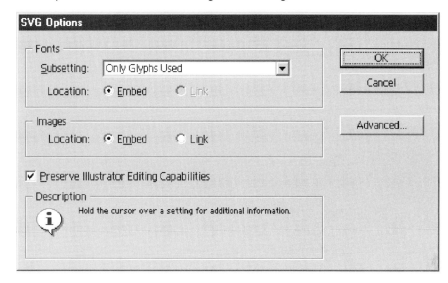

Fonts

- **Subsetting**: Defines which fonts are included.

  - **None**: Will not include any fonts with the file and is a good option if you are certain that the required fonts will be available on the users computer. This of course is not possible as far as the web is concerned, so would only be practical if you used common fonts such as Arial. The other situation where it would be safe to use would be on an Intranet network where company guidelines would define which fonts were available on all the computers linked to the Intranet. The benefit of using this option is a smaller file size.

  - **Only Glyphs Used** (only available when embedding fonts) This option includes only glyphs (characters and symbols) for text that exists in the current artwork. This will create a larger file size than the previous option, but it will not be excessive as no characters will be included that have not been used in the artwork. Naturally the more characters you use the larger the file will be.

  - **Common English**

  - **Common English & Glyphs Used**

  - **Common Roman**

  - **Common Roman & Glyphs Used**

  - **All Glyphs**

The last five options will be larger in file size than the first two options as entire font sets are being included regardless of whether or not they currently exist in the artwork. This option is useful when the text content of the SVG file is dynamic, for example in situations where the text will be delivered directly from the web server or a database, such as when you use a search engine on the web.

- **Fonts Location**:

    - **Embed**: Embeds the font subset directly in the file. This concept is similar to when you Place bitmap files in an Illustrator page and you choose to embed the image or link to it. Embedding fonts will create a larger file but will ensure that the fonts will be available for use.

    - **Link** will create a link to the original Illustrator file. This is useful if you have several SVG files that use the same fonts. Each file will link to the fonts and avoid having to embed the same fonts several times in different files.

- **Images Location**: Same situation as above but this time relating to images. Choose to either **Embed** the image directly in the file or **Link** to the exported bitmap image from the original Illustrator file. Embedding images increases file size but ensures that bitmap images will always be available.

- **Preserve Illustrator Editing Capabilities**: Check this box if you intend to open and edit the SVG file in Illustrator.

Select the options as in the picture above and click OK.

You now have a new file in the saved location called `Electra.svgz`. We are now going to view this file in a browser to see what it does. This is where the SVG plug-in is required. I assume you are working in Illustrator 10. If so, you should already have the SVG plug-in installed on your computer as this happens when you first install Illustrator 10. If for some reason you do not have the plug-in installed you can download the latest version by going to http://www.adobe.com/svg. One simple way to assess if you have the plug-in is to go to the Illustrator Help Menu (Help > About Plug).

In the dialog box that opens, scroll down the alphabetic list to see if the SVG plug-in is displayed as in the image here.

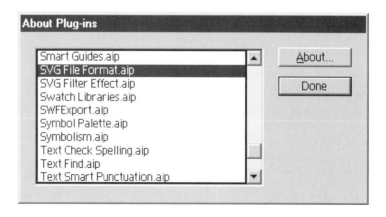

If so, you have the plug-in. You also need to have a browser installed.

1. A new file called `Electra.svgz` will have been created in the same location as your `Electra.ai` file. Double-click the svgz file to open it in your browser.

   Try zooming in on the guitar. This is where you may encounter another of those software incompatibilities. My browser, Microsoft Internet Explorer version 5.5 on a PC supports zooming on vector graphics. Some older browsers on PC and Macs don't support this function.

   We are going to zoom in to a point based on the letter "t" of the word "Electra"

2. CTRL/right-click near the letter "t". From the pop-up menu that appears select Zoom in.

   The browser zooms in on the guitar placing the point at which you clicked near to, but not exactly in the center of the screen. This gives you a certain amount of control over which part of the image is emphasized when zooming. Try that again by zooming in closer, but this time based on a different location.

3. You may have noticed an option to Zoom Out in the same pop-up menu. Try this now to zoom out of the image. The other option that becomes available once you have zoomed in is Original View. This option returns you to the view you saw when you first opened the page.

This introduction to the SVG format is intended to give you an idea of its capabilities and potential pitfalls. Knowledge of other Internet technologies such as Javascript and XML will enable you to greatly enhance the functionality of SVG. As with any technology, good or bad, its true success will ultimately depend upon the public's acceptance and willingness to use it as part of the everyday web tools.

Data Driven Graphics

The days of creating a web site and then forgetting about it for many months are long gone. Certainly any commercial or service-based web site is well aware of the need to keep the web site fresh and updated, much in the same way as a printed publication uses new material in every new issue.

This necessity means designers are burdened with the often laborious task of creating numerous versions of graphics for web banners, product and news pages, and a variety of other similarly formatted pages requiring frequent updating.

By way of example, imagine the following working scenario:

The Music Factory has agents and distributors worldwide. The design studio of the company is responsible for supplying web advertising images for each agent in each country. All the agents have their own unique web designs and interfaces. They also display text in their own language, of course, and require an assortment of different product images to rotate on a weekly basis so the advert doesn't start to look tired. Two of the many adverts are pictured below, one for the Brazilian agent and one for the French.

The interface designs are quite different, as are the languages and the slogan. The only common element is the format. If there are 50 agents worldwide and 10 different product photos are rotated for each of the agents, the designer is faced with making 500 different versions of the file.

The slogan for each country says, in the native language, "The finest musical instruments in *relevant country*" This slogan will change every two weeks also, so the figure of 500 files begins to grow even bigger. Not an enviable nor exciting task even for the most novice of designers.

ImageReady provides a fast and efficient solution to this problem. Using ImageReady you only need to create one PSD file. This file can contain each of the agents' interfaces, languages, and any other unique text or imagery associated with that agent on separate layers. The required version of the file can then be output automatically by defining the layers content as a **Variable**. Don't worry about this potentially scary programming type of word. We will look at variables in more depth shortly, but briefly it allows you to change elements to be displayed. For instance, one image can be replaced by another image or a line of text can be replaced by another line of text. Rather than physically inserting the new element into place in the PSD file, a script can be used to link to the database where all the elements are stored and the new PSD will be generated automatically.

Using a script is just one way of linking the variables to the database. Adobe GoLive, the web site creation application, can also be used as well as the new dynamic image server software by Adobe called AlterCast. AlterCast provides a powerful solution to updating web graphics. As well as linking the variables specified in ImageReady to the database, it can also output the required optimized files such as JPG or GIF and post them to the web. A script, created by the developer, performs this function. It allows users with traditional skills to concentrate on what they do best, so a designer can get on with designing and programmers can program without crossing over into each other's territory.

Understanding the use of variables

All this talk of databases and programming languages might leave the designer running for cover, but in fact this process is extremely 'designer friendly'. The only programming element designers need to get to grips with is the term 'variables'. The word itself has associations with JavaScript and other programming languages but it can be applied to any real life situation.

A variable can be thought of as a container. The container is given a name, usually a name that describes what the container will hold. A chocolate box will contain chocolates. The chocolate box itself is of little value, so the contents, which are of course chocolates in this case, become known as the value. This value will change depending how many chocolates have been eaten at any time.

Computer languages use this same principle to find answers to everyday mathematical questions. For example, someone working at a weather center would need to know for statistical purposes the average daily rainfall in any given month. More than one calculation would be needed as a calendar month can have anything from 28 to 31 days.

Of course we don't know how much rain will fall each day so we have unknown quantities to deal with also. This is where the use of variables is invaluable.

This is how programmers would create an automated solution to the problem.

- First they would create a variable (the container) and name it something relevant. *Rainfall* would be a good idea. This holds the amount of rain that fell in the chosen month (not literally), so the total amount of rain that fell becomes the value held within this variable.

- Now the programmer creates a variable named **DaysInMonth**. If the month being analyzed is July, then 31 will be the number used. 31 now becomes the value held in the **DaysInMonth** variable.

- And lastly, a variable needs to be created that will display the answer to the person requiring the information. A variable named *AverageDailyRain* will be created for the purpose. In the chosen programming language, the script would say something on the lines of the following:

    Divide the value held in the variable named Rainfall by the value in the variable named DaysInMonth and display the result in the variable named AverageDailyRain.

The result appears on screen and the weather analyst is saved the tedium of repetitive calculations.

We can now apply this principle to the way variables are used in ImageReady.

To simplify the exercise I have used just two agents, you can work with as many as you wish. For each image to be output, we only need to show the agent's interface, the line of text in the countries own language, and the product image. Let's run through this process in detail. From the download folder, open `variable_image.psd`.

The construction of the image is important. Every item that you want to be a variable, or in other words, will be expected to change, must be on its own layer. Here is the Layers palette setup relating to our master image. To make things even easier to work with I have made Layer sets to contain all layers specific to that country agent, so in my case just two, one for Brazil and one for France.

There are three kinds of variables in ImageReady. These refer to the kind of element you wish to change:

- **Pixel replacement variable**: Used to change the pixel area of a layer. This one can be used to change the image on the image layer.

■ **Text replacement variable**: Used to replace a string of text in a text layer. This will be used to change the slogan.

■ **Visibility variable**: Used to show or hide a layer's content. This can be used to show only the required interface and hide all the others.

Defining a Pixel Replacement variable

Select the layer for which you want to define a variable. (Variables cannot be defined for the background layer). We first need to define a variable for the image layer, so the image layer is selected.

Do either of the following.

■ Go to Image > Variables > Define: or
■ From the pop-up menu in the Layers palette select Variables.

The Variables dialog box opens so you can define the kind of variable.

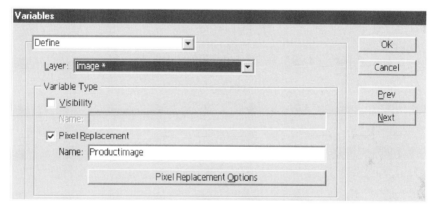

We are defining a variable, so leave Define as the option in the first drop-down box. The Layer drop- down box shows all the layers apart from the background layer, if you have one, which cannot be defined as a variable. I have selected the layer called image in this case.

To make the pixel area (the image) replaceable, check the Pixel Replacement check box. The Name field refers to the variable name. Though not essential, you will find it helpful to use a name relevant to the element you want to change. In this case I have named the variable "Productimage".

Naming of variables follows a strict convention. Names must begin with a letter, an underscore, or a colon. They must not contain spaces or special characters apart from periods, hyphens, underscores, or colons.

Next click the button labeled **Pixel Replacement Options**. The following dialog box allows you to define how the replacement image will be scaled, assuming the replacements are not the same size as the original.

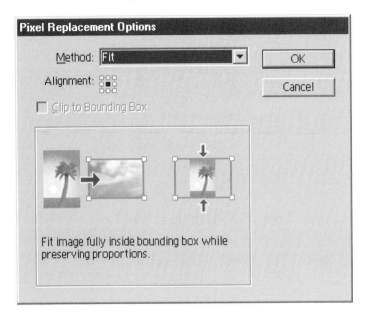

The options available are:

- **Fit**: Scales the image to fit within the bounding box of the original image. This may result in part of the bounding box area being left empty

- **Fill**: Scales the image to completely fill the bounding box. This may result in the image extending beyond the bounding box. Select the Clip to Bounding Box check box to clip areas of the image that fall outside the bounding box.

- **As Is**: To prevent any scaling. Select the Clip to Bounding Box check box to clip areas of the image that fall outside the bounding box.

- **Conform**: Scales the image non-proportionally to fit within the bounding box. This can result in the image becoming distorted.

In each case click a handle on the Alignment icon to define how the image should be aligned within the bounding box. Center is the default.

Click OK to confirm both dialog boxes and a variable for the image layer has now been defined.

In case you are wondering at this stage how we go about specifying a replacement image, we will look at how to define a **Data Set** shortly, which will do this job for us.

Defining a Text Replacement variable

The text slogan may change for each country, so next we are going to define each text layer as a variable also.

Select the text layer named "slogan France", then use the same steps as for the Pixel Replacement variable to open the Variables dialog box.

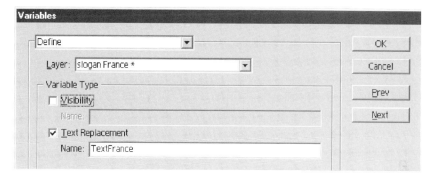

Because the selected layer was a text layer, the Text Replacement check box is checked automatically. Name the variable "TextFrance". The asterix appearing in the Layer drop-down box denotes that this layer has been defined as a variable.

Don't click OK yet. We are going to define another kind of variable. As well as the slogan changing, we will only require one country's slogan to be visible at a time, all the others must be invisible, so we need to define a **Visibility variable**.

Defining a Visibility variable

Check the Visibility check box. Name the Variable "France". Click OK to confirm the settings.

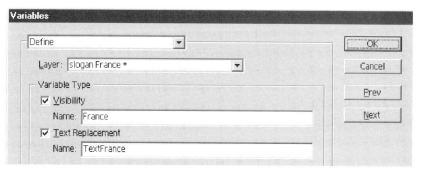

Finally, the interface for France also needs to be defined as a Visibility variable as only one interface will be visible at a time, just like the slogan. The picture below shows the layer named "Interface France" defined as a Visibility variable. Use the name as in the picture for the variable name.

All three kinds of variable have now been defined within the file.

Follow the same steps to define variables for the two layers relating to Brazil.

Using Data Sets

Data Sets provide the control to use the variables you have defined to output a file in a certain configuration. The **Data Set** describes a collection of variables and the data that is associated with the variables. By using different Data Sets, different images, text, and visibility settings can be uploaded to the template.

Editing the default Data Set

As soon as the first variable has been defined in the PSD file, the default Data Set is created. For this reason it is not possible to edit the default Data Set until a variable has been defined.

To edit the default Data Set, go to Image > Variables > Data Sets. Alternatively you can use the pop-up menu button in the Layers palette and choose the Variables option as you did earlier. When the Variables dialog box opens, select Data Sets from the first drop-down box.

The Variables dialog box pictured appears, displaying the default Data Set named Data Set 1. All functions relating to Data Sets can be performed in this box including creating, editing, saving, and deleting Data Sets.

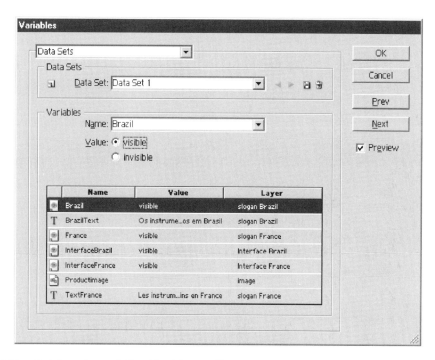

All the variables that have been defined in this PSD file appear displaying their variable name, the variable value (if one has been used) and the layer name.

Remember, the creation of this Data Set is an automatic function as soon as you define your first variable, so nothing else remains to be done so as far as this data set is concerned.

Creating a new Data Set

To output the required files in their varying configurations we are going to create new Data Sets, which will be associated with the variables that have been defined in the psd image.

Use the same step as you did previously to open the Variables dialog box. You will be looking at the same window as in the picture above.

Click the **New Data Set** icon as labeled above. This action causes Data Set 2 to appear in the Data Set drop-down box. Notice also that the Previous and Next Data Set buttons have become enabled as more than one Data Set now exists. Numerically naming Data Sets will become confusing as the amount of Data Sets grows, so a relevant name can be typed in the drop-down box to identify what the Data Set refers to.

Once a new Data Set has been created and named, the variables can have new values applied to them to define the required output file.

In the picture below, I have named the Data Set "Brazil" and then clicked the variable called Brazil, which becomes selected. This is the Brazilian slogan. The original value of this variable was visible. We need to keep this layer visible so nothing needs to be done. We can leave the value as it is.

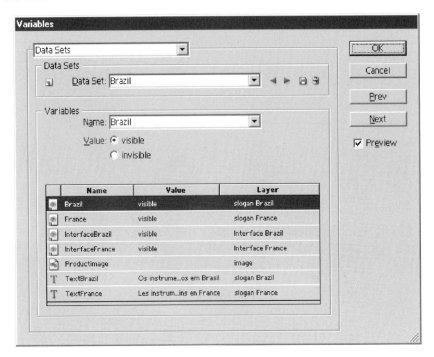

The same applies to the InterfaceBrazil variable; this can be left at its default visible value.

What we do have to do is hide the visibility variables relating to France. Select the variable named France and change its visibility to Invisible. Do the same for the variable named InterfaceFrance.

Finally we need to save the new Data Set.

Click the **Save Data Set** icon as in the labeled diagram. Click OK to close the dialog box.

Previewing Data Sets

The Data Sets can now be used to update and output files from the database. ImageReady will also allow you to preview the new files generated by the Data Sets just as if they had been actually updated from the database itself. This is a good idea to ensure everything works as you expect it to.

Make sure all the layers are visible in the Layers palette. From the toolbox, click the Preview document button or press the keyboard shortcut – Y

The Tool Options bar now displays a drop-down box containing all the Data Sets that have been created. Click the drop-down arrow and select the Data Set you wish to preview. In this case select the Brazil Data Set.

The result is pictured below. This is just the Brazil version of the image, all other layers have been rendered invisible by the variables

Different Data Sets can also be selected and previewed by clicking the forward and back buttons next to the Data Set drop-down box as in the above picture.

To leave preview mode and return to the original document, either click the same Preview button, press y or the Esc key, or click the Cancel Preview button in the Tools Option bar.

Modifying Data Sets

Data Sets themselves are not cast in stone and can be freely edited to suit your changing needs. You can rename, edit, or delete Data Sets.

- **Renaming a Data Set**: From within the variables dialog box, enter the new name in the Data Set field.

- **Changing the data in a Data Set**: From within the variables dialog box, select the Data Set in which you want to change the data, then select the relevant variable and edit the value as required. Click the Save icon to update the change.

- **Deleting a Data Set**: From within the Variables dialog box, select the Data Set you want to delete and click the trash can icon.

Replacing an image using variables

Although all the elements required for this range of web adverts are encompassed in multiple layers in one PSD file, we can still use variables to import a completely independent image from elsewhere. We only have one background product photo in the file at present which is used for everyone.

We're going to run through the process of changing that photo for final output. We've already created a variable for the image layer called ProductImage, so use any of the methods previously detailed to open the Variables dialog box, and then select the Data Set named Brazil.

Select the variable named ProductImage. Next to the Value field a Browse button appears. Click the button and navigate to the file you want to use. Select the file called image_B.psd.

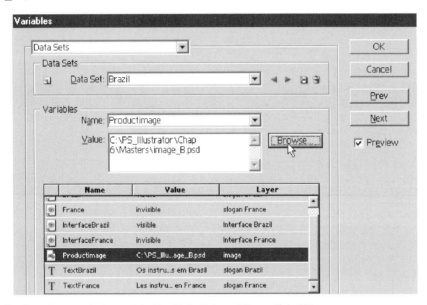

Click the Save icon again to update the Data Set, and then click OK.

Preview the image as before to see the new product photo image as part of the Brazil version advert.

Editing text in a text variable

Finally we are going to change one of the text slogans using a text variable.

Return to the Variables dialog box and select the Brazil Data Set. Select the variable named TextBrazil.

The text field labeled Value now allows you to type in your replacement string of text. If you feel like staying with the samba mood, type the text as in the picture below, or use your own words if you wish. (The line means "summer sale now on")

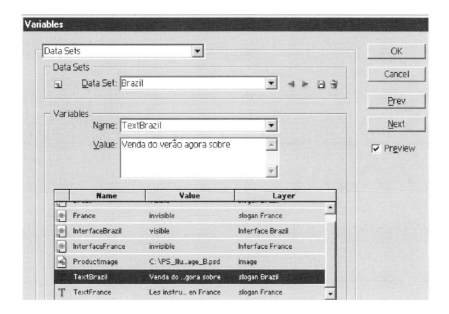

Save the Data Set again, and then preview it to see the new text.

Conclusion

In this chapter we have looked at how everyday web design projects are tackled using Adobe's ultimate suite of graphic applications in the form of Illustrator, Photoshop, and Image Ready. To call these applications merely "graphics" applications hides the true extent of their scripting and management capabilities that have been unveiled. You will encounter many of the workflow scenarios demonstrated here and come against many more that require a creative use of the three programs. Following the basic rules outlined, in terms of which programs to use, will ensure you are on the right track, but beyond that the scope for you to experiment is endless.

6 Producing Packaging Artwork

In this section we're going to look at several different approaches to creating packaging for a product. Our goal is to create a mock up for our client to show them what their packaging could look like, to do this we'll use Illustrator to create the flat artwork, and Photoshop to add in photographic images. We will be focusing on developing approaches that work efficiently and accurately, using numerically driven techniques wherever possible, to take full advantage of Illustrator's capabilities.

Throughout these projects we will take a look at a number of variations, but more often than not, will attempt to use techniques that are efficient and accurate. Where a keyboard shortcut is available, we'll use it, while making reference to the menu location of the actual command.

We want to take full advantage of the strengths of Illustrator and Photoshop: Illustrator to create vector based artwork that is very accurate and fully editable, and Photoshop to create photo realistic artwork with a high level of flexibility. Sometimes in order to create artwork that is highly flexible and allows for many changes, it actually can take a little more time and effort up front. The most flexible way of preparing artwork may not be the absolute fastest method. If it's a choice between finishing work sooner, but having less chance to change my mind, or taking longer but having more long-term options for change, I'd choose the latter option every time. This is the philosophy we're going to take for these projects: work efficiently by using shortcuts, use numerically driven methods wherever possible, and aim for highly flexible, editable documents.

The scenario

Our client is a manufacturer of golf balls, a new player in a very competitive market. They have tasked us with creating an eye-catching design – something that will stand out from the many choices available to golfers. Their research indicates that the majority of golf ball packaging designs are quite conservative. Most manufacturers have used solid colors with little use of graphics, and rely on their brand name to sell the product. One of our biggest challenges is to create awareness of this new brand. Our client wants to choose between a fairly conservative design and something a little more attention grabbing, so this is the brief that we'll work towards.

There are four main projects we'll complete:

- Creating the flat artwork in Illustrator and Photoshop.

- Creating the illusion of a 3D package in Illustrator.

- Using Photoshop to map the artwork to an existing image.

- Creating a two-color version of the artwork.

Project 1: Creating flat artwork in Illustrator

We need to create two different pieces for the golf ball packaging: a small box to hold three balls and a large box that contains five of the smaller boxes. In order to create accurate artwork for the boxes, we cannot rely on strictly visual creations, we need to know the measurements of each side of the small box, which is 1.625" x 5".

One of Illustrator's real strengths lies in working with a high degree of accuracy. The application's Illustrator's tools, dialog boxes, and palettes lend themselves naturally to working with specific dimensions, and objects that are created and transformed numerically.

You'll see the importance of accuracy become even more crucial when we move on to the next project, where the flat artwork will be used to create the illusion of dimension.

1. Create a new document in CMYK mode (CMD/CTRL+N).

2. Select the **Rectangle** tool (M), click once on the page to create the front of the box. Enter a Width of 1.625 and a Height of 5.

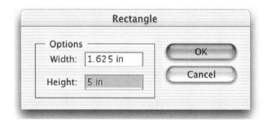

 If you get some unit of measurement other than inches go to Edit > Preferences > Units & Undo, *and change the setting to inches.*

3. With the rectangle still selected, use the Color palette to change the Fill to the values of CMYK shown below Cyan – 0%; Magenta 95%; Yellow 80 %, and Black 40%. Change the Stroke to none.

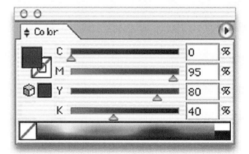

4. To create the side of the box we will duplicate the front, since the size is the same. You can use two methods to do this:

    ■ Hold down CMD/CTRL+OPT/ALT and start to drag the rectangle to the right. Once you've started to drag, also hold down SHIFT. This will copy the rectangle and will constrain the movement. Drag the copy so it lines up with the original.

■ Select the rectangle and from the Object menu choose Transform > Move. (CMD/CTRL+SHIFT+M) In the dialog box enter 1.625 in for the Horizontal position and 0 for Vertical. Click the Copy button.

Of the two methods, the second is more accurate since you are placing the duplicated rectangle by a specific measurement rather than by eye.

If you want to check for accuracy, press CMD/CTRL+Y to switch to Outline view. Zoom in on the edge that is shared by the two rectangles and you should only see a single line. If you see two lines very close to each other, as shown below, select one rectangle and use the arrow keys to nudge the shape until you see one line. (If the distance that the arrow keys nudge the object is too great, go to the General Preferences and lower the amount for Keyboard Increment).

5.   We'll create the top of the box by duplicating and then resizing the front of the box. Select the first rectangle with the Direct Selection tool, then press CMD/CTRL+SHIFT+M to open the Move command. Enter 0 for the Horizontal position and 5 for the Vertical position and click Copy.

6.   To accurately resize the top shape, we'll use the Transform palette (Window > Transform). In the Transform palette click on the middle bottom of the proxy. This will force the bottom of the shape to stay in a fixed position while we resize the box. Change the Height to 1.625 and press ENTER.

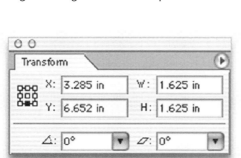

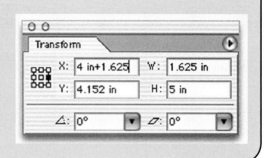

Here's an alternate method of duplicating an object that's both quick and accurate. In the Transform palette click on the right-hand size of the proxy. Then click beside the measurement in the X field. Type + 1.625 in, hold down OPT/ALT and press ENTER. *This will duplicate and move the selected object.*

7. If not in Outline view, switch to Outline view (CMD/CTRL+Y) so you can distinguish between the front and top of the box. We are going to create another rectangle, so select the Rectangle tool (M), position your cursor on the top left corner of the front rectangle and click once. Enter 1.625 for the Width and 0.325 for the Height. Press CMD/CTRL+Y to return to Preview view. Use the Swatches palette to fill that rectangle with yellow.

8. Duplicate the yellow rectangle onto the box side by using one of the previous methods. If you use the Move command, enter 1.625 for the Horizontal position and 0 for the Vertical position.

9. With the **Type** tool (T), click once (away from the existing shapes to avoid creating type within an object) and type BIRDIE. Set the type to Impact 20 pt. Hold down CMD/CTRL to activate the Selection tool and drag the type onto the box front. Position it just below the yellow rectangle and approximately a quarter of an inch from the left edge of the box.

10. Hold down CMD/CTRL and select the text as an object (so it is underlined) With the type highlighted, switch to the **Eyedropper** tool (I) and click on the box color. Then press ALT/OPTION to switch to the Paint bucket tool, then click on the type. This will change the color of the type to the same color as the box.

11. Go to the Color palette and hold down the SHIFT key while you drag the Magenta slider to the left. This will lower the percentage of all four colors at once. (Without the SHIFT key, only the Magenta slider would be affected). Lower the Magenta to about 80% (and the other colors will lower to approximately 70% yellow and 35% black). We want the text to be visible, but with only a slightly lighter shade of the box color.

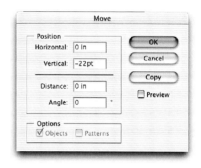

12. With the type still selected, open the Move command (CMD/CTRL+SHIFT+M). Enter 0 for the Horizontal position and –22 pt for the Vertical position. Make sure you type pt after the 22 or it will move 22 inches! Press the Copy button. Do not do anything else yet!

13. From the Object menu choose Transform > Transform Again (CMD/CTRL+D). That will duplicate the last operation, which in this case was to move and copy the text. Keep duplicating until you have 13 copies of the type on the box (a total of 14 words).

Don't mistake Transform Again (CMD/CTRL+D) for Duplicate. This command duplicates your last operation, not the selected object. In other words, if the last thing you did was to move an object to the left, Transform Again would move the same object the same distance (again). There would not be a copy unless that was part of your last operation. In this case since we moved and copied the word, Transform Again moves another copy each time you press the shortcut.

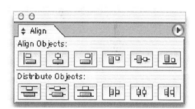

14. Holding down CMD/CTRL+SHIFT, drag the bottom BIRDIE down to just above the bottom of the box. Now we need to select all the other words. The simplest way is Select > Same > Fill Color. Then in the Align palette, click on the second button in the Distribute row (**Vertical Distribute Center**).

Now all the words will be evenly distributed.

15. Select the eighth BIRDIE down from the top and use the Type tool (T) to change that word to EAGLE.

16. Now let's create a graphic that will be repeated on different sides of the box. Use the Type tool to create text in some blank space away from the box. Type IN THE Enter HOLE! Set the type to Impact 40/42 and change the alignment to Centered. Fill the text with White.

17. Switch to Outline view (Cmd/Ctrl+Y) so you can see the text. With the **Ellipse** tool (L) we'll draw a circle that is slightly larger than the type. Hold down Opt/Alt to draw from the center outwards and Shift to make a perfect circle. Position your cursor approximately in the center of the type and drag outwards, creating a circle that is just slightly larger than the text.

18. Select both the text and the circle (Cmd/Ctrl+Shift+click on each), and from the Object menu choose Envelope Distort > Make with Top Object (Cmd/Ctrl+Opt/Alt+C). If necessary undo the operation and experiment with different sizes of circles until you get a result that you like. Because we filled the text with White, you may not be able to see the text after the transformation occurs. In order to see how the text looks, switch back out of Outline view (Cmd/Ctrl+Y) and drag the object onto the box somewhere.

> *When you use the Envelope Distort command, the objects that have been distorted cannot be edited directly. In order to be able to work with the original objects, choose* Envelope Distort > Edit Content *from the Object menu. Now you'll still see the distorted effect, but will be able to work with the original objects. Beware that it can look a little odd: you have to click where the original object is, not where you see the distorted result. Switch to Outline view (Cmd/Ctrl+Y) to see the original object again.*

19. Since we want to be able to easily reuse this graphic, we can turn it into a Symbol. This is one advantage of the Symbols palette, that it can be used as a type of library. Rather than painting with the symbol, we simply drag it on to the document. Select the graphic and drag it into the Symbols palette. To use the graphic in this document from now on, simply drag it from the Symbols palette onto the page.

When you add to the Symbols palette, that symbol is available only to the current document. If you want to make a symbol available to every document, you need to add the symbol to a specific document. This document, called the Adobe Illustrator Startup file, determines the contents of palettes such as Swatches, Brushes, Styles, and Symbols. This file is located in the Illustrator Application folder, in the Plug-ins folder. There are two documents, one for CMYK files and one for RGB documents. Anything you add to (or delete from) these documents becomes the default settings from then on.

20. Position the graphic on the front of the box, slightly overlapping the yellow box. Now we'll copy this design on to the top and the side. Using CMD/CTRL+OPT/ALT, drag a copy on to the side of the box and position it near the bottom. Use the same shortcut to drag another copy on to the top of the box. With the top design still selected, double-click on the **Scale** tool to open the Scale dialog box and enter 85% to scale it down slightly.

21. In order to make this design stand out a little more, we'll add a shadow to the graphic. Select all three graphics and from the Effect menu, choose Stylize > Drop Shadow. Change the Opacity to 80%, X and Y offset to .13 in, and pick black as the shadow color.

We're using Effects rather than Filters as they can be changed more easily.

22. Now we'll add the company logo. Open the file called `sm_target_logo.ai`, which can be downloaded from the friends of ED website (www.friendsofed.com). Select, copy, and paste into the box artwork. Position the logo at the bottom of the front of the box. Double-click on the Scale tool, enter 95%, and click OK.

23. With the Type tool (T), click away from any objects and type PRECISION GOLF BALLS. Set the type as Impact 22 pt with 24 pt leading, and fill with white. Move the text underneath the graphic on the box front.

24. With the Rectangle tool (M), click once outside the existing objects to create a rectangle with a Width of 1.45 and a Height of 2.5. Fill the rectangle with 100% Magenta, 80% Yellow. From the Object menu choose Path > Offset Path. In the dialog box enter 0.1 and click OK. This creates a second rectangle just larger than the first shape.

25. Using the **Area Type** tool, click on the path of the smaller box. Enter the following type: WARNING ENTER Repeated use of this product could dramatically increase your addiction to the great game of golf. Select the word WARNING and change it to Impact 20/24. Select the remainder of the text and change it to Arial Regular 14/16. Select the red rectangle and the text box and move them onto the box side. The end result should look something like this:

26. Save a copy of the finished artwork as small box art.ai.

Going large

Now to create the larger box, to do this we'll repeat many of these techniques, with a few new ones thrown in for good measure. This time around we'll use layers when creating the sides of the box to allow us to create two different boxes in one, and global color to let us change colors throughout the design very quickly. We'll also jump to Photoshop to create photographic artwork to use in our variations.

The measurements of the larger box are 6.625 x 10.625 x 1.625.

1. Create a new document in CMYK mode.

2. With the Rectangle tool (M) click once to create the top of the box. Enter 10.625 for the Width and 6.625 for the Height. Fill with some color (we'll be creating custom color shortly) and keep the rectangle selected.

3. In the Transform palette, click on the middle top of the proxy. In the Y field, click after the in and type in +6.625. Hold down OPT/ALT and press ENTER. This will create a copy that will become one of the sides of the box (in the next step).

4. Next, click on the middle bottom of the proxy. Change the Height to 1.625 and press ENTER.

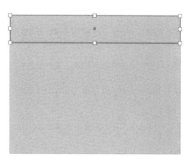

5. Now we'll repeat the same steps to create the last side. Select the large rectangle. In the Transform palette click on the middle top of the proxy. In the X field, click after the in and type in +10.625. Hold down OPT/ALT and press ENTER.

6. Click on the left middle of the proxy and change the Width to 1.625 and press ENTER.

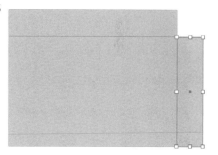

7. Now we will create layers and move the sides onto separate layers. Hold down OPT/ALT and click on the **New Layer** icon at the bottom of the Layers palette. Name the layer 'top'. Repeat this operation to create two more layers, one called 'long side', the other called 'short side'.

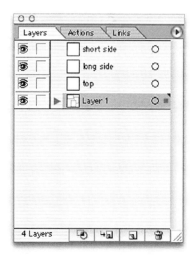

8. In order to move the sides onto the appropriate layers we'll use the Selection tool and the Layers palette. At the moment all three objects are on the same layer (Layer 1). Select the top of the box (the largest rectangle). Look in the Layers palette to the far right hand side of the name Layer 1 and you'll see a small colored square. By default this square is usually blue, but it could be some other color. This square indicates which layer the selected object is on.

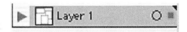

9. To move the object to a different layer, click and drag the small square onto the layer named top. The only visual clue on the image will be a change in color of the anchor points and/or bounding box of the selected object. Now repeat with the other two sides.

> *From now on we'll have to make sure we're on the correct layer before creating objects, placing graphics, adding type, etc.*

10. To give ourselves greater flexibility with color, we'll create a global color that can easily be changed. In the Swatches palette, use the pop-up menu to add a New Swatch. In the dialog box, name the color box color and check the Global box. Change the percentages to Cyan 90, Magenta 0, Yellow 100, and Black 30. Click OK. This new color will now be available in the Swatches palette.

    Although we created a process (CMYK) color, the Global color option means it is treated much like a spot color. Now we can create tints of the color, create swatches of those tints, and use the tints to create a gradient. By using this system, if we decide (or the client decides for us) to change the overall color scheme, we simply change the percentages of the original color and all the tint swatches and gradients will change throughout the document.

11. Let's create some tint swatches from this Global color that we'll then use to create a gradient. First make sure no objects are selected. Then click on the box color in the Swatches palette. In the Color palette you'll see a tint slider. Slide this to create a percentage of the color, or type in a number. Use 30% for the first tint. Now click on the swatch in the Color palette and drag it into the Swatches palette. This will create a new swatch that is a percentage of our global color. Repeat this operation to create a tint swatch of 55% and one of 75%.

12. In the Gradient palette we'll need to use the gradient slider to create our gradient. Use the pop-up menu to Show Options to see this slider. It will probably be showing a standard gradient of black and white. Click on the slider to display the color stops. We'll replace these with our colors, and add a couple of stops. For this to work effectively, you'll need to be able to see both the Gradient and the Swatches palettes. Drag the first color swatch (100%) from the Swatches palette on top of the first color stop on the gradient slider. The color should change. Drag the 55% tint swatch on top of the last stop on the gradient slider. You should see a gradient between these two colors.

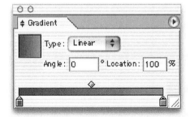

13. Now drag the 30% swatch onto the gradient slider, about halfway between the two stops. This will automatically create a new stop and add our chosen color. To duplicate an existing stop, hold down OPT/ALT and drag the stop to copy it to a different location on the slider.

14. Finally, click on the gradient swatch in the Gradient palette and drag it into the Swatches palette to save the gradient.

15. Let's see if this global color system will work for us! Select the top of the box and change the fill to the 75% swatch. Select the long side and fill it with 100%. Then select the short side and fill it with the gradient.

Now double-click on the original global color. In this dialog box, check the Preview box and change the percentages to create a different color. All the tint swatches, the gradient, and the objects using our global color will change on the fly. Cancel to leave the color as it was (but at least we've confirmed that it is possible to make a global change!)

16. Save (if you haven't already). Now we'll use Photoshop to create some images to place on our box in Illustrator. To make things easier, we'll create a Photoshop document from our layered Illustrator file. From the File menu, choose Export, name the file big box and choose Photoshop as the format. In the second dialog box leave it as CMYK and set the resolution as screen quality, since we're only making a mock-up. Make sure Write Layers is checked. This will separate the sides of our Illustrator box into three layers in Photoshop.

 Although there are various methods to take graphics from Illustrator and use them in Photoshop, this is the easiest method when the Illustrator document has layers and you want to use those same layers in Photoshop.

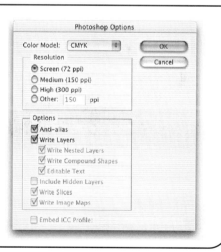

Adding images in Photoshop

Before we go too far in Photoshop, an important reminder: every tool has its own settings and Photoshop remembers the last settings used. So, if you change a setting for Tolerance, Style, Opacity, Feather, etc., remember to check the settings before you use the tool again.

1. Open the file in Photoshop. Make sure that the three layers appear – if they don't, something was amiss with the setting in the Save dialog box. Click on each layer and lock the transparent pixels by clicking on the first lock box, or by pressing the / key. This will ensure that we only change the existing pixels, which in turn will ensure we don't change the size of each side.

> *A lock stays turned on until you turn it off. It is important to note that for some oper-ations, Lock Transparent Pixels is very useful, while for some other functions, this lock will stop the operation from working. For example, if Lock Transparent Pixels is on, some filters such as Gaussian Blur will not work since those filters need to use the transparent areas to create the effect. The bottom line is: you'll have to decide on a case-by-case basis when to lock – and when not to.*

2. Open the file called `waterhole.psd`. Use the **Move** tool (V) to drag and drop the entire image onto our layered image. In the Layers palette, double-click on Layer 1 and rename it course photo. In the Layers palette, position this layer immediately above the layer called top.

3. Since the photo is larger than the top of the box, we need to make an adjustment. There's a couple of options here: we could scale the photo down to fit the box size, or have the box size clip the photo so it is only visible in the size of the box. Let's try the latter. From the Layers menu choose Group with Previous (CMD/CTRL+G) to create a Layer Clipping Group. Use the Move tool (V) to re-position the course photo layer until the flagpole is approximately 3 in from the right side and about 4.8 in down from the top.

> *To measure the exact location of the flagpole, use the **Measure** tool (I or SHIFT+I). Drag from the right edge of the box to the flagpole. Hold down OPT/ALT and drag from the pole to the top of the box. Check the Options Bar for the two measurements (D1, D2). To remove the measurement lines, click Clear in the Options Bar.*

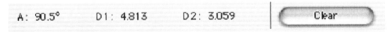

A: 90.5°   D1: 4.813   D2: 3.059   Clear

4. Open the file called oddgolfer.psd. We need to end up with only the man selected. Use whatever selection tools you wish, but it's likely that you will have the best results with the Magic Wand and Lasso tools, cleaning it up with Quick Mask. Use the Move tool to drag this selection onto our layered image. Name this layer "the man".

When it comes to making accurate selections, there are some real advantages to using Quick Mask. Quick Mask mode displays a colored overlay, where the color represents the areas that are not selected – or masked – and the selection does not have any color. Quick Mask can display details that the selection edges (or marching ants) simply cannot display. In this example, the Magic Wand was used to select the sky – it looks like a pretty fair selection.

In Quick Mask however, the colored overlay shows that it's not quite so good after all – there are small areas that were not selected that the marching ants couldn't display.

Along with using Quick Mask to check our selection, we can also fine-tune the selection by painting with black to mask areas that should not be selected, and white to add areas to the selection.

 Pressing Q switches between Regular mode and Quick Mask mode.

5. Position the man on the left-hand side of the image. Re-size the layer using Free Transform (CMD/CTRL+T). To manually scale, hold down SHIFT and use a corner handle to make the layer smaller. Or, in the Options Bar, click the chain symbol to keep the scaling proportional and enter a percentage of 75.

Well done! Let's save the image at this point before moving on. Take a break, stretch your legs, have a coffee...

6. You may see a slight fringe of white pixels from the original background. To remove this (or at least improve on the problem), from the Layer menu choose Matting > Defringe. Enter a value of 1 – 2 pixels and click OK.

This may resolve the problem. If you can still see a slight fringe, or if the edges of the layer look somewhat jagged after using Defringe, try this. Load the layer as a selection. From the Select menu choose Modify > Contract and enter an amount of 1 – 2 pixels. Then from the Select menu choose Inverse. These steps result in only the very outside 1 or 2 pixels of the layer being selected, which lets you apply a filter to only these few pixels. Try applying a Gaussian Blur (Filter > Blur > Gaussian Blur) of 1 pixel – or even less.

Even if you don't see a fringe or noticeable jagged edges, you may want to do this step anyway, since it can help the layer blend in with the image behind it.

7. Add an Outer Glow, choose Screen as your Blend mode, with an Opacity of 90%. In the Elements section, opt for a Softer technique, with a Spread of 4% and a Size of 8 pixels, as shown below in the Layer Style dialog box. For the color, click on the swatch and then move over to the image to pick up a shade of blue from the sky.

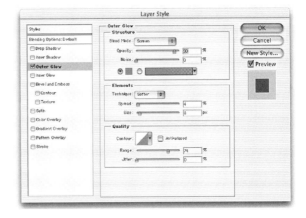

8. Add a new layer above the course photo layer. Use the **Pen** tool (P) to draw a path to represent a ball bouncing into the hole. Starting from the hole location, click and drag with the Pen to create a handle for a curve. Move over to the left and click and drag again to make a small curve. Position your cursor over the second anchor point, hold down OPT/ALT and drag a handle to create a second curve. Repeat this operation to create a third curve.

9. Pick red as the Foreground color and click on the Stroke Path button in the Paths palette. Double-click on the layer name to change the name to "shot 1". In the Paths palette, click in some gray space to deselect the path.

10. Duplicate this layer (CMD/CTRL+J), and then rename it "shot 2". Use the Motion Blur filter (Filter > Blur > Motion Blur) to add a slight blur to this copy – try an angle of 0 and a distance of 15 – 20.

11. Now we'll duplicate a portion of the course photo layer to create the long side of the box. Select the Rectangular Marquee tool (M) and in the Options Bar change the Style to Fixed Size and enter a Width of 10.625 in and a Height of 1.625 in. Make sure the course photo layer is the active layer and click and hold with the Marquee tool. You'll see the selection and can re-position it by dragging. Position the marquee to select only the sky in the photo.

 As a quick way of activating a layer with any tool selected, press and hold CMD+CTRL (Mac) or CTRL+ right-click (Windows) to pop up a list of layers. Choose the appropriate layer and let go of the keys/mouse. This eliminates the need to constantly go back and forth to the Layers palette to select a layer.

12. Duplicate the selected area as a layer (CMD/CTRL+J), and then rename it "sky side", make sure this layer is above the long side layer. Press CMD/CTRL+T to use Free Transform and enter 180 in the rotate box in the Options Bar and press ENTER. Switch to the Move tool (V) (or hold down CMD/CTRL) to position the layer above the long side layer and Group with Previous (CMD/CTRL+G).

13. Open the file called flamingogolf.psd. Select the Marquee tool (M) and change the fixed size to a Width of 2 in and a Height of 1.625 in. Click and hold to make a selection.

You may notice that there is a slight problem with our images. We need our selection to match the side of the box, but we also need to see all of the golfer and the flamingo. A simple solution is to temporarily change the image size so that the same size of selection will select a larger area. Use the Image Size (Image > Image Size) command and change the Width to 2. (Make sure Resample Image is checked).

14. Use the Marquee tool again to select the golfer and the flamingo. Use the Move tool (V) to drag this selection into our main image. Rename the layer "bird man".

15. Rotate the image by pressing CMD/CTRL+T and entering 180 in the rotate box in the Options Bar and hit ENTER.

16. Move the bird man onto the left side of the sky. We want this image to blend in with the sky, so we'll add a layer mask. Click on the **Add Layer Mask** icon at the bottom of the Layers palette. Select the Gradient tool (G) and reset the colors to default (D). Starting at the edge of the photo, drag over to the golfer's hands. (Experiment with different lengths of gradients until you get the effect you want – there's no need to undo, simply re-paint a new gradient over the previous one).

Avoid the temptation to delete parts of a layer – if you do, those pixels are gone and cannot be retrieved once the file if closed. Instead, use Layer Masks to hide parts of a layer by painting with black. Then if you need to show those pixels again later, simply paint with white. Here's the key to using Layer Masks: use Black to hide (mask) areas, white to show areas, gray to partially hide or show, depending on the shade of gray.

17. Open the file called oneball.psd. We're going to select the ball and move it into our main image. Chances are, an automatic selection with the Magic Wand won't work well here, so we'll make a Marquee selection.

18. Select the **Elliptical Marquee** tool (M or SHIFT+M) and change the Style back to Normal. Position your cursor in the approximate center of the ball. Hold down OPT/ALT to drag from the center outwards. If you need to re-position the marquee as you're dragging, keep the mouse button and OPT/ALT held down and press the SPACEBAR, which allows you to move the marquee. Release the SPACEBAR to continue creating your selection. Try to end up with a selection just inside the edge of the ball. (If necessary, go to Select > Transform Selection and use the handles to adjust the selection, then press ENTER).

19. Use the Move tool (V) to drag and drop the selection onto our main image. Rename the layer "huge ball" and position it in the Layers palette above the sky side layer. Move it visually so it hangs over the right end of the long side and Group with Previous (CMD/CTRL+G).

   Now we'll colorize the ball with an Adjustment layer. Again, a potential roadblock: if we add an Adjustment layer above the huge ball layer, it will affect all layers below it. We need to restrict the effects of the Adjustment layer to only the huge ball layer.

20. In the Layers palette, load the huge ball layer as a selection. Click the Adjustment layer icon and choose Hue/Saturation. In the dialog box, check the Colorize button and change the settings to Hue: 235 Saturation: 69 Lightness: 0 and click OK. Notice how the Adjustment layer has a layer mask that is based on our selection.

Normally we could restrict the effects of the Adjustment layer to only the layer immediately below by creating a Layer Clipping Group. In our case this wouldn't work since the layer we're trying to affect is already in a group. If the ball was not in a clipping group: hold down Opt/Alt when you click the Adjustment Layer icon. In the dialog box, check Group with Previous Layer – now the Adjustment layer will only affect the layer immediately below it.

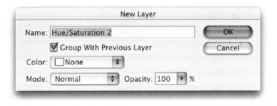

Hang in there – Last few steps...

In the man layer, the number 2 on the flag in his golf bag is a little distracting. Let's cover that up with a gradient.

21. Activate the man layer, and use the **Polygon Lasso** tool (L or SHIFT+L) to select the colored area of the flag. Add a Feather of 1 pixel. Use the Eyedropper tool (I) and click on the light blue in the flag to make it the Foreground color. Hold down OPT/ALT and click on the dark blue at the bottom of the flag to choose it as the Background color. Select the Gradient tool (G) and check the Options Bar – we want to use the first gradient (Foreground to Background). Click and drag a gradient within the selection. Deselect (CMD/CTRL+D).

22. Since we are altering the flag, why not add our client's logo? Choose File > Place, and select `sm_target_logo.ai`. Use the handles to scale the logo down and rotate slightly to fit within the flag. Press ENTER. (The Place command automatically creates a new layer and rasterizes the vector graphic to the resolution of our document).

23. Now we'll use a portion of the course photo layer for the short side of the box. Select the Rectangular Marquee tool (SHIFT+M), change the Style to Fixed Size and enter a Width of 6.625 and a Height of 1.625. (We have to select it lengthwise and then rotate a copy to fit the side). Make sure the course photo layer is the active layer and select a portion of the golf green. Copy (CMD/CTRL+J) the selection to a new layer. Rename the layer "green side", and then use Free Transform to rotate 180 degrees. Move the image on top of the short side layer and in the Layers palette, position the layer above the short side layer.

OK, so we have finished the photographic artwork for the big box. Now we have to take this multi-layered document and create three flattened files, one for each side, to place into Illustrator. Although we could do this in a number of ways, here's a method that's both efficient and safe – so we don't end up flattening and saving the wrong thing. We will repeat this procedure for each side of the box.

Creating flattened artwork from the layered original

1. Show only the layers for the front of the box: top, course photo, the man, shot 1, shot 2, `sm_target_logo.ai`. (A simple way to do this is to OPT/ALT click on the eyeball beside the top layer – to show only that layer. Then drag through the eyeballs of the other layers you want to show).

2. Add a new blank layer at the top of the Layers palette (CMD/CTRL+SHIFT+N). Hold down OPT/ALT and choose Merge Visible (CMD/CTRL+SHIFT+E). This will copy all the visible layers into the blank layer to create a flattened version of the layers.

3. In the Layers palette, CTRL/right-click on this flattened layer and choose Duplicate Layer. In the dialog box change the Destination to New.

4. In the newly created document, go to Image > Trim. In the dialog box choose Transparent Pixels and click OK. Flatten the image and save as `topimage.psd`.

Repeat this operation for each side: Show only the layers you need, create a new layer, OPT/ALT Merge Visible, duplicate layer to new document, trim, flatten, and save. Create two flattened files, called `longside.psd` and `shortside.psd`.

If it helps you to organize the layers for each side, you can create a folder (set) for each side of the box. Link the layers for one side and then from the Layers palette pop-up menu choose New Set from Linked. If you decide later on that you don't want the set, choose Delete Layer Set from the pop-up menu, and select Set Only to keep the layers.

This may seem like a lot of work just to create the artwork for the sides, but this method offers a great deal of flexibility. By keeping many separate layers, we keep our options open for moving or changing images, changing colors, etc.

Quick keyboard commands to create artwork

Compared to all that work, it will be a walk in the park to create the photographic art for the sides and top of the small box! We'll just select two portions of one photo to create the two sides and a third area to create the top. To make life even simpler, we'll use a string of keyboard commands to speed things up.

1. Open the image called `flamingogolf.psd`. Use the Marquee Selection tool (M) and change its options to a Fixed Size of 1.625 in wide by 5 in high. Position the marquee to make a selection with the golfer roughly in the center of the selection.

2. Now, we need to: copy the selected area, create a new document, OK the new document size, paste, and merge down. So, press the following keyboard combination: CMD/CTRL+C, CMD/CTRL+N, RETURN, CMD/CTRL+V, CMD/CTRL+E. Save the document as `oddfront.psd`.

3. Return to the original document. If the Rulers are not showing, press CMD/CTRL+R. From the Vertical ruler, drag a guide that lines up with the right edge of the selection. With the Marquee tool, start to drag the selection, and then hold down SHIFT to constrain the movement. Move the selection to the right until the left edge lines up with the guide. Repeat the above keyboard commands. Save this document as `oddside.psd`.

4. To create the top, change the Marquee tool Fixed Size to 1.625 in by 1.625 in. Position the marquee in the top left-hand corner of the image to select the shaded sky. Repeat the same keyboard commands and save as `oddtop.psd`. We'll use these three files later.

Adding the photographic art to the boxes

Now we'll move back into Illustrator, add the photographic elements to the three sides of the big box, copy a few graphics from the smaller box, and add a few new graphics. Throughout these operations, it is very important to make sure you're on the correct layer before you place, paste, or create anything. (If you don't and items end up on the wrong layer, it can be a bit of a chore to get them where they belong, particularly when you have a graphic made up of several objects).

1. Select the top of the big box. Go to File > Place and choose the file called topimage.psd. Position this graphic on top of the box front so the edges line up.

2. Switch to the artwork for the small box. Select the IN THE HOLE! graphic, warning text, target logo, and PRECISION GOLF BALLS text. Copy, switch back to the big box and paste.

3. Position the PRECISION GOLF BALLS text as shown, remove the carriage return after PRECISION and change the point size to 44.

4. Position the IN THE HOLE! graphic just to the right of the flag pole.

5. Move the warning text down near the bottom as shown. Using the **Rectangle** tool (U), draw a rectangle slightly larger than the text. Fill with white, press CMD/CTRL+[to send the box backwards (not to the back). In the Transparency palette, change the Opacity to 60%. Readjust the box position if necessary.

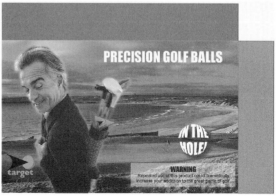

6. Now we'll add a new graphic. Click on the image with the Ellipse tool (U) to create a circle of 1.25 x 1.25 inches. Fill with our custom color and Stroke with Black 5 pt. In the Appearance palette, use the pop-up menu to Add a New Stroke. Change the color to white and the weight to 2 pt. Use the same method to add another new stroke, this time yellow, 2 pt. Then choose Effect > Distort & Transform > Roughen. In the Roughen dialog box change Size to 15, Detail to 13, and Smooth.

In many ways the Appearance palette acts like a History function, as it shows the hierarchy of appearance attributes in the artwork. At any time you can select an object and see a description in this palette making it easy to modify appearance attributes at any time. If you've used Effects (such as Roughen) you can double-click on that part of the palette to re-open the dialog box to check and/or alter the settings. Unlike Photoshop's History palette however, the Appearance palette does not disappear when you close a document.

Just in case we want to apply that same look to another object, let's make that appearance into a Style. Styles can save the designer time and patience by not having to try and get the same effect over several objects. Make sure you can see both the Appearance palette and the Styles palette. In the Appearance palette, click on the swatch at the top of the palette (Path) and drag it into the Styles palette. If you want to name the style, double-click on the swatch in the Styles palette.

7. With the Type tool (T), click on the circle to add some text (just make sure you see the I-beam surrounded by a dotted rectangle. If the I-beam has a dotted oval around it, you will be creating area path text and the look of the circle will disappear). Type the number 15, and choose a font and size that will take up approximately half the circle. Add the text BALLS in the same font but a smaller size. Select the circle and the two pieces of text and use the Align palette to horizontally align by the centers.

8. Select the circle and the two pieces of text and drag them into the Symbols palette. Now we'll be able to easily add the same graphic to other layers – if we tried to OPT/ALT drag to copy the layer, we'd end up with three objects on the wrong layer and would have to drag each one to the correct layer.

Now we'll place the photo we prepared and add the same two graphics to the short side layer.

9. Select the short side object – that will automatically activate the correct layer. From the File menu choose Place and select `shortside.psd`. Position it directly on top of the object. From the Symbols palette drag first the 15 BALLS symbol and then the IN THE HOLE! symbol onto this layer. Select both graphics and in the Transform palette, enter 90 in the Rotate field and press ENTER. Double-click on the Scale tool and enter 75 for Uniform scale. Now select the 15 BALLS symbol and use the Scale tool to scale to 60%. Position the IN THE HOLE! symbol just to the left of the flag pole, and move the 15 BALLS symbol to the left side of the photo.

10. In order to reuse the PRECISION GOLF BALLS text from the front of the box, we'll copy and paste between layers. Once again, this is often easier than dragging a copy and then re-positioning it. Select the PRECISION GOLF BALLS text. Copy. Select any object on the short side layer. Paste. Use the Type tool to add a carriage return between PRECISION and GOLF BALLS. Change the size to 32 pt and position the text roughly between the two graphics.

    To finish off the artwork, we'll add the last photo and paste and edit the text.

11. Select the long side box to activate the long side layer. Select File > Place to add the `longside.psd` image and position it directly on top of the long side object. Since the text is still on the Clipboard we can paste it onto this layer. After pasting, use the Transform palette to rotate the text 180 degrees. Edit the text to NOT YOUR AVERAGE GOLF BALLS. Use the Selection tool with OPT/ALT to drag a copy of the text below the original text. Change the text to from target golf and change to a smaller size and a different font.

If you paste an object and cannot see it because it is below another layer, you can always switch to Outline view (CMD/CTRL+Y). Since the fill of an object is not visible in Outline view, all objects are easy to see and select, regardless of what layer they are on. Then you can move the object to the appropriate location.

12. Save the document, and then save a copy called `big box original.ai`.

Project 2: Creating the illusion of dimension

Although it is not possible to create actual 3D artwork in Illustrator, we can create the illusion of dimension using the Transformation tools. We're going to use the Scale, Shear, and Rotate tools using specific measurements. Then we'll make some minor modifications to help with the illusion. We'll repeat the same basic operations to both the small and large boxes.

There are two real keys to this operation:

1. Make sure all objects on each side are selected.

2. Use a specific reference point for the transformations.

Actually, there's a third key – knowing what numbers to enter for the percentages and angles. Luckily, various people have figured this out and shared their findings with us so we can use the correct values. I'd love to take credit for this but I can't. I first saw these numbers in an Adobe manual way back in the days of Illustrator 88 and had the foresight – more likely good fortune – to write down the numbers and save them away for future use. Let me tell you, these are not numbers the average person would probably figure out on their own!

Transforming the small box

OK, here we go! For each part of the box we're going to follow the same basic procedure: select the shapes, then use the Scale, Shear, and Rotate tools – in that order. The only thing that will change is the values. Each time you use the transformation tools, you will hold down Opt/Alt and click on the point shown here and enter the value indicated for that specific side of the box. (If you didn't Opt/Alt click this specific point, the transformation tools would use the center of the object as the reference point and the process wouldn't work).

Each time you use the Scale tool you will leave the Horizontal value at 100 and change the Vertical scale to the value indicated. Every time you use the Shear tool you'll use Horizontal Shear and enter the angle given.

Note: Don't worry if things don't look right during the steps – it'll look just right once it's finished.

1. Select the top of the box and the graphic.

2. With the **Scale** tool (S) selected, hold down Opt/Alt and click on the indicated point. In the Scale dialog box, click on the Non-Uniform scale button. As mentioned, you'll leave the Horizontal value at 100 and in this case, change the Vertical scale to 70.711. (I told you you'd never come up with values like this!) Click OK.

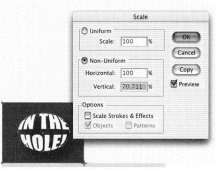

3. Switch to the **Shear** tool (sorry, there's no shortcut for this tool). and click on the indicated point (while pressing OPT/ALT). In the Shear dialog box enter 45 and click OK.

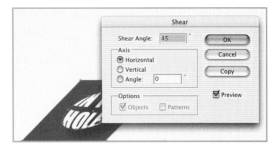

4. Press R to select the **Rotate** tool. With OPT/ALT pressed, click on the indicated point, enter -15 and click OK.

5. Now we'll repeat the same steps for the front of the box: select all the objects for the front of the box. Use the Scale tool with a Vertical scale of 96.592, Shear -15, and Rotate -15. Remember to hold down OPT/ALT and click on the indicated point with each tool.

6. Now for the side of the box, using the same routine with these numbers: Scale Vertical 86.602, Shear 30, and Rotate 30.

7. If you have a stroke on the sides and top of the box, you may want to zoom in very close on the corners where the sides join. Chances are, the corners of the strokes are a little too pointed, causing a poor looking joint. To fix this, select the object and in the Stroke palette, use the pop-up menu to Show Options. Then click on either the **Round Join** or **Bevel Join** buttons (whichever works best).

To help with the illusion of dimension, we'll adjust the colors slightly and add a shadow.

8. Select the rectangle shape (the front of the box) and copy (CMD/CTRL+C) then Paste in Front (CMD/CTRL+F). This creates a copy of the shape directly on top of the original. (If you have used layers, the shape might not be on the very top – if it isn't, press CMD/CTRL+SHIFT+]).

9. Change the fill to white and in the Transparency palette lower the Opacity to 20% to give the effect of lightening the front of the box. Now select the side rectangle and again press CMD/CTRL+C, CMD/CTRL+F to Copy then Paste in Front. This time change the fill to black and in the Transparency palette lower the Opacity to 20%.

10. To create the shadow, use the Pen tool (P) to draw a rough shape as shown, then fill with a black to white gradient and use the Effect menu to Feather the object using a value of 0.25 in.

Send the shadow to the back of the layer.

11. Try this variation to create more of a highlight effect on the front of the box. Select the shape you pasted in front and change the fill to the original color of the box. Using the **Mesh** tool (U), click on the rectangle and add some mesh points as shown.

12. Click on the mesh point and click on white in the Swatches palette. Now click on the white swatch and drag in into the area between some mesh points (called a mesh patch). Now in the Transparency palette, change the mode to Screen and the Opacity to 30.

 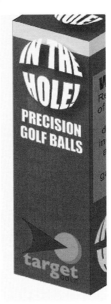

13. Save the transformed box.

Transforming the large box

Many of the steps will be the same as with the previous section, with the only slight change being the fact that we are working on layers. Since we used layers to create the large box, we can take advantage of them to help with the transformation of the objects, and to give us some display options once we're finished.

We'll use the same procedure as before, with the same values. The only difference is in the naming of the sides of the box – with the small box we referred to the top, front, and side whereas this time we'll transform the long side as the top, the top as the front, and the short side as the side. Confused? Don't worry, it will all become clear as we work through it.

1. In the Layers palette, hold down OPT/ALT and click on the eyeball beside the long side layer. This hides the other layers. Press CMD/CTRL+A to Select All (since only this layer is visible, no other objects can be selected – this way you don't have to worry about missing anything).

2. Select the Scale tool (S). Hold down OPT/ALT and click on the bottom right-hand corner of the object. Change the Vertical scale to 70.711. Click OK.

3. Switch to the Shear tool. Hold down OPT/ALT and click on the bottom right-hand corner of the object. Change the Shear to 45. Click OK.

4. Press R for the Rotate tool and, again, click on the bottom right-hand corner of the object while pressing OPT/ALT. Change the angle to –15 and click OK.

5. Hold down OPT/ALT and click on the eyeball beside the top layer in the Layers palette. You may have to repeat this operation to show only the top layer. Press CMD/CTRL+A to Select All.

6. Repeat the same transformation steps – Scale, Shear, and Rotate, but this time you'll use the top right-hand corner of the object as your reference point. Here's the values you'll use: Scale Vertical 96.592, Shear -15, Rotate -15.

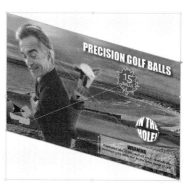

7.   Now we'll finish off the last side of the box. Show only the short side layer. For this layer you'll use the top left-hand corner as the reference point for the transformation tools. Here are the numbers for this side: Scale Vertical 86.602, Shear 30, Rotate 30.

If we show all the layers, here's what we should have so far...

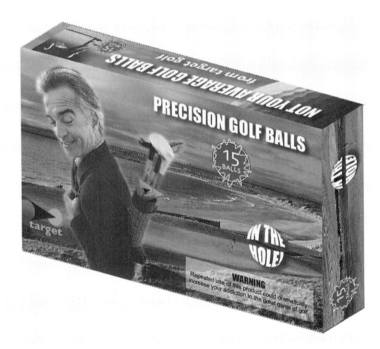

Now we can take advantage of the layers in this document to display the box in different ways. Realistically, we'd need to add a few more graphics to make the box look a little more interesting, but here's the theory anyway...

Click on the triangle beside the top layer to reveal all the sub-layers, in the Layers palette. Click on the eyeball beside the layer called topimage.psd to hide only that layer. Now the green box underneath is visible. Repeat this for each of the other two layers, revealing the sub-layers and hiding the sub-layer with the photographic image. Now we have a more traditional box without the images. By showing and hiding these sub-layers we have two different display options in one document. In fact, we have multiple display options. Since we created a global color we could easily change the color of all sides of the box just by editing the global color.

Let's show all the photographic sub-layers so we can make a couple of minor tweaks.

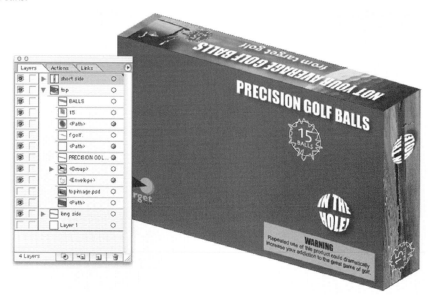

8. In the Layers palette, show all the sub-layers for the long side layer. Click on the circle to the right of the bottom sub-layer called <Path>. This will select the green box on this layer. Copy (CMD/CTRL+C) then Paste in Front (CMD/CTRL+F), and make sure the object is at the top of the layer (CMD/CTRL+SHIFT+]) – you should see a green box covering everything up. Change the fill to black.

9. In the Transparency palette, use the pop-up menu to Show Options, then choose Make Opacity Mask. An Opacity mask functions much like a Layer mask in Photoshop: use black to hide objects, white to show objects and gray for partial transparency. By default the new Transparency mask is black, so the object is hidden. Click on the Opacity mask thumbnail and use the Pen tool (P) to draw over the shape of the box side (don't worry about being too accurate, in fact, you may want to make this masking shape a little larger than you need). Change the fill to the black and white gradient. Select the Gradient tool (G) and, starting on the edge of the large golf ball, drag about an inch past the end of the box. Now click on the left thumbnail (the object rather than the mask) and change the blend mode to Multiply and the Opacity to 50%.

Although Transparency masks can offer many interesting possibilities, they can take some getting used to. In some ways, you're almost drawing blind as you create the masking object. Once you are comfortable with the process, masking does give you a lot of flexibility though. If you want to toggle the mask on and off, hold down SHIFT as you click on the mask in the Transparency palette. If you need to move the object independently from the mask (or vice versa), click off the chain symbol between the object thumbnail and the mask thumbnail.

10. For the short side, we'll just duplicate the box and change the transparency settings. As before, show all the sub-layers for the short side layer and repeat step 8 on these sub-layers. From the Swatches palette, pick the black and white Radial Gradient. Use the Gradient tool (G) to drag from the top left-hand corner down about 75% of the way to the opposite corner. In the Transparency palette, change the blend mode to Multiply and the Opacity to 20%.

11. Save the finished product.

Project 3: Mapping flat artwork to an image in Photoshop

Now that we've mocked-up an imitation 3D version of our two boxes, we'll take it a step further by adding the artwork to a couple of photographs of actual products. Since our client has supplied us with samples of their competitor's packaging, we'll take a few digital photos and add our artwork to them. (Don't worry, you don't have to run out and buy golf balls, we've provided the images for you).

This project will involve moving the Illustrator artwork into a Photoshop document – we'll do this in two different ways – then transforming the artwork to fit the boxes. We'll use Layer functions such as masks and adjustment layers to finalize the work.

Creating the small box

1. Open `tallbox.psd` in Photoshop. We'll be adding layers to this document to map the artwork onto this image.

2. Switch to Illustrator and open the `small box art.ai`. Since this file does not include layers, we'll select the object for each side and copy and paste into Photoshop. Select the two objects that make up the top of the box with the Selection tool (V). Copy (CMD/CTRL+C), switch to Photoshop, and paste (CMD/CTRL+V).

    Depending on how your Illustrator Preferences are set up, one of two things will happen in Photoshop:

    -   A new layer will be created and the artwork will appear with a bounding box, allowing you to resize the artwork before it is rasterized.

    -   A dialog box will open, giving you the option of pasting as pixels, paths, or a shape layer. If you choose pixels, you will again see the bounding box. Choosing paths or shape layer means the artwork would remain vector.

    To determine in Illustrator which of these results you get, go to Edit > Preferences > Files & Clipboard. In order to be given the option when you paste into

Photoshop, AICB must be checked in the Clipboard settings. You can also specify whether you want to preserve the overall appearance of the selected objects or copy the selected objects as a set of paths.

3. Once you have your image in Photoshop, use the handles to make the top of the box slightly larger than you'll need – always better to start large and get smaller. Rename the layer "boxtop".

4. Repeat the same operation for the two sides: select and copy in Illustrator, paste and resize in Photoshop. Rename the layers "boxfront" and "boxside".

5. Hide the boxfront and boxside layers so only the photo and the boxtop layers are visible. Make the boxtop layer the active layer and type V to activate the Move tool. Drag the layer so it is positioned roughly over the top of the box in the photo. Type 7 to change the layer Opacity to 70%. (This will let us see both our layer and the underlying image to help us transform the layer).

> *As long as the Move tool is active, pressing a number from 1 – 9 will change the Opacity between 10 – 90%. Press 0 to return to 100%. If on the other hand, you have a painting tool as your active tool, the same shortcut will change that tool's Opacity rather than the layer Opacity.*

6. In Free Transform mode (Cmd/Ctrl+T), hold down Cmd/Ctrl and click and drag one of the corner handles. Distort the layer so the corner of the artwork matches up with the corner of the top of the box. Since the edges of the box top in the photo are slightly rounded, make the artwork slightly larger than the photo – we'll fix that later. Use this technique to make all four corners of the layer match the photo. Press Enter to finalize the transformation (or press Esc if you want to start over). Type 0 to change the layer Opacity back to 100%.

7. Repeat the same technique with each of the other two layers: show only the layer you're working on and the Background photo. Make sure that the visible layer is active, and press V then 7. Press Cmd/Ctrl+T and hold down Cmd/Ctrl to distort the four corners. Press Enter to finalize the transformation and type 0 to return to 100% Opacity.

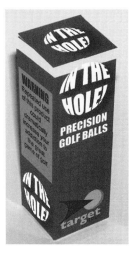

*When using Free Transform: if you are not happy with the last move you make while using this command, you can press C*MD*/C*TRL*+Z to undo that last step. Don't worry if the quality of the artwork looks poor while you are transforming – that's just a preview. Once you finalize the transformation the quality will improve. If you need to magnify your image to help you see what you are doing, viewing shortcuts such as* C*MD*/C*TRL*+ and – will work to zoom in and out, and the* S*PACEBAR* will let you scroll your view.*

8. We need to make the top of the box match up a little better with the real box top, since it has a slight curve to it and has a cut out for the flap. Hide the boxtop layer and use the Magnetic Lasso tool (L or SHIFT+L) to select around the edges of the top of the box. If necessary, switch to the Lasso tool (SHIFT+L) to add to (SHIFT) or subtract from (OPT/ALT) the selection. (Once again, you can use any selection method you like, just make sure you have an accurate selection that follows the curve on the right, the cut out area at the back, and the slight curve on the left).

9. Show the boxtop layer and click on the Add Layer Mask icon. Since there was a selection when we added the Layer Mask, it automatically masked that selected area. If necessary, select the **Brush** tool (B) and use black to hide areas or white to show areas that should not be hidden.

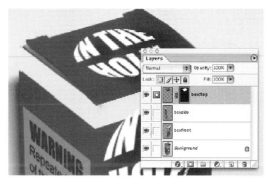

10. Check the front and side of the box to make sure the sides match up. If necessary, you can use Free Transform again to make minor changes, or add a Layer Mask to hide parts of the sides.

11. Let's tweak the lighting a little bit to help with the overall effect. In the Layers palette, load the boxfront layer as a selection. From the bottom of the palette, add a Curves Adjustment layer. (Since we have a selection, the Adjustment layer will only affect the selected area – in this case the whole layer). In the Curves dialog box, click on the center of the line. Drag that point straight up until the Output number reads around 144 and click OK. This will lighten the colors slightly.

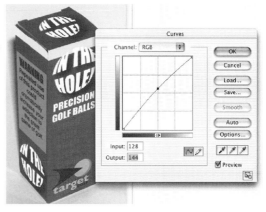

12. Now we'll alter the effects of the Adjustment layer by painting a gradient in the mask. Select the Gradient tool (G) and set your colors to default (D). In the Options Bar, open the Gradient Picker and choose the second gradient – Foreground to Transparent. Also change the blending mode to Multiply so the gradient will be added to, rather than painting over the existing mask. Start at the bottom of the front of the box and drag about halfway up. This will create a gradient that will mask the effects of the Curves Adjustment Layer at the bottom, gradually revealing the effects. (It will be subtle, but you should be able to see the change. If it helps, SHIFT click on the mask thumbnail to hide and show the effects of the mask).

13. We'll also add an Adjustment layer to the boxside layer. Load the layer as a selection. Add a Curves Adjustment layer and click to add a center point, but this time we'll pull the point down to around 100, to darken the colors.

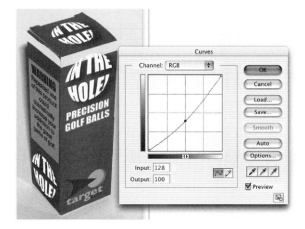

There is only one last thing left to do to finalize the effect. We'll try to simulate a very slight reflection from the flash of the camera. To do this we'll load a selection based on both the front and the side of the box.

14. CMD/CTRL and click in the Layers palette on the boxfront layer. Now CMD/CTRL+SHIFT and click on the boxside layer. You should end up with a selection that combines both sides of the box.

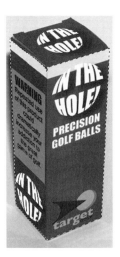

15. Add a new layer (CMD/CTRL+SHIFT+N) and call it "glare". Make sure it is at the top of the Layers palette. Press G to get the Gradient tool and then D, X to make white your Foreground color. The Gradient tool should still be set to Foreground to Transparent, but we need to change the Style to Radial and the blending mode to Normal. Start at the joint of the two sides and pull straight down to approximately the height of the warning label. To reduce the intensity of this glare effect, change the blending mode of the glare layer to Overlay and the Opacity to 70%.

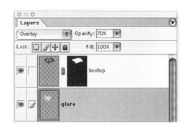

Here's an optional step you can try if you like. Add a new layer at the top of the Layers palette and merge the visible layers into the blank layer (CMD/CTRL+OPT/ALT+SHIFT+E). From the Filter menu choose Render > Lighting Effects and play with the settings to create a more dramatic effect. Here's the settings I used – and after using the filter I used the Fade Filter command to lower the effects to 70%:

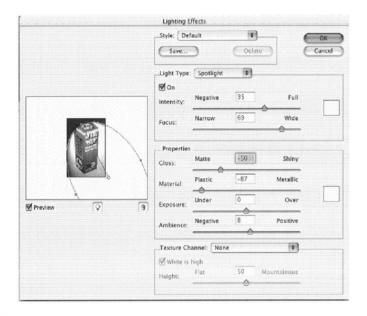
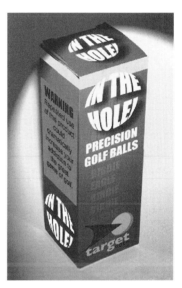

16. Save your work before proceeding.

Creating the large box

Now we'll use the same techniques to apply our Illustrator artwork to the larger box in Photoshop. As we saw earlier, if an Illustrator document includes layers, we can export these layers as a Photoshop layered document. Unfortunately, there are some exceptions to this rule. If the Illustrator artwork contains transparency, blending modes other than Normal, or some effects, you cannot export the separate layers. Instead, one flattened image will be created. In the case of our large box Illustrator artwork, there are many of these things happening. So here are our choices:

- Manually copy and paste the layers between Illustrator and Photoshop as we did with the small box.

- Try to isolate and change the problem objects until we're able to export layers.

- Flatten Transparency in Illustrator then re-create the layers and export layers.

- Export the image as one layer then drag and drop between Photoshop documents.

Since we've already been through the process of manually copying and pasting layers between Illustrator and Photoshop, we'll skip that one. The second choice isn't really much of a choice as we'd have to sacrifice some of the effects we created. Flatten Transparency is an ideal solution when you are printing an Illustrator file and the transparency, blending modes, or effects are causing problems. In our case it would help to preserve the look of the artwork and would ultimately give us our separate layers, so that's a possible solution. There is one drawback to using Flatten Transparency: you lose the separate editable objects unless you keep a copy of the original vector art before you use Flatten Transparency. To avoid that problem, we'll simply export a one layer Photoshop document and then drag and drop in Photoshop.

1. In Illustrator, open the file you saved previously called `big box original.ai`.

2. Go to File > Export and choose Photoshop as the format. Call it `big box layers.psd`. In the second dialog box, you'll see that Write Layers is checked, but grayed out. That indicates that something is stopping the separate layers from being written.

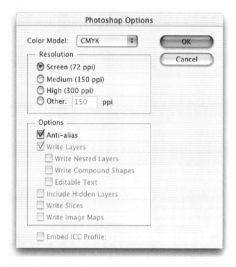

3. In Photoshop, open the file called `boxphoto.psd` and the file you just saved. Make sure you can see at least a portion of both documents so you'll be able to drag and drop between them.

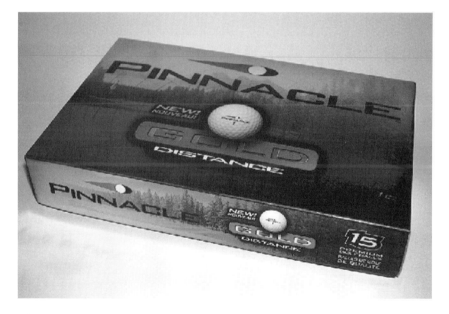

4. Select the long side of the box artwork in the `big box layers` image with the Marquee tool (M). In the Options Bar, enter a Fixed Size of 10.625 x 1.625. Click and hold with the Marquee in the top left-hand corner of the image to select the long side of the box. With the Move tool (V), drag and drop into the `boxphoto` image. Name this layer "SIDE".

5. Return to the `big box layers` document and change the Marquee Fixed Size to 10.625 x 6.625. Position the cursor at the top left-hand corner of the box front and click. Drag and drop this into the `boxphoto` image. Name this layer "FRONT".

6. Activate the SIDE layer and hide the FRONT layer. Go to Edit > Transform > Rotate 180. Press V for the Move tool and 7 to lower the Opacity to 70%. Open Free Transform (CMD/CTRL+T) and CMD/CTRL+click on a corner handle to resize the layer to fit the long side of the box. As before, make the layer slightly larger than you need. Press ENTER when you're finished. Press 0 to put the Opacity back to 100%.

7. Repeat this procedure for the top layer.

8. Now let's fix up the areas where the layers are a little larger than they should be. Activate the side layer, and then hide this layer, and also the front layer. Use the Polygon Lasso (or the regular Lasso with OPT/ALT held down) to select along the edges of the long side of the photo. Your goal is to follow the edges of the photo as closely as possible.

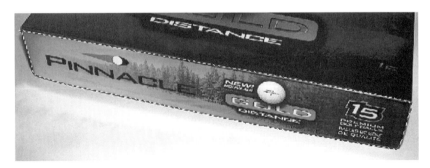

9. Without deselecting, show the layer and click on the Add Layer Mask icon. If necessary, zoom in and use a small hard paintbrush to adjust the edges – use black to hide and white to reveal.

10. Repeat these steps to fix up the front layer.

There may be a slight gap between the top and the side of the box. To fix this we'll add a new layer and paint in some blue.

11. Create a layer (CMD/CTRL+SHIFT+N) – call it "paint". On that layer, use the Lasso tool (L) to make a selection slightly larger that the gap between the layers. With the Eyedropper tool (I) pick a shade of blue from the top area of the side layer and fill the selection (OPT/ALT+DEL/BACKSPACE). Deselect (CMD/CTRL+D). Make sure this layer sits just above the Background layer.

Take a look at the original photo and you'll see a very slight reflection of the long side of the box – it's subtle, but it's there. Let's make a similar reflection of our box.

12. Duplicate (CMD/CTRL+J) the SIDE layer. On the copied layer, CTRL/right-click on the Layer Mask and from the menu, choose Apply Layer Mask. From the Edit menu choose Transform > Flip Vertical. Move the copied layer below the SIDE layer. Open Free Transform (CMD/CTRL+T) and move your cursor just outside the handles until you see a rotate symbol. Rotate the layer so if roughly follows the angle of the bottom of the box. Press ENTER. Lower the Opacity of the layer to 30%.

13. Now we'll apply a Gaussian Blur filter (Filter > Blur > Gaussian Blur) with a setting of around 6 pixels. Press CMD/CTRL+F to reapply the filter until you like the look – we're aiming to make it pretty blurry without completely losing all detail. Finally, add a Layer mask and use the Gradient tool (G) to drag a black and white gradient, starting at the right side of the layer and dragging across just past the opposite end of the layer.

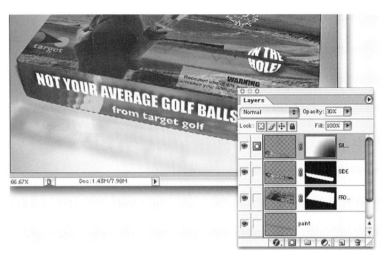

14. Finally, we'll add a little contrast to the top of the box. Use the Lasso tool (L) to make a very vague selection of the right-hand side of the box – about the last third of the box.

15. CTRL/right-click to bring up the context sensitive menu and choose Feather. Enter a very high amount like 45 pixels to help this effect blend in. Then from the Layers palette add a Levels Adjustment layer. In the Levels dialog box, move the middle gray triangle to the right until the middle number changes from 1.00 to around 0.50. Click OK. The selected area should be considerably darker than the rest of the image.

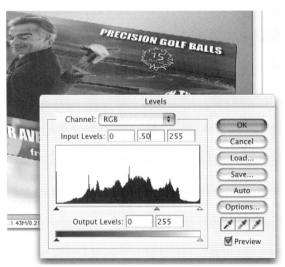

16. Now we'll experiment with different blending modes to see the effect. Rather than worry too much about what each mode does, we'll simply let our eyes decide by scrolling through the modes using the keyboard. First, activate the Move tool (V), then press SHIFT +. Each time you press this shortcut you will jump down to the next blending mode. To move back up the list, press SHIFT -. Experiment until you find a mode that will tone down the effect just a bit. (Chances are, it will be a mode such as Overlay or Soft Light).

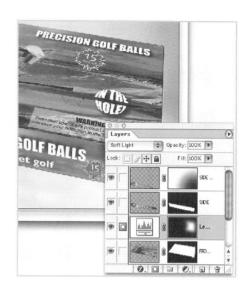

There you have it – well done! Now, don't forget to save your file.

Let's compare the results of our Illustrator and Photoshop boxes. Although the Photoshop version looks more photo-realistic, we end up with a raster image with all its inherent restrictions – resolution, file size, and limited editing. In contrast, the Illustrator version doesn't have the same photographic look, but does offer the advantages of vector: notably scalability and flexibility. Your choice will depend on what's most important to you, photo-realism or flexibility.

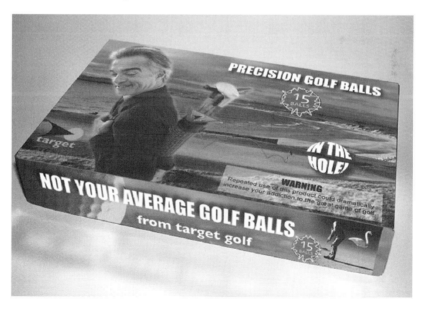

One step beyond ...

Your mission, should you choose to accept it, is to apply the same theory to map the artwork to another photo, but a more challenging image. This time you'll need to transform the artwork to match the top and side, but then make sure you haven't covered up the other elements of the photo, namely the golf glove, tees, and the smaller box.

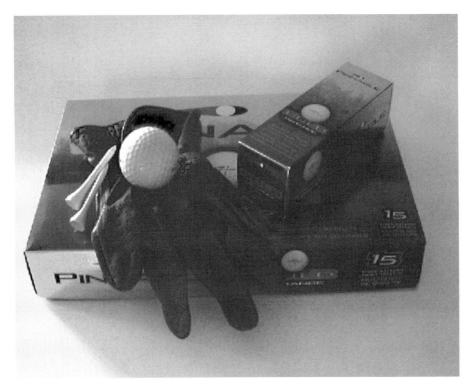

We won't give you the step-by-step instructions this time, but here's a summary to help you get going:

- Drag and drop the artwork onto the image.

- Use Free Transform to adjust the layers to fit the box, temporarily covering up the other parts of the image.

- Open the files we created previously of the flamingo golfer (oddfront, oddside, oddtop) and add them to the document.

- Use the Free Transform technique to map those images to the smaller box.

- Add a Layer Mask to each layer to hide the layers so that other parts show again.

- Lighten or darken areas.

- Add some highlights, shadows, or reflections where necessary.

Your Layers palette should look something like this, and your final image hopefully resembles this one:

Project 4: Creating two-color artwork

In this project we'll create some simple artwork to address the issues involved with two-color printing. Previously we were assuming there were no real limits to our client's budget, so we didn't worry about color and did everything in CMYK. Now we're going to change that assumption and prepare artwork that uses only black and a spot color. As soon as spot color enters into the equation, the rules change. Now we have to plan a little more carefully and make a few more decisions up front.

Particularly in Photoshop, creating spot color documents is much more challenging than working in CMYK as we have to work with Spot Color Channels. Layers play less of a role and we often end up with documents that don't offer many opportunities to change our mind. As such, we have to move with caution. (In Illustrator, spot color is not that much more difficult than working in process color, but still needs planning).

As much as the Pantone Matching System is a universal printing ink system, it is not unusual for different software programs to use slightly different naming systems. This simply means we need to be aware of this and make sure the name of our Pantone color is exactly the same in both Photoshop and Illustrator. One approach that works well is to start in Photoshop and then place the resulting file into Illustrator. This way, the spot color in the Photoshop document is automatically added to the Illustrator file, eliminating any naming issues.

Rather than creating the same artwork we did before, we'll just use a couple of elements to see the implications of spot color work in Photoshop. We'll place the finished file into Illustrator and work with the spot color to add two or three more objects.

Before we start, one final note: in every print job it is important to consult with your service bureau and/or print shop before you start. With spot color it is particularly important, since there are some decisions you'll need to make that would be very difficult to change later. You need to find out the answer to some key questions before you start:

- Is it necessary to trap the file? If so, who will do that job?

- What are the color settings you should be using in Photoshop?

- What are the options you should use when saving the Photoshop file in DCS format?

Any and all advice you can get before you start can only help! With that in mind, here we go.

Creating two color documents in Photoshop

1.   Open the file called `waterhole.psd`.

2.   Select the Marquee tool (M) and change the Options to Fixed Size 10.625 x 6.625. Click and hold to select the portion of the photo you want to use.

3. Go to Image > Crop. Save as `grayimage.psd`.

We need to convert the image to Grayscale. Rather than simply changing the mode to Grayscale, we'll use a method that typically creates a better grayscale image (better is a relative term, but normally this method creates an image with better contrast).

4. First, from the Image menu, change the mode to Lab Color. In the Channels palette, click on the Lightness channel. Now change the mode to Grayscale and save.

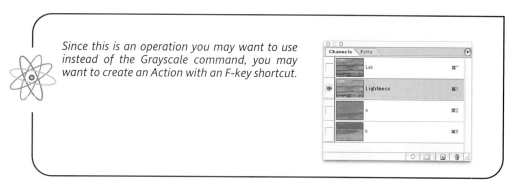

Since this is an operation you may want to use instead of the Grayscale command, you may want to create an Action with an F-key shortcut.

5. Use the Lasso tool (L) to make a selection of the green of the golf course (don't worry about being incredibly accurate). CTRL/right-click, and from the Context Sensitive menu choose Feather and enter a value of 2.

6. Go to Select > Save Selection. Click OK in the resulting dialog box. This will create an Alpha Channel we can use to reselect the same area.

Now we'll add our Spot Color channel – first the wrong way, and then the better way.

7. With the selection still active, use the Channels palette pop-up menu to choose New Spot Channel. In the dialog box click on the color swatch and in the Color Picker, click Custom. Type 348 (there's no box to type this in, just type blindly and click OK.

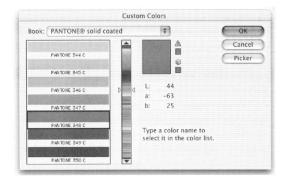

Notice how a new channel is created, with an area of black where the selection was:

This creates a solid patch of our Pantone color, but just as a solid area, without any shades or contrast.

That's not what we really want, so we'll have to go back a few steps and use a slightly different approach.

8. Use the History palette to move backwards to when you saved the selection to create the Alpha channel.

9. With the selection still active, copy it (CMD/CTRL+C). (If the selection isn't active for some reason, CMD/CTRL click on the Alpha channel to load the selection) and deselect (CMD/CTRL+D).

10. Now we'll add the spot channel again, but this time with nothing selected. Use the Channels palette pop-up menu to choose New Spot Channel. In the dialog box click on the color swatch and in the Color Picker, click Custom. In that dialog box type 348 and click OK. Since we didn't have a selection, a blank channel is created.

11. Load the Alpha channel (go to Select > Load Selection, or CMD/CTRL click on the Alpha channel in the Channels palette). Now paste (CMD/CTRL+V) the selection you made previously to the Clipboard. You should see a mostly gray image with some green in the area that we pasted.

Working with Spot Color channels is essentially the same as creating color separations: everything you want to print in black is on one channel, while everything on the spot channel will ultimately be printed in our spot color. So our job, in effect, is to manually separate the image into the two colors by pasting elements on to the appropriate channel. If we want less ink, we lighten areas – darken to make the ink darker. With both the gray and the spot channel showing we see an approximation of the printed result. Here's the key: black represents 100% of an ink, white represents no ink, and shades of gray mean some percentage of ink.

12. Hide the Gray channel and look at only the Spot (green) channel – you'll see only the pasted information.

13. Make sure both channels are visible again and click on the Gray channel to make it the active information. In this case we want a little less black ink so we'll lighten the Gray channel. With the selection still active, open the Levels command (CMD/CTRL+L). Move the black output triangle to the right to lighten the black pixels, in effect removing some of the black ink. We do need some black information to help define the shades in the image, so we can't go too far.

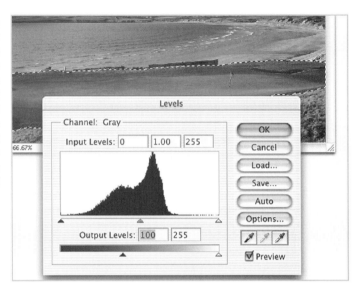

Now activate the spot channel and use the Levels command again, this time moving the white output triangle to the left to darken the green pixels. Deselect (CMD/CTRL+D).

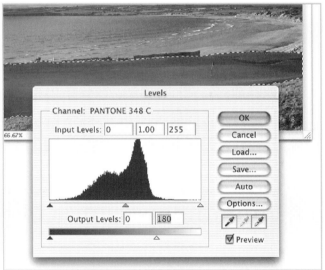

Wherever we have both black and the spot color in the same area, we are creating the equivalent of a duotone. In order to create areas that are only black or only color, we need to actually remove those areas on the opposite channel.

14. Make sure the Gray channel is the active channel. Press D and then X to make white your Foreground color and then select the Type tool (T). Type "PRECISION GOLF BALLS" using Impact 65. From the Layers palette, add a Drop Shadow.

> *Adding text to spot color images is tricky. To get the best color results, we often have to make selections from our type layer, which means we can't change our mind. So, be sure you have the right font, size, and spelling, because in the next steps you'll be unable to change it.*

15. CTRL/right-click on the effects symbol beside the Type layer and from the context sensitive menu choose Create Layer. This will put the Drop Shadow on its own layer (click OK to any warning dialog box).

16. In the Layers palette, CMD/CTRL-click on the Type layer to load it as a selection. Make the drop shadow layer active, and then press DELETE. If you deselect and hide the type layer, you should see only the shadow and a see-through area where the type should be. (You'll see why in a moment).

Load the Type layer as a selection and make sure both the type layer and the drop shadow layer are hidden. Click on the Background layer to make it active. This is a crucial step you may have to repeat: CMD/CTRL-click on a layer to make it into a selection, then hiding the layer and activating the Background layer.

17. We want the writing to print only in green, without any black ink. Here's how we do that: activate the spot channel; and fill the selection with black (remember, this represents 100% ink).

PRECISION GOLF BALLS

Now activate the gray channel and fill with white – to remove all black ink from that area.

18. Now we'll add the drop shadow to the text. CMD/CTRL click on the drop shadow layer to load it as a selection – but make sure it is hidden. Also make sure that the Background layer is the active one. In the Channels palette, ensure that the Gray channel is active and fill with Black. You should now see 100% green text without any black in it, with a shadow.

If you view only the Gray channel, you should see what looks like white text with a drop shadow and a slightly lightened version of the golf green.

Viewing the spot channel should show only the black text and the pasted golf green (looking somewhat darker than the version on the Gray channel).

Before saving this for separations, we need to do a couple of things. First, we'll save a layered version in case we need to make some changes. Of course we can never make complete changes since we filled selections and therefore our text isn't really editable. Second, we need to delete the Alpha channel we created previously.

In order to save this as a placeable file that contains the color separation information, we are going to use Photoshop DCS format (this stands for Desktop Color Separation, a special version of EPS that pre-separates the file).

19.   Go to File > Save As, name the file `twocolors.eps`, and choose Photoshop DCS 2.0 as the format. In the second dialog box we need to make some choices, which usually requires the advice of our service bureau or print shop. In our case we'll change the DCS setting to Single file with Color Composite. This means we'll have a version we can place into Illustrator and we'll be able to see a low res preview (If we chose a setting with no composite, we would not be able to preview the image in Illustrator).

Again, it is important to emphasize the importance of discussing the DCS settings with your service bureau and or print shop – they will know the settings that work best with their equipment.

Creating two color documents in Illustrator

Now we'll use the Photoshop artwork in an Illustrator document and add a couple of objects. We're not going to worry about creating finished artwork, we simply want to look at some of the key issues when working in Spot Color in Illustrator. As challenging as it can be to create Spot Color files in Photoshop, in Illustrator it should be relatively straightforward. The only thing we have to be careful about is using strictly our Spot Color – it is very easy to choose an RGB or CMYK color, or to unwittingly create a process color by adding transparency, blends, or effects to a spot color object.

Let's go ahead and place in our spot image and create some more elements.

1.   In Illustrator, create a new document – we'll use CMYK mode even though ultimately we're only using a spot color. Change the page setup to a wide (landscape) page.

2.   Before adding any artwork, we'll clear out our Swatches palette to make sure we don't use any process colors by mistake. From the Swatches palette pop-up menu, choose Select All Unused. Hold down Opt/Alt (to avoid a warning dialog box) and click on the Trash can in the Swatches palette. Don't be surprised if some swatches remain in the palette. You will always see None, Registration, White, and Black. Sometimes you may have other colors remaining after deleting the unused colors – go ahead and manually delete those too. (Remember, each new document refers to the Illustrator Startup File to determine the contents of the Swatches palette. So, when we delete color swatches, we're deleting them from this document only.)

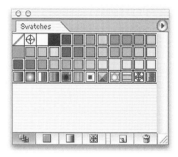

Rather than adding the Pantone color to our Swatches palette, we'll simply place our Photoshop DCS file, as this file contains our color and it will automatically be added to the palette.

3. From the File menu, choose Place and indicate the file we previously saved, `twocolors.eps`. A dialog box appears, warning us about linked EPS files – this is a generic warning that pops up every time we place an EPS file. It is worth noting that there can indeed be issues with linked EPS files and transparency – we will not be using transparency since it creates problems of a different kind for spot colors. After placing the file, the Pantone color should automatically appear in the Swatches palette.

The display of the Photoshop spot color file is only a low quality (72 ppi) preview. Don't use this to make decisions about quality or color, the preview should only be used for layout issues.

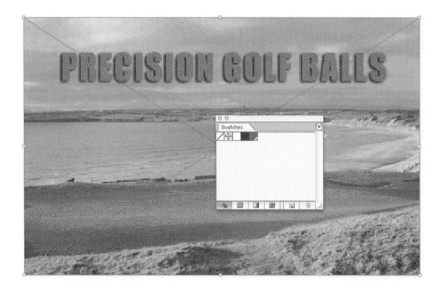

Some examples of the kinds of problems we could run into in Illustrator if we weren't careful are: If you created an object filled with 100% of your Pantone color, positioned over a black filled object, and changed the Transparency of the top object to 40%, we'd need to flatten the Transparency, to avoid possible printing problems. Well, in doing so, we would actually create a problem, since one of the steps the Flatten Transparency command takes is to convert all spot colors to process to simulate the transparency. Similarly, if you were to Blend between a black filled object and an object filled with the Pantone color, Illustrator would create intermediate shapes filled with process colors. What we need to do is to avoid the issue by careful planning, and by simulation – if you want to make an object look transparent, then fake the transparency using a Pathfinder command such as Divide, filling the resulting objects with percentages of Pantone. Avoid blending between objects unless they're both filled with percentages of the same Pantone color.

4. Using the Type tool (T), add some more type to the file, filling with the Pantone color. Note how the color may look slightly different on screen – that's OK since the important thing is that the objects are being described using the exact same Pantone number (and name).

5. Now let's create a gradient using our spot color. In the Gradient palette, click on the gradient slider to edit the existing gradient. From the Swatches palette, drag the Pantone color swatch on top of the first color stop, replacing white. Repeat this operation, replacing the black stop, giving you a gradient from 100% Pantone to 100% Pantone – not much of a gradient! Click on the right hand stop and in the Color palette, lower the tint of the spot color to 0%. This will create the equivalent of a gradient that starts with 100% Pantone and changes to white, but by using 0% of the Pantone color, we'll get a better result when we print. Finally, drag the swatch from the Gradient palette into the Swatches palette.

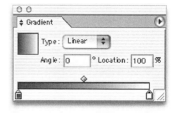

6.   Draw an object and fill with the gradient we just created.

7.   Let's assume that we're done and that this artwork is ready to send off to print. When we save the finished file, we need to make sure that we check the box Include Linked Files in the save options.

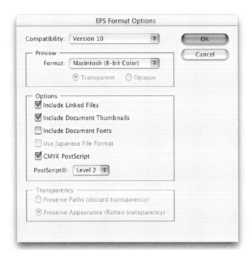

Remember, our goal here was to discuss the implications of working with spot colors in Illustrator, rather than recreating complete artwork. But hey, if you want to create all three sides of the box in Photoshop and Illustrator, go for it! Just remember that it can require a significantly higher amount of planning to end up with the results you want.

Conclusion

Over these last four projects we've looked at techniques for producing packaging artwork, using Photoshop and Illustrator in tandem. Our aim all the way through has been to work at maximum efficiency, so let's recap some of the key factors that have emerged in these projects.

We could sum these factors up with two words – flexibility and accuracy. It's best to use techniques that allow you to make late amendments - even if they take longer initially to create. When using Illustrator take full advantage of the Appearance palette, which enables you to add to existing objects and edit changes, and use Effects rather than Filters wherever possible, as Effects are more versatile. Similarly, in Photoshop its best to use Adjustment layers and Layer masks to achieve effects, as once again these options allow for ongoing changes.

Illustrator thrives on accuracy, its much better to use methods that are numerically driven rather than manual movements, to achieve the most precise end result. Your whole workflow can be greatly accelerated by accuracy and good planning: We all know the importance of naming layers in Photoshop, but how often does this simple step get skipped, leading to a loss of time, energy and temper?

The final point to remember is those handy shortcuts, such as Illustrator's Global Color option to easily change colors, or using the Outline view to remove all fills and strokes and see only the wire frames of the artwork. Keyboard shortcuts are vital too, you probably know a fair few of these already, and maybe you've picked up some new ones over the course of these projects, keep using these and keep aiming for flexibility and accuracy to get the most out of Photoshop and Illustrator working in perfect harmony

Appendix A
Managing files with WebDAV

Where teams of people work on joint projects, and information and files are shared, a system of workgroup management is not only desirable but also often necessary. Through workgroup management associates can pass files to each other but only one person can edit a file at one time.

Photoshop and ImageReady support **WebDAV – Web Distributed Authoring and Versioning**. This is a server technology that can be used to connect to a WebDAV server and from there manage files within the workgroup and prevent unintentional overwriting of files. Workgroup management using a WebDAV server is conducted via the Web. All project associates are allowed to download any files being managed by the WebDAV server, but only one person **can check out** the file. Checking out a file means the file can be edited by the person who checked it out. Until the file has been **checked in** again, other associates can download but not edit the file. This system ensures that the file is always accessible without the risk of it being inadvertently overwritten.

You need to be able to connect to a WebDAV server to take advantage of this workgroup management in Photoshop. An organization's IT department will usually look after setting up the server which goes beyond the scope of this book. We are going to look at the essentials of how to manage, locate, check in and check out files when working with a WebDAV server.

To begin with, go to Edit > Preferences > File Handling to set up the workgroup management preferences. We are going to concentrate on the bottom half of the dialog box, as it is the relevant section.

To display the Workgroup pop up menu, check the Enable Workgroup Functionality check box.

The following choices are available from the **Check Out from Server** drop down box:

- **Never:** This opens the local copy of the file without checking it out and without displaying a dialog box.

- **Always:** Automatically checks out the file when you open it.

- **Ask:** Opens a dialog box when you open a file that has not been checked out.

From the Update from Server drop down box select one of the following:

- **Never:** Opens the local copy of the file without displaying a dialog box and without downloading the latest version of the file from the server.

- **Always:** Downloads the latest version of the file from the server without offering further options.

- **Ask:** Opens a dialog box asking if you want to download the latest version.

Working with WebDAV

Different methods will apply to logging on to WebDAV servers depending on the server. Check with your IT administrator for precise authentication procedures. In some cases a user name and password will need to be entered for every transaction. Alternatively, authentication may be required only once per session. In either case, type your user name and password into the authentication dialog box when it is displayed.

To log off, go to File > Workgroup > Logoff All Servers.

To view a managed file, you can open a copy of the file from the WebDAV server. This action creates a copy of the file on your hard drive, which becomes known as a local copy. If the local copy on your hard drive is a checked out file, it can be reverted to the version of the file on the server. If it is a non-checked out file, you can update it with changes from the file on the server. Updating (File > Workgroup > Update) or reverting to the file on the server (File > Workgroup > Revert) discards all changes made to the file.

Checking out a file is preferred, as it will stop other associates editing the file on the WebDAV server. If the file is already open, go to File > Workgroup > Check Out. If the file has not yet been opened go to >File > Workgroup > Open. Then, navigate to the desired file and click Check Out. Before checking out a file, you can verify if a local file is available to be checked out through the Verify State command (File > Workgroup > Verify State). You can only verify open local files.

Once work on a file is completed, you can check in the file to update the changes to the server and so permit the managed file to be checked out by other associates. You can either check in the file with or without updating the server (File > Workgroup > Check In or File > Workgroup > Cancel Check Out). Changes to the managed file can be saved to the server (File > Workgroup > Save) while you are still working on a checked out file. This allows other associates to view your work without releasing your lock on the file.

Finally, you can also add files to the server (File > Workgroup > Save As) but when you add a file to a WebDAV server you automatically create a managed file.

Appendix B
What is XML?

What has XML got to do with Illustrator or Photoshop? Well, for a start Illustrator's most modern of file formats – SVG – is entirely constructed from XML. Another important application of XML is in the dynamic modification of artwork. Adobe AlterCast and GoLive are both capable of making amendments to an already prepared Photoshop PSD, or an Illustrator SVG file using XML.

As you progress further into the world of advanced Illustrator and Photoshop usage, you will find dynamic graphic design becoming more and more of a factor. You may find that in your working life, you spend more time creating templates rather than final artwork, or even simply scripting a series of instructions (such as AlterCast XML Commands) to allow your images to manifest themselves on demand. At the moment this may sound like an Orwellian vision of the future, but it will undoubtedly improve your workflow efficiency.

The aim of this appendix is to give you an overview of XML, to introduce its basic concepts, structure, and elements, so that by the end of this section you'll be able to open up an Illustrator SVG file and be able to understand much of what's going on there. Don't worry if you're new to all programming languages – XML is reassuringly simple.

From HTML to XML

You are probably already familiar with the language commonly used to create web pages – **HTML**, and you are most likely aware that this is not a programming language in the normal sense, but a markup language: HTML stands for **Hyper Text Mark-up Language**, which basically refers to the way in which this language specifies how information should be presented by web browsers. In this case, hypertext might be defined as simply text that can possess active links to other documents.

If you find the concept of a markup language confusing then think of it in terms of traditional print media design. In the days before the advent of desktop publishing, designers would mark up their original copy with style information, to be inputted by the typesetter.

HTML was born out of the need to present online documents with a degree of marked up presentation, just like traditional design work. HTML is fine for the purpose that it was designed for; an approachable means of marking up a document, without having to learn any particularly complex language, but it's quite limited in it's scope and range of achievable ability. As a result many people have tried pushing HTML beyond its original role. In the mid 1990s, we started to see web browser manufacturers adding their own proprietary extensions to HTML, additional bolt-on augmentations to the language had extended the original capabilities to include much that we now see on the web of today.

Eventually it became apparent that the only solution would be to leave HTML and develop a language that can be expanded in ways that was making HTML creak under the strain. In fact, a language purely designed to be extended, and one that was pretty much nothing at all unless you actually did extend it. This language was **XML – Extensible Markup Language**

Beyond hypertext

The World Wide Web consortium (W3C) developed the specification for XML, and within a short space of time, XML was adopted as a beneficial technology by many diverse organizations.

Like HTML, XML is simply that – a markup language, but it differs in that it is a **meta** language, which may be used to create further markup languages. In other words, XML alone is not generally useful as an end in itself. What we do with XML is to define further languages with it, suitable to a specific task.

HTML contains elements; the tags surrounded by angled brackets, which all have a defined purpose. The purpose is written in the HTML specification, and defined in what's called the **DTD – Document Type Definition**. Each browser has access to the HTML DTD, enabling it to interpret HTML correctly in order to display it appropriately as words and picture.

XML also consists of elements, which are also surrounded by angled brackets, but the difference is that the purpose of these elements is specific to each individual application, defined by the application's designer. The second main difference between XML and HTML is that whereas HTML concerns itself only with the presentation of information, XML separates presentation from content.

Some rules of XML

Let's look at some examples of XML now:

```
<text>Some amusing errors by history students:
The Pope was inflammable.
Suffragettes were the things the Germans shot underwater to kill the
British in the First World War.
Alexander the Great entered Troy disguised as a wooden horse.
Mary, Queen of Scots, was playing golf with her husband when news was
brought to her of the birth of her son and heir.</text>
```

Notice a few things. The element `text` opens, and closes with a matching closing tag (the closing tag is the same name as the opening tag, but with a slash before the name). Also, the `text` element clearly 'contains' some text.

Now, let's turn up the complication knob. Firstly, although we have included line-ends in our text, simply by pressing the return key, XML sees this as simply 'white space' – the equivalent of a normal space or several spaces. Tabs, too, are seen as white space. All white space is generally ignored under normal circumstances, and collapsed into the equivalent of one space. This is also how HTML works, as you probably know.

So, we need to introduce some delineation in our text. Seeing as we are dealing with a specific subject matter (amusing exam paper mistakes by students), let's form some kind of logic pertaining to the topic. Overall, the biggest level, at least at this stage, is our topic itself, which we might call 'exam-bloopers' for want of a better term. If we're going to use this as our XML element name, we can't use any spaces – hence the dash. The next level down in our logic, we have a sort of introduction line (or perhaps paragraph), and then we proceed with the list of actual bloopers – the individual amusing mistake entries. So, already, we have a hierarchy of containers within containers.

Structured appeal

If we were to look at our container hierarchy, with no content whatsoever, it would look like this:

```
<exam-bloopers>
<p></p>
<blooper></blooper>
<blooper></blooper>
<blooper></blooper>
<blooper></blooper>
</exam-bloopers>
```

As you can see, the `root` element in this case is our `exam-bloopers` element, and from it (inside it) we have branches, in the form of `intro` (shown by `<p></p>`) and several `blooper` elements. Both the `intro` and `blooper` elements are on the same level as each other. If either element were to have branches of its own, they would represent a further level along the tree.

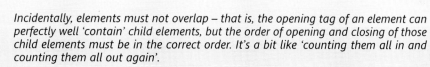

Incidentally, elements must not overlap – that is, the opening tag of an element can perfectly well 'contain' child elements, but the order of opening and closing of those child elements must be in the correct order. It's a bit like 'counting them all in and counting them all out again'.

So, another rule of XML is: Elements may contain text, or further elements. Let's see what our example would look like in this context:

```
<exam-bloopers>
<p>Some amusing errors by history students:</p>
<blooper>The Pope was inflammable.</blooper>
<blooper>Suffragettes were the things the Germans shot underwater to
kill the British in the First World War.</blooper>
<blooper>Alexander the Great entered Troy disguised as a wooden
horse.</blooper>
<blooper>Mary, Queen of Scots, was playing golf with her husband when
news was brought to her of the birth of her son and heir.</blooper>
</exam-bloopers>
```

Here, you can see how we've demarcated each item within its own element. Notice also, that as a result of our relatively sensible element naming, we also know at a glance what kind of information each element contains – even before we have arrived at the content. This is quite an important point to contemplate. It might not seem so, but it is precisely this that helps set XML apart from many other markup methods and file formats. XML is inherently self-documenting, this makes it easy to index, and hence searchable for specific types of information. In addition to this, XML is not too confusing for the human eye to decipher. Many file formats are not so easy to work with.

Attributes of elements

An element may have attributes. These are simply a textual name, followed by an equals sign, followed by a value of some sort in quote marks. Although the element of a certain name corresponds to a container of information of a certain type, one often wants to add information of a lower level of abstraction. What this means is that an element is a 'thing', whereas an attribute is 'about the thing'. For example, if I say 'cat' and you say 'gray', the cat is obviously the thing that is gray, as opposed to the other way round. Let's look at a possibly familiar HTML example.

```
<img src="aspidistra.png" alt="Aspidistra" width="100" height="250" />
```

The element is img. The src is not part of the element name – it is merely an attribute. It tells the browser, upon encountering the 'img' element, where exactly to link to the expected image file (the src attribute and value are required). Similarly, the alt, width, and height are all attributes of the img element. They needn't be presented in this order at all. Some attributes are required, some will derive default values when not present, and others are entirely optional.

An attribute must always have a value. Attribute values must always be quoted. Those are the rules. Just as with element names, attribute names are also case-sensitive. What goes in them is largely up to you – the element that you invent would typically accommodate attributes (or maybe it doesn't need any), and the logic and reasoning behind those attributes are also of your own devising.

Element or attribute?

Something that people often find confusing is the difference between whether to enclose an item of information in an element, and whether it should be carried as an attribute. There's no hard or fast rule in this respect. At one end of the scale, all your information could be contained as text surrounded by elements. At the other end, everything could be an attribute. Your system might work equally, either way. The problem arises when expandability or unpredictable source material arrives and tests your system logic. With experience, you soon detect the sort of information that truly is at home as an attribute of an element, and the sort that should be kept as text enclosed by elements.

Let's return to our example and add some attributes.

```
<exam-bloopers id="collection01">
    <p id="intro01">Some amusing errors by history students:</p>
    <blooper id="blooper01">The Pope was inflammable.</blooper>
    <blooper id="blooper 02">Suffragettes were the things the Germans
```

```
shot underwater to kill the British in the First World
War.</blooper>
<blooper id="blooper 03">Alexander the Great entered Troy
disguised as a wooden horse.</blooper>
<blooper id="blooper 04">Mary, Queen of Scots, was playing golf
with her husband when news was brought to her of the birth of her
son and heir.</blooper>
</exam-bloopers>
```

Here, we have added an `id` attribute to each and every element. This is not such a bad idea really, and the id attribute is rather special in that it is expected that every element might have one. There is also an additional complication to the `id` attribute alone – the value of each 'id' attribute within an XML document must be unique. That is, you can't have two id attributes with the same content between their quotes. Even if the elements are the same – id attributes must be unique. There is a nice and versatile mechanism that turns up later on in JavaScript, that allows you to find an element by id. If there were two id's with the same content, this operation would fail.

By now, you may have noticed that these element names say nothing whatsoever about how the XML source will be displayed ultimately. This is intentional. This is one of the powerful aspects of XML. It separates presentation from content. This is a pivotal aspect of XML, and also points to one of the major failings of the design of the HTML language, where presentation isn't necessarily separated from content.

Separating presentation and content

To demonstrate the importance of separating presentation and content let's look at some simple HTML. Let's keep it simple, so I'll strip out the html head and body elements and just dive right in to a pertinent snippet.

```
<h1>Breaking News</h1>
<p><b>This just in: </b> Tree <i>fell down</i> in forest. No-one
around to hear it.</p>
```

OK, now that seems to be perfectly legal HTML. It is (as a snippet, that is). What can possibly be wrong with it? Well, if you run this into a browser, you might get something like this:

The problem is this: the h1 element is being used as a headline. If you know your HTML, then you know that any text within the h1 element will render in the browser as the biggest type size available to the browser from a predetermined set of six sizes. Likewise, h2 would give you a smaller type size, and h3 smaller still. Why is this a problem? It's a problem because of the implicit assumption that an element will always produce a certain kind of visual result. Web designers wanting a large, big, bold line of type will know to use the h1 headline style – whether it's a headline or not. The fact that it is assumed that you would like your headlines of a certain size, and boldness, is built into the element (or more accurately, built in to the way the browser treats the content of the element).

Style sheets alleviate this to an extent, as they simply define the visual appearance of certain elements. However, in HTML, style sheets are simply not mandatory – it will attempt to guess your presentation according to what sort of element you've used, if no style sheet is found, based upon some artistic notion that the browser has.

We could create a style sheet for our XML elements, saying something like:
"Make all p elements Helvetica Bold, 12pt, blue".

We could then add another rule:
"Make all blooper elements Helvetica Roman, 10pt, black".

Then, we could go one step further and add one saying:
"Make all exam-bloopers elements have a very light cream background".

Well, we're not really making the elements themselves those things, we're making the result of what they contain, when viewed on a browser, appear in those specific ways.

What we've done here is to keep 'what it is' – content, and 'what it appears like' – presentation, separate. The content is in the XML file. The presentation information is in the style sheet. Change the style sheet and you change the appearance. Even if you can't touch the XML source, you can change how it will be presented. Even if the XML will change on a daily, hourly, minutely basis, you don't care – you know how it will look, given a known set of likely elements. Even if the XML is dynamically created on demand, you can affect the design merely by attending to a style sheet.

In HTML, style sheets exist in the form of CSS – Cascading Style Sheets. While we won't get into them in a big way here (other books are the best place for that), suffice to say that a CSS file contains rules. Rules that define the way elements look. XML works in a similar way. You can apply CSS to XML via a few intermediate steps. How this is done, we won't bother ourselves with, but you now have the freedom to design XML elements that pertain to what is supposed to go in them, and leave the question of how they're supposed to look to a completely different phase of the process.

Self-documenting data

Another important aspect of XML is its ability to self-document, to classify its information. This makes it an excellent way to store data. In one way or another, pretty much everything these days seems to be sweeping over toward an XML domicile. OK, so maybe not an entire world where every concept and physical manifestation is constructed from XML, but certainly a large and diverse wave of topics are finding their home in XML. The reason for this is often the sheer logical and organizational benefits offered by XML.

An analogy of the way XML classifies data would be the world of libraries. Nobody would ever get very far if a library simply consisted of a building with books in it and no accompanying logistic system. There are organizational systems that ensure that certain books belong in certain places, and those places are known for all. Cataloguing which books are where involves information about those books – not the information within those books, but merely 'about' those books. This 'meta-information', if you like, such as Author, Publisher, Title, Publishing date, ISBN, are often kept in some sort of filing system. This filing system will typically have a means of accessing it usefully – it is organized probably along the same sort of lines that the books themselves are too.

As a result, you can find what information you're looking for, by browsing bookshelves, or if you know exactly that a certain item of information is within a specific book, you can ascertain whether that book exists, where it is, etc. XML works in a similar hierarchical way, and its strength lies in its ability to exploit metadata to create fully searchable information.

Brief introduction to SVG

With the release of Illustrator 9 (and also via a plug-in that was available for Illustrator 8 for a while), Illustrator can now create SVG (Scalable Vector Graphics) files. Illustrator 10 offers considerably stronger and broader support for the SVG file format. This is an exciting development, as SVG is an XML application.

Now, let's take a brief look at some pretty basic SVG. You need to be able to see SVG in your browser, in order to view the results of what we're about to embark upon, so let's check that you're ready. One rather nice way of checking if you're all kitted out, by way of introduction, is to go to Adobe's own SVG demo page (http://www.adobe.com/svg/demos/main.html) where you may select from many impressive demonstrations of SVG. Of course, a considerable amount of work has been put into these demos, and we're going to only touch the surface here, but it goes to show what can be achieved by way of whetting the appetite.

Installing an Adobe SVG viewer

If you experience difficulty in viewing what you think you should be viewing, it's possible that your SVG viewer is not installed. Ordinarily, installing Photoshop 7 or Illustrator 10 would also install the Adobe SVG Viewer browser plug-in. However, your clients are not as likely to be in this situation as you (as a content provider), so there need to be ways of allowing any web user the facility to view SVG. There is. Adobe SVG Viewer (version 3 at time of writing) is available as a separate download on its own, as a browser plug-in (http://www.adobe.com/svg/viewer/install/main.html), or even as part of the current Adobe Acrobat Reader download. This works equally for MacOS or Windows operating systems.

The Adobe SVG Viewer plug-in is also available for Linux (http://www.adobe.com/svg/viewer/install/old.html), which is a version 3 beta at the time of writing. However, it is worth noting that this is unsupported by Adobe. I expect that this may be because there are so many varieties of Linux, and so many different ways that people might have configured their machines, that it's not quite so predictable from a helpdesk point of view as the two other main OS platforms. It doesn't mean that it's out of date, or not current, just that there's no help available if you get stuck.

A first SVG document

Once you are satisfied that you or your audience have SVG viewing capabilities, let us begin. Here is a very simple piece of SVG. Using any standard text editor, such as Notepad, type in the following:

```
<?xml version="1.0" standalone="no"?>
<!DOCTYPE svg PUBLIC "-//W3C//DTD SVG 20010904//EN"
    "http://www.w3.org/TR/2001/REC-SVG-20010904/DTD/svg10.dtd">

<svg>
    <text x="25" y="50">Cheers!</text>
    <rect x="5" y="36" width="80" height="20"
            fill="none" stroke="red" stroke-width="5px" />
    <circle cx="45" cy="46" r="30"
            fill="none" stroke="green" stroke-width="8px"/>
</svg>
```

Remember to save as an SVG file (.svg), and then use a web browser to view the document. This SVG markup results in this:

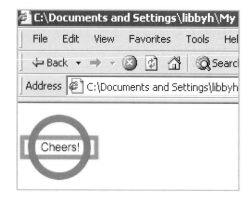

The first line simply defines the file as XML; the next line is the document type **DOCTYPE** declaration.

```
<!DOCTYPE svg PUBLIC "-//W3C//DTD SVG 20010904//EN"
    "http://www.w3.org/TR/2001/REC-SVG-20010904/DTD/svg10.dtd">
```

The purpose of this, having already established in the first line that we're looking at an XML document, is to indicate to the software reading this document what those element and attribute names that we're about to encounter actually mean. The 'meaning' is to be found in the SVG DTD (Document Type Definition), and this line tells us where to find it. The reading software now knows, therefore, that it's looking at an XML file, and it knows that it is an SVG kind of XML file. It also knows where to find the SVG DTD. Not all SVG files, or indeed XML files, will have their DOCTYPE line present. So don't worry if it's not present in any final XML you encounter.

The next element we see is an `svg` element.

```
<svg>
    <text x="25" y="50">Cheers!</text>
    <rect x="5" y="36" width="80" height="20"
          fill="none" stroke="red" stroke-width="5px" />
    <circle cx="45" cy="46" r="30"
          fill="none" stroke="green" stroke-width="8px"/>
</svg>
```

In this case, this represents the whole of the SVG document itself. In other words, everything else rests inside the `svg` element. Everything else is a child of the `svg` element, the `svg` element is the 'root' element.

Three elements, are the children of the `svg` root element: the `text` element; a `rect` element; and finally a `circle` element. The first child of the `svg` root element is a `text` element.

```
    <text x="25" y="50">Cheers!</text>
```

This in turn contains some text, the jolly greeting of "Cheers!" which will be treated as text on the screen. Of course, it has to know where to put it. Luckily, we've specified a pair of coordinates using 'x' and 'y' attributes.

The `rect` element has attributes to specify its top left corner coordinate, and its width and height.

```
    <rect x="5" y="36" width="80" height="20"
          fill="none" stroke="red" stroke-width="5px" />
```

This is all the information it needs to draw a rectangle. However, if we left it at that, the default would be for the SVG viewer to paint a solid black rectangle, smack on top of the text. What we need in this example is to give the rectangle shape no fill at all by specifying the attribute `fill` with a value of "none". We also specify a red `stroke`, with a `stroke-width` of 5 pixels.

Making it move

Let's take a look at a dynamic graphic effect, with respect to our amazingly simplistic example. Animation, for most people, conjures up the idea of graphics that move about on the screen. In SVG, this is of course true, but additionally, 'animation' is a wider term than simply motion. SVG uses the term 'animation' to describe any changing aspect that causes some sort of visual alteration over time. For example, the size of an object can be animated – it stays where it is, but gets smaller or bigger over time. Alternatively, you could animate other (perhaps more subtle) aspects, such as transparency or color. For example, the shape itself might stay where it is, but the color could change over the passage of time, or fade away completely.

First, let's create a simple animation. Let's make the circle decrease in size. In your text editor input the following (it's the same as before – only this time we've added an animation section):

```
<?xml version="1.0" standalone="no"?>
<!DOCTYPE svg PUBLIC "-//W3C//DTD SVG 20010904//EN"
    "http://www.w3.org/TR/2001/REC-SVG-20010904/DTD/svg10.dtd">

<svg>
<text x="25" y="50">Cheers!</text>
<rect x="5" y="36" width="80" height="20"
    fill="none" stroke="red" stroke-width="5px" />
<circle cx="45" cy="46" r="30"
    fill="none" stroke="green" stroke-width="8px">
    <animate attributeName="r" attributeType="XML"
        begin="2s" dur="4s"
        from="30" to="9" fill="freeze" >
</circle>
</svg>
```

We have animated the radius of the circle, so that it grows smaller before your eyes. Incredible!

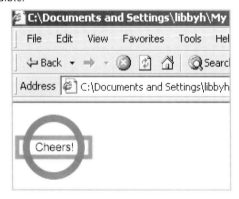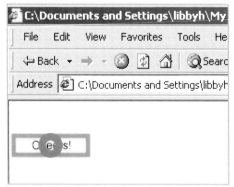

After two seconds, the animation kicks in, and after four further seconds, the circle has shrunk from a starting radius value that matches the initial radius value (30), to a much smaller value of '9'. Then it stays like that. You can see all this happening in the `animate` element, which is a child of the `circle` element.

```
<animate attributeName="r" attributeType="XML"
        begin="2s" dur="4s"
        from="30" to="9" fill="freeze" >
<circle>
```

You might also notice that the `circle` element is no longer an empty element (that is, one that ends in '/>'). It now contains a further element (the `animate` element), so the correct syntax is now to open the circle element with an opening circle element tag (`</circle>`), and close it afterwards with a closing circle element tag (`</circle>`).

In the `animate` element, we specify which attributes of the parent element (the `circle` element) we want to alter. In this case, we specify an `attributeName` as having the value of 'r', which is the attribute in the parent (`circle`), that will be affected. The `attributeType` is set to a value of `XML`, simply because this is an attribute of an XML element (as opposed to perhaps a property of a style sheet in a CSS).

The `begin` attribute specifies how much time to wait from the start, before taking any effect (two seconds in this case), and the `dur` attribute is the duration of the effect. The words `from` and `to` specify which value the attribute will start with (needn't be the current value, but if it is different, it will appear to 'jump' to it when the animate starts), and which value it will end with. The `fill="freeze"` phrase is simply a way of telling the animation engine that we're done.

As you can see, SVG is quite readable, and makes a reasonable amount of sense even if you've never actually learned anything much about it. Of course, there's a lot to learn, and this appendix will only give you an appetizer. Nevertheless, this is where the aforementioned 'self documenting' nature of XML comes into play. Reading and making some sort of sense of our simplistic SVG documents here is not a difficult task, all in all.

Index

Notes

Notes

Notes

Notes

friendsof

DESIGNER TO DESIGNER™

friends of ED writes books for you. Any suggestions, or ideas about how you want information given in your ideal book will be studied by our team.Your comments are always valued at friends of ED.

For technical support please contact support@friendsofed.com.

Free phone in USA: 800.873.9769
Fax: 312.893.8001

UK Telephone: 0121.258.8858
Fax: 0121.258.8868

Registration Code: | 09343UR9K5GZ1601 |

Photoshop 7 and Illustrator 10 – Registration Card

Name ....

Address ....

City ....State/Region ....

Country ....Postcode/Zip ....

E-mail ....

Profession: design student ☐ freelance designer ☐
                    part of an agency ☐ inhouse designer ☐
                    other (please specify) ....

Age: Under 20 ☐ 20-25 ☐ 25-30 ☐ 30-40 ☐ over 40 ☐

Do you use: mac ☐ pc ☐ both ☐

How did you hear about this book?...

☐ Book review (name)...

☐ Advertisement (name) ....

☐ Recommendation ....

☐ Catalog ....

☐ Other ....

Where did you buy this book? ....

☐ Bookstore (name) ....City...........................

☐ Computer Store (name)..

☐ Mail Order...

☐ Other...

How did you rate the overall content of this book?
   Excellent ☐   Good ☐
   Average ☐   Poor ☐

What applications/technologies do you intend to learn in the near future?...
....

What did you find most useful about this book? ....
....

What did you find the least useful about this book? ....
....

Please add any additional comments ....

What other subjects will you buy a computer book on soon?
....
....

What is the best computer book you have used this year?
....
....

Note: This information will only be used to keep you
updated about new friends of ED titles and will not be used for
any other purpose or passed to any other third party.

friendsof

D E S I G N E R   T O   D E S I G N E R ™

N.B. If you post the bounce back card below in the UK, please send it to:

friends of ED Ltd.,
30 Lincoln Road, Olton,
Birmingham, B27 6PA. UK.